Praise for **Boy Alone**

"A candid, brave, painful and very well-written memoir about a truly tragic family situation."

—Peter Matthiessen, author of *The Shadow Country*

"Extraordinary. . . . devastating. . . . Greenfeld has shown us, with power, honesty and heart-rending sensitivity, the severely autistic population as it ages, and the clock ticks." —David Royko, *Chicago Tribune*

"Precise and poignant. . . . [A] luminous account of true brotherhood, lived and written in an age of indulgence and self-pity."

—Stefan Kanfer, *City Journal*

"This is a truly beautiful and powerful book. Karl Greenfeld has written his own angle on the story of his autistic brother, Noah, made famous in the works of their father, Josh Greenfeld. Karl turns his sibling saga into a lyrical exploration of love, mystery, family, and what makes us human. He also dances around hope and reality, fact and fiction, in a way that will startle you. The result is a masterpiece of literature and memory that will leave you breathless."

—Walter Isaacson, author of *Einstein: His Life and Universe*

"*Boy Alone* unlocks the heart and lets the emotions pour out: grief, despair, anger, love, devotion and wonder. Whether you are a parent or a sibling of someone with autism or just looking in from the outside through this rarely opened window into the complex life of a family coping with autism, you will never forget this book."

—Portia Iversen, co-founder of the Cure Autism Now foundation and author of *Strange Son*

"In his extraordinary memoir, Karl Greenfeld details what it is like to grow up next to a "beautiful" boy with whom he can never play and never connect and who never returns his love, but who, nonetheless, is the most important fact of his life. Greenfeld's story goes beyond autism, however; it is also a brilliant depiction of male adolescence and a meditation on what family means and what we owe one another in this life."

—Michael Thompson, Ph.D., coauthor of *Raising Cain*

"A vivid, compelling, painfully honest sibling story. My heart went out to Karl. I couldn't put this book down."

—Rachel Simon, author of *Riding the Bus with My Sister*

"Deep, dark, and devastating, *Boy Alone* is remarkable in its ruthless honesty, exceptional writing, and eye-opening subject matter. A fascinating and powerful read."

—Janice Erlbaum, author of *Have You Found Her*

"Sibling rivalry—and love—of a ravaging kind is the subject of this unsparing memoir of the author's life with his severely autistic brother. [An] affecting chronicle of a family simultaneously shattered and bound tight by autism."

—*Publishers Weekly*

"Recent autism memoirs range from accounts of strenuous 'healing' to reflection on accepting the condition. Such a reaction isn't found in Greenfeld's book. . . . Karl resolves the conflict he sets up . . . with a surprise twist that may remind some readers of *The Sixth Sense*."

—Polly Morrice, *New York Times Book Review*

© GUY AROCH

About the Author

KARL TARO GREENFELD is the author of *China Syndrome, Standard Deviations,* and *Speed Tribes.* He is the former editor of *Time Asia* and editor-at-large for *Sports Illustrated.* His writing has appeared in numerous *Best American* anthologies, including *Best American Short Stories 2009.*

Also by Karl Taro Greenfeld

China Syndrome: The True Story of the 21st Century's First Great Epidemic

Standard Deviations: Growing Up and Coming Down in the New Asia

Speed Tribes: Days and Nights with Japan's Next Generation

BOY ALONE

A Brother's Memoir of Growing Up with an Autistic Sibling

KARL TARO GREENFELD

HARPER PERENNIAL

NEW YORK • LONDON • TORONTO • SYDNEY • NEW DELHI • AUCKLAND

HARPER PERENNIAL

A hardcover edition of this book was published in 2009 by Harper, an imprint of HarperCollins Publishers.

HarperCollins books may be purchased for educational, business, or sales promotional use. For information please write: Special Markets Department, HarperCollins Publishers, 10 East 53rd Street, New York, NY 10022.

FIRST HARPER PERENNIAL EDITION PUBLISHED 2010.

Library of Congress Cataloging-in-Publication Data is available upon request.

ISBN 978-0-06-113667-2

10 11 12 13 14 OV/RRD 10 9 8 7 6 5 4 3 2 1

For Noah

CONTENTS

PART I

A CHILD

1.

A boy sits by himself on a stained white carpet, the corner of a frayed blanket stuffed into his mouth, his head bobbing, the fingers of both hands twiddling at ear level. He seems neither to miss company nor show any eagerness to seek it. If you say hello, he will not look at you nor turn in the direction of your voice. If you take up position in his line of sight, he will look away.

We lived in Croton-on-Hudson in a white house atop a black driveway along which wild blackberry bushes bore fruit in the summer. I used to walk up that driveway, stopping to pick the berries. No one else in my family knew they were there, and I never told anyone about them.

I don't recall the precise beginning of concern. I was born in Kobe, Japan, on November 26, 1964; Noah was born in North Tarrytown, New York, on July 1, 1966. As soon as I was aware of myself, there he was. How could I have seen that Noah wasn't like other boys? What did I know of childhood development, normal or otherwise? I recall all the worry and conversation about Noah as steady background noise to which I would occasionally tune in. The two of them, my parents—my father a head taller than my mother—are sitting at the dinner table drinking tea after dinner, and their voices are low. Our living, dining, and kitchen areas share one sprawling space at the top of a four-step rise from the entryway. I can sit on these steps, just out of sight, and listen.

They talk about Noah. Something is wrong with Noah. Noah should be doing this by now but he is not. Karl—they said my name!—he's already doing *this*. And when Karl was two he was doing *that*. But Noah—they are already back to Noah—he's not doing *this*. This is serious, I know, a grownup conversation, with none of the careful enunciation or broad gestures that my father and mother use when they are talking to me. Their talk with me is meant, in part, to entertain me. This talk, this adult talk, is different.

I can also hear Noah. He is mumbling, repeatedly, a kind of dirgey stream of consonants, n-n-n-n-n, muh-muh-muh-muh, da-da-da-da-da. He doesn't talk. Not in words, anyway. The boy down the street, Mark, is younger than Noah and he talks. I play with Mark. I can't really play with Noah, not anymore.

My parents are saying that Noah used to talk.

I'm surprised. Noah talked?

What did he say?

Did he talk to me?

I stand up. My pockets are stuffed with Matchbox cars. I take Matchbox cars with me everywhere.

Noah is sitting in the den, on a tan sofa with a wood frame that faces the television. He is kneading his blanket like it is Play-Doh. He never watches television. I watch television every Saturday, the *Lone Ranger*—the cartoon, not the live-action show—and my mother makes me butter sandwiches on toast. I also have Lone Ranger pajamas.

"Talk!" I order Noah. "Talk. You can talk."

He doesn't acknowledge me. He doesn't really look at me. He never really looks at me.

"Mommy and Daddy said you could talk," I shout at him.

He never says a word.

2.

On April 24, 1969, my father wrote in his diary, "My sons: Karl is truth. He looks like a boy, reacts without deviousness, his life never far from the surface. Noah is beauty, sensitive rather than sensible, his life throbbing away in some subcellar. Karl laughs, audibly, openly. Noah smiles, silently, mysteriously. Yet I can't deny it, Noah seems to regress more and more. He refuses to listen or to understand what we say to him, and has all but stopped talking. It's time to see the doctors again."

3.

My father is a writer, and he rides the train to work in New York City. He wears a tan raincoat that smells like water. Our train station is at the bottom of the hill, beside the gray river. My father once took me on the train. We rode one stop, got off, and took a taxi back home.

Once, my father got a haircut while he was in the city, and when he came through the front door I didn't recognize him and I started to cry.

Noah didn't notice the difference.

My brother and I each have our own bedroom with a mattress on the floor. In mine, I have my toys piled in bookcases. Noah doesn't like most toys. But if a toy is made of plastic, he will chew on it. He seems to like the texture, the malleability between his teeth. My mother believes chewing on these toys is dangerous, something about the coloring being poisonous. Whenever Noah receives a plastic toy as a gift from our parents' friends, it ends up in my room because I won't chew on it. Often, we each receive the same toys from fair-minded adults, and I end up with two of them. Two Spirograph sets, for example, when what I really wanted was a Billy Blastoff.

Noah is not interested in me. When I have nothing else to do, I will tickle him or wrestle with him. But that quickly becomes boring because Noah doesn't resist or tickle back. He just lies there giggling until I stop, and then he doesn't notice that I've stopped or he doesn't care.

I'm normal, my parents have said so in their hushed conversations. And Noah isn't normal. And the rest of the kids on Hillside Avenue, they are normal, except for Dana, who shot someone in the eye with a slingshot. That can't be normal. But how can everyone be normal but Noah? How can Noah be the only one not normal?

I have other friends on the block. I have a swing in the front yard and a cat named Brodsky. The Robinsons next door have a swing set with a slide and a dog named Alexander. Tom lives next door on the other side, and he has a train set in the basement. Kirsten lives at the house at the bottom of our driveway, and her father built her an entire toy kitchen out of wood. I liked playing in the toy kitchen with her until Dana made fun of me. Kirsten's older brother Arno has a ten-speed bicycle. He can ride all the way to the toy store by himself. I took three dollars from an envelope in the cabinet and gave it to him because he said he would buy me a Matchbox Mini Cooper. Instead he bought me a Volkswagen bus.

I go to the Scarborough School, and my best friend there is named Robe. He has a younger sister, Pierre. One day when his mother was picking him up from school and I was waiting for the school bus, she asked if Noah and I would like to come over some day and play with Robe and Pierre.

"Why do you want Noah to come over?" I asked.

"Isn't he three?"

I shrugged. What did that have to do with it?

I like fossils and dinosaurs, astronauts, the Lone Ranger, Matchbox cars, and now, lately, Hot Wheels. My father watches football and basketball, but I don't understand what they are doing. When I ask him how they play, he says, follow the ball.

I watch the ball, but I still can't figure out what is going on.

But at school, all the boys say they like football and baseball and basketball. Our favorite player is Joe Namath. I'm not sure exactly who or what he is.

4.

I don't consciously worry about Noah. He is a fact of my life, as much a part of it as our house or my parents or our blue Oldsmobile. Vaguely, there is a sense that something is wrong, that something in the center, at the heart, is not as it should be. But I can't put words or thought to it any more than I could elucidate my inchoate notions of God or the soul. But it is there, always, like an arrhythmic baseline underneath an otherwise happy family melody.

We live in a crescendo of questions: First, Is something wrong? Then, What is wrong? Then, What is it called? Then, What can we do? And most disappointing of all is the fact that as every query is first conceived, then formulated, then verbalized, we all already know the only answers are bad ones. The result is that always—gathering, accreting, growing steadily louder—is the idea that something, somewhere, is indeed *very* wrong. The family's every day together, even those of relative tranquillity when Noah is behaving well, are exhibits in a case of steady disappointment.

I now understand that my parents were every day confronting the reality of Noah's autism. First, he wasn't turning over, then he wasn't crawling, walking, talking. And then, most vexing, after the miracle of speech begins when he is eighteen months or so, he recedes, sentences becoming phrases, phrases becoming words, words becoming nothing. He wets himself and makes bowel movements in his pants until he is six. He sleeps irregularly and wakes constantly, keeping my parents up as if tending to a newborn. And always, my parents are struggling to find out what is wrong with Noah.

5.

JUNE 6, 1969

"Our fears about Noah continue to undergo dramatic ups and downs. Because of his increased opacity, the fact that he doesn't respond when we call his name and fails to relate completely to his immediate environment—a pattern of retardation or autism—we took him to a nearby hospital. There, in a team approach, a child psychologist, a psychiatrist, and a speech therapist will all test him and then compare notes. The doctor in charge of the overall program preexamined Noah. She used phrases such as 'autistic tendencies' to describe him, thus intensifying our worst fears. Especially Foumi's. In her heart she knows something is wrong with Noah. What disturbs her most are his sudden outbursts of laughter. I guess we both fear that what we dread is so, that Noah is not a normal child, that he is a freak, and his condition is getting worse."

6.

Come on, Noah. Climb off that swing, put down those smooth stones from the Japanese garden. No matter how many times you run them through your fingers, you're not going to find a gem. Just come with me.

I am five, you are three. I can read, you can't speak. I can tie my shoes, you can't slip on a sock. You still sleep in a crib.

You can't come with me. We don't grow up so much as grow apart.

In the morning, we eat breakfast before you. If you see bread on the table, you will refuse to eat or drink anything until you get your bread. So my father and I eat our eggs and toast and listen to your keening and mindless, repeated syllables, the sounds as regular and meaningless as a washing machine. Then my mother climbs the stairs and helps you from your crib, and you come down and you are smiling and bobbing your head. You and I share our mother's black hair, yours is thinner than mine. You have a narrower, more refined nose than me and high, almost elfin cheekbones. My father says that you look like my mother and I look like him. So that means you look like a girl and I look like a boy. What I won't understand until later is that this means you are beautiful and I am . . . just a boy. When we go to the supermarket, when you are seated in the cart, housewives will stop my father to tell him that you are so beautiful. They never did this for me. "He looks like that because he is pure," my father will write, "he is not touched by anything in this world. Everything he feels, everything he is, comes from inside himself. That's what autism means. It means being locked in the confines of the self, being one's own entire world."

It is like a trick, this beauty, that seduces so many teachers, specialists, psychiatrists, and even your family into believing that somehow there must be a way through to you, that God would not have made you so lovely on the outside and so messed up in the middle. And in the morning, in that first instance when you come bounding into the sunny kitchen and gaze around at all of us, my parents are fooled again into believing, despite all their better judgment and wisdom, that perhaps today will be different. You talk in his dreams, my father says.

But you don't fool me. You are my brother. And my rival. And I can feel the room tilting toward you whenever you walk in, all the attention and parental love drains into you, never to come back out. You possess gravity out of all proportion to your size. And perhaps your indifference to your own importance makes you even more beloved. I am learning that I can never compete with you; despite being older, bigger, smarter, faster, I will lose every race for our parents' time and attention.

If you could come with me, then it would all be different. We are playing in the front yard, in the few minutes between breakfast and when Bus 13 comes to take me to school. It is a sunny day, mid-September, and I have bendy, rubber figures of space monsters tied to the ends of strings. My mother has planted a patch of ferns by the porch, and I like the way the monsters look amid their broad, green leaves. But when I play in the garden, I step on the plants, so my mother has tied strings to the figures and told me to dangle them in the plants, which is actually better because I can stand up and watch green and blue Lord Neptune march through the boreal forest.

Then it is time to go. And that's when I think that, if you could come with me to school, it would all be different. Then you would be like me, then it would all be fair and we could even play with Lord Neptune together. Well, maybe not with Lord Neptune. But I would let you play with Gorgon, Mentoricon, or the other monsters.

Instead, my father comes down the stairs and says we have to go right now to catch Bus 13.

When I come home, I find you have chewed Lord Neptune's helmet so that it is flattened and the wire that allows his neck to bend now sticks out of the back of his head.

7.

A boy sits by himself . . .

8.

My father is a slight man, balding, with a fringe of wiry brown hair. He wears thick-frame glasses over bulging brown eyes and has a long nose and thin lips. I remember him smiling more than anything else, and laughing, and trying to make me smile and laugh. But he also always had a preoccupied air, a distractedness, a projected sense that even though he was playing with me, he should be doing something else: writing. He is a writer, and I now know that means feeling that every moment is stolen from your work.

He was born in Malden, Massachusetts, in 1928 and moved to Linden Boulevard in East Flatbush, Brooklyn, when he was in fifth grade. Today, when he plays Monopoly with my daughters, I can still see the competitive kid from the poor Jewish family, the younger brother of his big sister Irma, as he counts the number of spaces until Kentucky Avenue and then says, "Seven, seven, an easy number, come on, seven." He stands up when he plays, his pink and green choo-choo train money in his fist, checking his property to see how much houses cost. It is a curious sight, this wiry old man, his thin arms clutching bills in one hand and the dice in the other. I can imagine the young man—the compulsive gambler—who loved shooting craps and lost a college semester's tuition playing poker and, further back, the competitive boy up on the roof of his old tenement, playing this aggressive brand of Monopoly with his block mates. My daughters, Esmee and Lola, are soft compared to him; they are being raised amid more affluence, in part because of that competitive Jewish boy's success, but they are also young girls and less spirited in their board-game play. Esmee, my oldest, when she lands on my father's Connecticut Avenue with four houses on it will burst into tears at his dunning. My father collects.

When I was a child, I was put through this same initiation into competitive board games. My mother would urge my father to let me win, yet my father couldn't.

I used to watch him work in his little office downstairs. I would ask him if I could play with his books, and he was powerless to order me to leave him in peace.

"What are you doing?" I ask.

"Working," he says, vainly hoping a four-year-old can take a hint.

"What are you working?"

"Writing," he says, not looking up from his Royal upright. Magazines and newspapers from New York City send up black cars to pick up his stories and book reviews. A driver in a hat will trot up the stairs, and my father will hand him a manila envelope.

"Are you writing a story?" I ask.

"Yes," he says, "about Noah. And you. About all of us."

"Can I play with your books?"

He is rarely serious, yet he is often impatient. Now he is both. He takes a stack of dull yellow and red galleys down from his desk and sets them on the floor and resumes typing.

I stack the books up in a pile on the floor, near his desk. Then I leave the room.

He has been a writer since finishing at the University of Michigan in 1949 and then serving in the army; he was a playwright, a novelist, a magazine writer. He put in six months as a book reviewer at *Newsweek* in the early 1960s before he was fired. He would write dozens of stories for a slew of men's magazines—*Sport*, *Climax*, *Saga*, *Argosy*, *True*—as well as stories for the glossies: *Esquire*, the *Saturday Evening Post*, *Redbook*. I remember coming upon a crate of these old titles in our basement, stories by my father about Curtis LeMay and Joe Stilwell and the 1927 Yankees. In 1960, after he was awarded a Guggenheim when his play *Clandestine on the Morning Line* was produced in Washington, D.C., he attended the MacDowell Colony, an artists' retreat in New Hampshire, where he met a Japanese painter, my mother, Foumiko Kometani. U.S. immigration law didn't allow for a lingering romance, and they were married in downtown Manhattan later that year. Two years later, after *Clandestine* was produced off-Broadway while my mother worked as a secretary at an insurance company to get up a stake, they left for Japan, going by way of Holland, Belgium, France, Spain, Italy, Greece, Egypt, Yemen, India, Ceylon, Vietnam, Singapore, and Hong Kong. My mother, then terrified of flying, insisted on one literal ground rule: no planes.

They returned to New York about a year after I was born; Noah was born just before we moved to this house in Croton-on-Hudson. My father's first novel *O for a Master of Magic* was published in 1968; it sold, as my father jokingly reminds me, exactly 753 copies. By the time I was born he had already conceded that he would not succeed at his chosen field—theater—and was already considering other careers: advertising, magazine writing, editing. But if before children he pursued his writing mostly for art's sake, now that he has us he writes for the money. Never with any resentment, for what father feels resentment toward his children? Still, he feels some lingering disappointment that life has turned out this way, though with Noah's regression, he will soon grow too realistic to feel any disappointment over a conflict so trivial as art versus commerce.

He is a kind man, always eager to make me laugh, to joke with me and pass along riddles—"What looks like a box, smells like a lox, and flies?"—though the corollary to this is that he is also prone to teasing and occasionally making fun of me. (The answer is a flying lox box.) "All right for you, Karly," he'll say when we're playing checkers and he is about to triple jump me. "All right for you."

That he is an odd fellow is something I am aware of even in kindergarten. He is unlike the other fathers. For one thing, he is often the only dad who comes to midday school events. As a writer, he is free when other fathers are busy. The other dads are stolid, prone to wearing suits and dark trousers, and they have short hair parted to one side. My father's wiry hair is unruly, and he often wears caps or floppy fedoras. He is often the loudest at any gathering, and he tends to make embarrassing comments about me. I will later determine that part of his seeming different is his Jewishness, which still, in the late 1960s, seems out of place here in the suburbs. He is the only dad on our block, on Hillside Avenue, who is Jewish. (My mother is the only Asian.) He is also an oddly appearing person, shuffling in his gait, too skinny in his carriage, taking flamingo-like steps on four-inch-diameter legs. There is nothing soothing or calming about his physical presence. He is an agitation. But that is not all; there is also a strange combination of ingratiating overeagerness and disdainful hubris, a mixture that is manifested by my father managing to be both intellectually overbearing and archly dismissive at the same time.

Yet he is a writer, and I recall even then, at a very young age, being impressed by that alchemy of sitting at a typewriter and turning thoughts to words and then, via those chauffeurs, words into money. Later I will discover that the reason he wrote so many book reviews and essays—for *Time*, the *New York Times*, *Playboy*, *Life*, the *Village Voice*—was that because of Noah, he couldn't travel on assignment. All I knew was that my father was always around.

He was ill prepared for the burden of Noah. Yet prone as he is to noticing defects and studying flaws, he quickly observes there is a strangeness to his second son. Knowing the downside, of course, is his specialty, pointing out the likely pitfalls one of his gifts. A later generation would label him negative or hypercritical—remember, at this point in his career, he makes his living as a book critic—yet he can't help his honesty. It is no virtue, not deployed as it is, willy-nilly and without regard for consequences. Instead, this aberrant behavior is a kind of borderline insanity. He cannot keep his opinions to himself. He insults guests and will tell his friends, novelists, writers, why their latest book is wanting.

The first years with Noah are a protracted study in that probing and speculative honesty. He sees that Noah is not turning over, sitting, crawling, walking, doing anything on schedule except talking. And the more he discusses what is not happening, he is at the same time trying to convince himself that perhaps it is a phase, that maybe Noah is progressing by his own schedule. My father lays out the worst case in the hopes that it will not come to pass, as if by acknowledgment of a problem he will somehow jinx it away. I have since seen him in this mode many times. If I have written an article or story or book and am waiting to hear from an editor or publisher, he will go through with me repeatedly all the reasons the journal or publisher or magazine may not accept the work. He is preparing me for possible disappointment while, all along, quietly hoping for success.

Noah, of course, confirms the pessimistic point of view, and I see my father lose a little of his swagger, his shrugging indifference to society, as he now realizes he is far more deeply invested than he ever imagined. In his mind's eye, he is still that young man living in Greenwich Village, working on a play, dreaming literary dreams. "What the hell am I doing in Westchester with two baby sons?" he writes. "Over all the beers I guzzled at the Remo and the Kettle of

Fish and Johnny Romero's and the Riv and the White Horse and the Cedar Street Bar and Gilhooleys; over all the cups of coffee I sipped at the Figaro and Rienzi and Limelight and the Lion's Head; over all the martinis I nursed at the Waverly Lounge and the Jumble Shop and the Dicken's Room; over all the red wine I drank at Felini's and Mary's; and during all the nights of prowling down all the elephant paths of the village and long days of numb sun sitting on the concrete lip of the 'snake pit' in the center of the park and walking down its spoke-like bypaths grimly searching joyous companionship . . . during all those years when 14th Street was my uptown Rubicon—I never dreamt that I would wind up a Westchester resident. A father. A family man with two sons."

That vision of his younger self was of course already obsolete as he hit forty, but the arrival of two children, and the onrushing awareness of the profound disability in one of them, will sink rather than merely mothball such notions.

I am now the same age as he was in 1969; I now have two young children of my own. So I can empathize with his dilemma, and now marvel at his sanguinity in the face of disappointment. Parents take for commonplace development in their offspring. A child crawls then stands then walks; he learns to speak and then read, each progression one of life's greatest contradictions: a miracle that is taken for granted. Yet as I watch my daughters acquire each new skill—climb the jungle gym, swing from monkey bars, master arithmetic—it is with relief as much as appreciation. For I know what it is like for a child to stop developing, to regress. It happened right next to me. Yet developmental delays don't present in symptoms like nonproductive coughs or angry red spots; there is no checklist of nonmanifestations that can then be collated into a diagnosis, not at first anyway. Initially, it is merely a sense.

That boy, sitting by himself on the white carpet, indifferent to his surroundings. He seems a little . . . off.

9.

It is an idea, quickly banished, for what parents haven't been stricken in odd moments by paranoia, by irrational fear that their child isn't right? (Never? Then as a parent you are among the lucky ones.) But it is almost always dismissed as soon as the next milestone is reached. Parents are given a yellow card—the Child's Growth Chart—when they take their child to his or her first vaccination. It is like a little time line, at two months the child should be raising his head, at three to five months he should be reaching, at five to eight months he should be sitting up, at eight to twelve months crawling, at twelve to fifteen months walking, all the way to drawing faces, skipping, and telling stories at four to five years. Above the little graph are illustrations of a baby sitting, pointing, climbing steps. Each band of months supposedly wide enough to accommodate all of us. For those whose crawling and responding to their names falls to the right of the normal latitudinal band, there will be concern, worry, and extra appointments with pediatricians and specialists. (We actually live our entire lives in such narrow schedules, I have found, and that little yellow card could be extended through puberty—at fifteen to eighteen years the child should lose his or her virginity, at eighteen to twenty-three years the child should earn a bachelor's degree, and then marry, raise children, and retire. Each delay or deviation will be reliably commented upon by our peers.)

Noah has managed to miss every single one of those developmental ranges, besides speech, which he would soon lose. It is my mother who is the first to comment that she feels something is wrong with Noah. His suckle, she observes, is too weak; he is vomiting his milk after each nursing. She mentions it to my father in passing, but she is prone to worry, especially about matters of health and safety—remember, she refused to fly in an airplane until I was born—so such worries are easily dismissed amid the settling in of life with a new baby. They worry about how I am adjusting, about my sibling jealousy. I moan and whine all day long, my father laments. Like most parents of newborns, they are not sleeping through the night, waking up every few hours for Noah's feedings, so concerns about Noah's slack nursing style are of equal concern with relearning infant diaper changing and bathing him in a sink.

But the worry is there, and in hindsight, as Noah's problems became impossible to ignore, it becomes easier for both my parents to add a detail or a layer foreshadowing the trials to come. My mother would talk of the decision made by the Chinese American physician, chosen by my parents in part through their own twisted brand of reverse discrimination because of her Asian ancestry, to induce labor and the mercury contained in the drugs administered. Neither of my parents had really wanted a second child, nor had my mother even wanted a first, for that matter. Abortions in the United States in 1965 were a dicey affair. In Japan, they were legal and almost free. Both my parents said had they still been in Japan, they would have aborted the pregnancy very early on. My father, product of the Freudian Industrial Complex that dominated psychoanalyses in the mid-twentieth century, would later wonder if Noah's early problems were a reaction to his having been unwanted as a fetus.

10.

Or was the worry really there? Any more so than it was for me after I brought Esmee and then Lola home? My wife, Silka, German-born and Dutch-raised, the second oldest of four handsome siblings—and the shortest at five feet eleven inches—is predisposed to assume any kinks or flaws or lags will be quickly evened out by time. She never doubts her genetic good fortune and can't help her optimism. Lives, as she has seen them, work out. Children, as she has known them, grow up. She never for a moment doubted the steady progress of our children's development. Because of Noah, she told me, I watched too closely, if that is possible. Let them be, was her mantra.

Why wouldn't my parents have had this initial impulse? My mother was the middle sibling of five. My father the youngest of two. Neither grew up living amid anyone who had brought in a bad genetic parley. So why would they have worried any more than you or I about our children who then turn out to meet each of their targeted developmental milestones within the allotted time frame?

My father's predisposition to study the pitfalls meant that he would have been checking constantly. My mother's response would have been more instinctive. Maternal instinct is an early warning system that should encompass studying the offspring for impending problems as well as knowing when to gather up the child in the face of an oncoming predator. A mother studies her child endlessly, watching him sleep after nursing and burping, caressing his tiny feet and legs, laying a pinkie in his palm to feel his little hand close. This is all a loving inspection, of course, an appraisal of the genetic package, a discreet itemization of reflexes, muscle tone, skin color. In the animal kingdom, the mother does nothing to ensure the survival of the runt of her litter after the first few days. If the human runt is found to be wanting, flawed, defective, unlikely to thrive, then what?

So the child is vomiting, but he is beautiful. More beautiful, I have been told repeatedly by both my parents, than me. He looked like my mother, delicate, almost feminine. I was born heavier, hairier; in photos I have an almost Brando-like thickness to my features. My brother is soft, sharp, his features fine and foxlike. "Noah, I think, is cuter—and more sensitive," my father writes. "Words I never thought of applying to Karl." Both my parents are taken with his looks and take the appropriate delight in this beautiful baby. It is a common description of autistic children that they are physically beautiful. "The child is usually exceptionally healthy and attractive," wrote Bernard Rimland in his landmark 1964 book *Infantile Autism: The Syndrome and Its Implications for a Neural Theory of Behavior*; Leo Kanner, in his 1943 paper on autism, would comment on their "strikingly intelligent physiognomies." It would be a more literary than scientific observation that perhaps the isolation of the individual—the purity—makes for an unsullied and pristine person, and haven't we been conditioned to associate innocence with beauty? If it is the subjective observation of proud parents or the quirky trait of the autistic child, Noah's beauty has become one of our family's myths, a fact that my parents include in every account, as clear to them as the little white house on Hillside Avenue. In photos Noah is lovely, but wasn't your child? Didn't your baby strike you as beautiful? My own children seemed abundantly pulchritudinous to me, though I recently found photos of my oldest at a few days old and noticed she had my Brando-like heaviness; she was unlovely, yet you could never have convinced me of that. Who would tell a parent his baby was ugly?

Noah's beauty keeps coming up because what else do my parents have as memories? His *not* doing things? By six months he is late, slow, missing all his deadlines like a lazy writer who doesn't need the money. And they are intelligent parents, unlikely to insist their baby abide by the strict time line provided in the Growth Chart, but the feeling, it is there—the weak suckle, the vomiting. (I was shocked when I recently reread Rimland's book to find at the very beginning, "Very little that is unusual is noticed in the first months, except, perhaps that feeding may be a problem.") My father comments on his strange laughter, that he laughs far more often than he cries, normally not a concern, but then there is the observation that he cries so very little, and doesn't seem to mind being left alone. But what parent really worries that their baby doesn't cry enough? "It is some time before it occurs to a busy mother," wrote Clara Park in *The Siege*, "that a baby can be too self-sufficient."

11.

At nine months, however, he still isn't turning over.

During a routine visit to a pediatrician for his third triple shot, my parents offer that they are slightly worried. They expect the doctor to assure them they have nothing to worry about, that each baby develops at his own pace. Instead, he asks questions—Is Noah talking? Does he pass objects from hand to hand? Is he reaching?—and imagine the panic that begins to set in as my parents answer each time: no. The doctor voices concern about Noah's motor development, saying that if Noah doesn't develop in the next three months, he should see a specialist. He tries to reassure them by saying that he has "strictly a gut reaction" that Noah is fine. "But we came home," my father writes, "and began looking at Noah through worried eyes, and it was easy to see a mongoloid idiot lurking in his beautiful Eurasian face."

Over the next few days and weeks, they tell each other that he is moving more, that he is becoming more agile, that they need worry less and less. My father's instinct, by his own admission historically unreliable, is that Noah will be all right. "Noah is so lovely," my father writes, "he will look so much lovelier when he sits up . . . but if gradually his form of retardation manifests itself increasingly, I will not love him a mite less, and he will be even more my son."

We now know, of course, in the diagnostic criterion, that slow motor development is the most likely indicator of a potential developmental issue. There was no *DSM IV* Diagnostic Criteria for Autistic Disorder in 1967, no *Handbook of Autism and Pervasive Developmental Disorders*, no chart telling parents and pediatricians that if a child merits a yes in "six (or more) items from (1), (2), and (3), with at least two from (1), and one each from (2) and (3)," then the child is likely to have a developmental disorder. In Westchester County in the mid-1960s, most pediatricians believed they had never seen a case of autism, so rare was the disorder considered—1 in 10,000 was the accepted prevailing frequency. Noah was born into this prehistory, just two decades after Leo Kanner's publication about the first clinically observed cohort of autistics, the gang of eleven described in "Autistic Disturbances of Affective Contact." (The children were introduced to Kanner as "idiots or imbeciles," a few of them residing in a "state school for the feebleminded.") There was no resource my parents could tap for information or guidance. New York, the eastern seaboard, was dominated by the theories of the mind espoused by Freudian analysts.

That era seems both distant and familiar. Yet in terms of the lives and prospects for the severely autistic, it is another world. Oh that my parents had more than *Doctor Spock's Baby and Child Care* for a reference. And I spend days wondering, what if we had known then what we know now about autistics and the urgency of early intervention. Would Noah have emerged? Developed? Would I have had a brother instead of a fraternal obligation?

I can never answer those questions, but as I journeyed through the labs and clinics talking to our generation's best scientists who are working on the pathology, genetics, and treatment of autism, I can't help wonder about my brother's disappearance.

12.

He is such an enigmatic infant, and between nine months and a year he begins speaking, first simple requests and words, the usual, mommy, dosh (Josh), juice, apple, and then soon, almost too soon, without the usual pairing of words, "eat apple" or "daddy go," he jumps to complete sentences, saying "I wanna eat strawberries" and

"Can we go home?" and "I sit down and eat," but never answers any question. My parents gladly note the milestone and banish some of their worry. To this day, my father says he can still hear Noah's voice speaking, adding that he recalls Noah speaking paragraphs, describing a journey down the street or the neighbor's dog. My mother believes my father is exaggerating, that he is confusing his own dreams—literally his dreams, for Noah was frequently speaking in my father's dreams—with reality. My mother says no, it was a few phrases, little sentences, but he spoke. But it was odd, she still recalls, not speech in the same manner as I took it up, uttering each word and then gazing around as if I expected praise. Noah said the words, any word, and then it was as if he hadn't said it at all, and then he might never use the word again. He wasn't building a vocabulary, she now says, these were like little clearings of the mind where language would shine through, and then it would grow cloudy and the words would be gone.

At the next appointment with a pediatrician, a specialist in neurology, they are told that since Noah is talking now, there was less cause to worry. Noah is "hypertonic," a word that seems to mean the opposite of what the doctor went on to say, that Noah was a floppy baby, a slow developer. He assured them that time would be the maturing agent. Yet a week later, at another visit with a pediatric neurologist at Albert Einstein Hospital in the Bronx, they receive yet another diagnosis of concern. Noah's slow motor development—the primary cause for alarm—might be a symptom of intellectual retardation. This specialist orders a series of X-rays of Noah's skull and brain. A technician hurriedly weighs down Noah with sandbags and asks my father to secure Noah's head beneath metal bars. He must keep still, the technician tells my father instead of Noah, who is terrified. She tries and fails to get a clear, complete image, and then begins to cruelly push Noah around, trying to force him toward the middle of the X-ray table. He keeps wiggling out, sliding to the edge of the table, the sandbags shifting off him. My father stands there, watching the technician, "young, dumb-faced, closed-mouthed, vacuously chewing gum," and suggests that she go and get my mother.

My mother has the presence of mind in the X-ray room to show the girl that "only patience—not force—could do the job."

That night, my parents cannot sleep. They discuss the possibilities, and in the morning they constantly look into Noah's eyes for signs of light. For the next few days, they will observe his every movement for "a hint of development," whatever that is, and seek to find fault in the doctor, as if, my father wrote, he were a messenger in a Greek play.

13.

My mother, at first, refuses to consider that Noah might be retarded. He is slow, meandering, leisurely, different. What was it the second doctor said? "Hypertonic?" Why can't it be that instead of retarded? Retarded is a much harsher word, implying slow and defective. Hypertonic has a jet-age whiff about it; if you have to choose a diagnosis, why not one that sounds like a health drink? Yet even that was a telltale sign. Leo Kanner wrote in 1943 that this was a common trait among those eleven autistics he had documented: "The average infant learns during the first few months to adjust his body to the posture of the person who holds him. Our children were not able to do so for two or three years. We had an opportunity to observe 38-month old Herbert in such a situation. His mother informed him in appropriate terms that she was going to lift him up, extending her arms in his direction. There was no response. She proceeded to pick him up, and he allowed her to do so, remaining completely passive as if he were a sack of flour."

My mother is reluctant to admit mistakes, denies her errors, and refuses to accept blame for even her most trivial missteps. (She will even reject the notion that one of her more difficult traits may be that tendency to deny fault.) To concede to herself that her son is disabled, was, in a sense, to cop to the most colossal failure possible. Her own genetic material had come up short. She would eventually insist that my father's faulty genes had been to blame—there were more crazy great uncles and schizophrenic cousins in his line than hers—but at that point, when Noah is a baby, she cannot accept the tentatively offered diagnoses of the first few pediatricians they saw. These men know they are messengers of disastrous news and so temper their diagnoses so as to minimize the despair. A diagnosis of autism at that point, in the late 1960s, was viewed as telling the parents the kid was hopeless; there were no known effective treatments. When the third pediatrician tells my parents that Noah's motor development is the classic sign of mental retardation, he goes on to caution that the intellectual gap only widens as the child matures. If Noah is now functioning at about half the level of a "normal" baby his age, then extrapolate that forward and you end up with an adult with a sub-50 IQ.

But then why is he speaking? my mother asks. Why does he talk at a typical level? Consult any Growth Chart—when it comes to language, to talking, Noah is right on schedule. And what is more important than language? Isn't that what separates us from animals? What allows for all human achievement?

My mother is stubborn, a fighter, and far less likely than my father to concede the wisdom of doctors and psychiatrists. She is a mother and she knows her sons. Observing it all, as she does, through a cultural and linguistic filter, she learns to trust faces and manner, her feelings about a person, rather than the more easily manipulated superficialities of words. She can tell, in an instant, if a doctor or teacher or psychiatrist is a phony.

It is funny. In Japan, among Japanese, she has a harder time detecting the bullshit, but in America, she has a knack for weeding out the liars. Perhaps that's why she escaped Japan when she did, as a young woman in her late twenties, in an era when very few single women, or anyone for that matter, would leave Japan.

14.

She was born in 1930 in Osaka, Japan, where her father, Yoshimatsu Kometani, owned a small factory that manufactured weaving machines. His first wife had died in labor with a stillborn daughter. In early photos, my mother, the eldest of the three children borne by his second wife, my grandmother, always has a sullen expression, beleaguered, a product, she says, of being a woman in a sexist society. She says she didn't smile for the first fourteen years of her life. Still, her family, despite its commingling of half siblings, was a prosperous conclave, my grandfather amassing a fortune in real estate, thirty houses scattered across Kobe by December 1941. World War II and life under Japan's military regime were, besides Noah, the formative experiences of my mother's life. We who have never lived through a war, and especially through being on the losing side in a total war, can never imagine being eyewitnesses to that kind of calamity. And Japan, a conformist society even during its zaniest times, was from 1930 to 1945 a rigidly patriarchal police state tolerating no deviation from the imperial fascist line. My mother still recalls her father being ordered to stop smiling by a passing military officer, who chastised him for not being serious enough during those earnest times and ordered him to bow in contrition. Like so many Japanese, the family went hungry in the last days of the war, subsisting on pine needle tempura and barley porridge. My mother still recalls walking to school amid the rubble and corpses of the previous evening's bombing raids. It has left her fervently pacifist; she remains one of Japan's foremost liberal and feminist voices. After the war, she attended the Osaka Women's University as a Japanese literature major—she had dreamed of studying art, but in postwar Japan such opportunities were limited. In her spare time, already planning to leave Japan, she studied English, stenography, and typing; she also attended a missionary Bible study class to improve her English. She worked in an Indian trading company for a few months after graduating, and then took a position as a secretary at Bank of America. At twenty-five, she moved on to an American trading company in Kobe and from there jumped to JC Penney. On the weekends and the evenings, she painted in the long upstairs veranda of her parents' house on Mount Rokkô, her heavily textured, abstract paintings gaining entry for three consecutive years into the Nika Exhibition, the annual show of one of Japan's foremost artist groups.

Yet the defining act of her life is one that seems so unlikely. My mother in her daily life can come across as hidebound and frightened. She is afraid of driving, flying, swimming, riding elevators, and even walking on the sidewalk of busy streets or climbing a stepladder. She has never learned to ride a bicycle or a horse and lived in Los Angeles for eight years before she learned to drive a car. Yet as a single Japanese woman she moved to the United States in her late twenties, in 1960, a year when she may have been one of, say, a half-dozen single Japanese women to emigrate to the States. It was an astonishing act of bravery that to this day I have trouble identifying with my paranoid, overcautious mother.

For her, she says, it was a matter of survival. In Japan, despite the relative opening up that accompanied the American occupation and postwar democracy, she still felt so constrained by the mores of Japanese society that, as she puts it, she couldn't breathe. "I couldn't stand the whole system," she now says. "If you wanted to become a great painter, I thought, you couldn't stay in Japan. I wanted to go to Paris, of course, but nobody would sponsor me. To go, you had to say you converted to Catholicism. I wouldn't sell my soul." Desperate to emigrate from Japan, she wrote, she says, "100 letters" to art academies and institutions around the world. Finally, in 1958, the Pennsylvania Academy of Fine Arts offered her a scholarship. My mother wrote back asking the school to hold her place for a few years so she could save enough money for room and board. In the meantime, she received a fellowship at the MacDowell Colony in May 1960, which she accepted, planning to go from there to the Pennsylvania Academy. In April 1960, in Yokohama, she boarded the *Yamakuni Maru*, a freighter bound for San Francisco. From there she took a train to New York and then caught a lift to the MacDowell Colony.

Her first night at the MacDowell Colony, her sponsors—during this period, because of foreign currency restrictions, Japanese émigrés were allowed to expatriate from Japan only $250, requiring a host family to financially vouch for them—John Cassidy, a buyer for JC Penney who regularly visited Japan, and his wife, pointed out my father, in his black beret and overcoat, smoking his French cigarettes, and warned her: "Look out for guys like that. Avoid him."

They married that autumn.

My mother was always a tidy presence in our house. Soap smelling, clean, well turned out. It is embarrassing that I resort to stereotypical descriptions of a Japanese, but she has always been hard to explain or categorize. Part of this is a lack of context. I was able to fix my father's points in the universe even from a young age: writer, Jewish, jocular, bohemian. He was a familiar type in postwar America—another "minor writer," Norman Mailer once called him, "a gnat weight." It wasn't until I went to Japan as an adult after college that I finally began to understand my mother. Like most voluntary emigrants, she had a toughness that was a by-product of her nonconformity. She left Japan, she relates, because she had no choice. Yet how to reconcile her cultural bravery with her physical cowardice? She still sends me newspaper clippings warning about the dangers of eating shellfish, drinking beverages containing artificial flavors, taking too many pain relievers, swimming in polluted water, or crossing busy streets. My own wife, Silka, also an emigrant, from fellow Axis power Germany, is, I suppose, similarly courageous in her willingness to walk away from her home country. But in our era, the journey from Europe to America—even if she did go, ironically, via Japan—is far less culturally arduous than the journey from Asia to America in 1960.

When I lived in Japan in the late 1980s and early '90s, I finally came to understand the enormity of what my mother had done. There were thousands of Japanese girls resigned to their lives of smothering desperation who spoke better English than my mother yet couldn't conceive of moving from Japan. Tokyo in the 1990s was, of course, a far cry from Kobe in the 1950s, the opportunities for women were vaster and more genial, but still, most Japanese women in their twenties were afraid even to travel alone, much less seek to settle in a foreign country.

I came to admire her courage and iconoclasm. And to begin to understand how she is both unique and typical of her culture.

She is short and throughout my childhood was always slight, weighing in at about one hundred pounds. She had black hair, of course, which was usually worn long and parted in the middle; later, she would grow bangs, and now, as an older woman, her hair is permed into curls and sometimes dyed in the curious shade of purple common to elderly Japanese women.

As a young mother, she is so slim she can fit into a wicker baby chair my parents purchased before leaving Yokohama so that I would have a place to sit on the boat crossing back to the United States. She is not a pretty woman; even as a boy I can discern that. If we have certain conceptions of classical Asian beauty, or an idea of the perfectly ovoid faces that to the Western mind represent Asian femininity, then my mother is slightly too coarse-featured. She has, she says, "an ordinary face." Her only distinctive feature, and she would be hard-pressed to call it distinctive, is the "lazy but graceful arc formed by each of her widely separated eyebrows."

As a boy, my standards for beauty were, of course, those gathered from advertising, media, and popular culture, and in the 1960s there were no Japanese appearing in any mass media, save, perhaps, for Yoko Ono, who had a vaguely villainous look about her. But she is patient with me, more patient and gentle than my father, who when we misbehave will sometimes spank or slap Noah and me. My mother will never hit me, and she takes the time to help me with my projects, cutting out pictures from magazines and shapes from construction paper and gluing them together. At one point, I recall, she helps me to build a house for our cat Brodsky out of cardboard. I have never seen a cat use such a structure, but she is always willing to collaborate with me on these projects.

She wears denim pantsuits or corduroy trousers. Occasionally, for special occasions, she will wear a sari-like dress she and my father purchased in India before I was born. She is steadfastly practical and frugal, a trait held over from wartime Japan. For someone who turned her back on Japan, she remains in so many ways steadfastly Japanese.

There remains in my memory a period, however brief, before the family's energy was consumed by worry about Noah, when my mother was more carefree. She still dreamed about being a painter. She had her first son and then her second. That was two more children than she had wanted, but still, eventually these boys would start school, and perhaps my mother could then return to her art. She could just begin to see, a few years away, a glimmer of hope and light. Our basement downstairs had been finished with a glass wall so that it caught the afternoon light; it is intended to be her studio.

And in that first year, Noah seems just another baby. She is already scheming, subtly, to go back to her painting. There is a lightness to her, to our whole family. My father will write; my mother will paint. What a happy little creative commune they will be!

A Japanese infancy and early childhood, I believe, must be among the happier varieties. I am indulged by my mother; Japanese parents are shameless in how they dote.

I want an apple, a wafer, a banana. My favorite food is a grilled-cheese sandwich. I am taken to Carvel for custard. We visit a sloop moored on the Hudson River. I can watch my father trimming our trees, my mother planting white flowers, my baby brother in his little crib. The backyard smells of burning leaves and wet grass, and there is a pond beyond our back property line where we can go and I try to throw rocks in the water. My father tells me I should never come here alone. In the front yard are white pebbles and a few stones arranged in a Japanese-style rock garden. My father hangs a swing from the porch, and my mother pushes me in it gently as Noah watches from the wicker baby chair.

This lasts three years, into my fourth.

15.

Then I feel a shift. A plunge. The lightness is replaced, and the family suddenly seems to move more cautiously, heavily, as if we are submerged. That is the feeling: before we were walking downstream, propelled by the current. Now we have reversed and are going against the flow.

Noah is two, and he still doesn't walk. When he does take tentative steps, holding my father's hand, he is a walking contradiction, calling out the names of every child on the street—Ian, Dana, Arno, Kirsten, Tom—and saying hi to each of them. Yet I can call his name a dozen times and he won't even turn to me.

My parents are assiduously trying to toilet train him, to exercise him, to make him go, as if he were a toy that just needed winding and priming and then some internal gears would mesh and transfer energy and he would begin marching toward development. It is a sense, my father says, that Noah is not engaged, that he is here but not with us. He finds it occasionally disturbing and struggles to discern if this is his paranoia or if this is real. "Noah remains a puzzle. He seldom sleeps; he never seems to listen to us. All of his sensitivities seem directed only toward himself," my father wrote on January 2, 1969. "This morning Noah threw his juice on the floor. But he did not cry when we chastised him. Nor did he cry when I threatened not to take him with me for a car ride this morning. He hears only what he wants to hear, communicates only what he cares to."

My father can sporadically will himself not to worry—"I just don't want to start the new year with the same old problem: worrying about the kid"—only to find my mother now concerned.

I have begun nursery school, in a church basement, which I attend wearing pull-up diapers for the first few weeks until I am toilet trained. I am finding a social life now; there are the children on our block whom I play with, and now this new cohort at school, where we play with blocks and color paint and where I am introduced to board games and playing cards and puzzles. I find puzzles extremely confusing and am frustrated by their complexity. I cannot correctly assemble any of them, and I try to avoid playing with them. This will continue well into kindergarten at the Scarborough School, where I find a puzzle with each piece shaped like a fish so it is very easy. Every day at puzzle time I quickly rush to the steel cabinet and grab this puzzle and then sit there, with a wonderful sense of mastery, putting the same one together and apart.

At the exact instant I am finding there are vast numbers of people in the world—Mark and Dana on the block, my friend Robe at school—and special days, Halloween, Christmas, my birthday!—it is easy to miss that my brother, whom I barely was coming to know, is disappearing. There was barely a year, maybe only six months, when you, Noah, were there. When you could speak and walk. (You never crawled.) We could wrestle with my father together; we could play with each other. I could lead us in little games—follow the blanket through the room. I could tickle you. I could push you around the way a big brother pushes a little one around. It was just a few months when I could take my rightful place as big brother, abusive, peremptory, imperial but also protective and instructive.

So much is happening—I am in the world for the first time—that I almost don't notice that you have gone.

16.

ATTENDING ADMISSION NOTE

JULY 16, 1969
Noah Greenfeld

This is the first examination of this three-year-old youngster who is admitted with the chief complaint of delayed acquisition of developmental milestones complicated by regression involving expressive language function.

Noah is the result of a nine-month uncomplicated pregnancy that was terminated by induction of labor and a normal delivery. The birth weight was 7 lbs., 11 oz. The immediate neonatal period was characterized by a weak suck at the breast. In addition, there was recurrent vomiting for the first month of life.

The acquisition of developmental milestones revealed a significant delay in motor milestones in that the child sat alone at 8 months, crawled at 18 months, stood alone unassisted at 2 years, 3 months, and walked unassisted also at 2 years, 3 months. Noah first began to speak with words at 8 months of age; in phrases at 18 months, and also spoke in complete sentences at 18 months of age. Shortly after he began to walk at 2 years, 3 months, he stopped speaking. In addition, for the past 8 months he has ceased to be responsive to his immediate environment.

Coordination is stated to be average for walking, running, and throwing. The child is not yet toilet trained.

Past medical history and review of symptoms revealed that Noah had mumps and chickenpox before the age of three, and the parents have noted that the urine is pink since the first year of age.

Behaviorally the youngest is stated to have a low frustration threshold, poor attention span, temper outbursts, is impulsive and underactive, and has multiple fears.

The family history is essentially negative.

Physical examination revealed a youngster who showed no true purposeful activity, and his motor function was often without direction. The child would jump up and down or on other occasions stare inappropriately at his right hand. On occasion the child babbled, but his babble was without inflection. At no time was there any evidence of true expressive language patterns.

His head circumference measured 49.8 cm., and there was no evidence of an intracranial bruit. The occiput was flattened. The gait was on a wide base with a tendency to toe outward. This gait was associated with a prominent hypotonia and associated hyperextensibility of joints. This decrease in muscle tone was present in both the upper and lower extremities. The hypotonia was associated with hyperreflexia; this was more prominent in the lower extremities. The Babinski responses were normal. There were no pathological reflexes. Sensory examination was normal to touch and pain. Cranial nerve examination and the funduscopic evaluation were benign.

IMPRESSION: Atonic diplegia—evidence to support this clinical impression is the prominent hypotonia associated with marked hyperre-

flexia and psychomotor retardation. The history of regression as evidence by loss of previously acquired speech patterns is most unusual in this condition, and the possibility of degenerative disease of the central nervous system must be ruled out.

17.

Now both my parents have to concede that Noah has regressed. They make what Clara Park describes as the "lacerating pilgrimage . . . the disruptive and expensive treks from specialist to specialist, city to city, trying to buy hope." Or what Pearl S. Buck, years earlier about her own retarded and autistic child, calls, "That long journey of which parents of such children know so well . . . Driven by conviction that there must be someone who can cure . . . we go to doctors, good and bad, to anyone, for only a wisp of hope." They begin to hear dreaded words: retarded, autistic tendencies, childhood schizophrenia. After hearing those words, my father wants to cry. As he rides a train into the city for a meeting; after he returns home. Back in our kitchen, he and my mother get into an argument about whether hereditary factors are to blame. It is now apparent to my father that Noah is a disturbed child, "a burden, withdrawing in steps; the moments of connection, of entry into the outer world, becoming less and less . . . we both rack our brains trying to figure out just when he began to stop talking."

My mother recalls how Noah bumped his head on the playroom floor and after that kept repeating, "Oh, my head!" When was that? Last summer? Were those the last words he spoke? Or maybe it was the cold weather, the literally cold world, my father says, that froze his fragile sensitivities. None of this makes sense, of course. All children konk their heads. It is cold every winter.

18.

I now start to watch my family, often from above. From our black, industrial-tiled living/dining room rises a carpeted stairway to the second floor. My room is at the end of the hall; my parents are to one side of me and Noah to the other. I can sit on these stairs, just above the living room, and watch the family as they sit at the dining table or read the newspaper in the living room. Once in a while, I fall down the stairs, sliding on my buttocks until I land on the ground floor in tears.

But I am every day becoming steadier on my feet. Noah continues to wobble, to walk erratically in his pigeon-toed, uneven steps. Now I feel confident and can sit nearly at the top of these steps and watch and observe, a little king atop his castle walls. Noah, if he is downstairs, can't yet muster the coordination to climb to join me, and my parents are too preoccupied to notice where I have perched, within earshot, my pockets stuffed with Hot Wheels. My father will come to the kitchen for coffee; my mother will sit at the table, drinking green tea, in between massaging Noah, working his legs and arms like a trainer, trying to interest him in a toy or a ball, to make him crawl on his hands and knees or run, to make him respond, to get through to him, to get some reaction, any reaction.

It is while I am sitting there, watching, listening, that I begin to feel that Noah is not like other children. This is the heaviness. My mother is no longer as light and easygoing. My father, when he tries to joke with me, it is too clear he is forcing a break from his worry and concern. I don't know this word, but any child knows it when he sees it: they are *preoccupied*. If before I was jealous of the attention they gave to Noah, now, I realize, I am not jealous. My parents had told me Noah was sick. We were sitting in our kitchen, or they were sitting there, around our dining room table, after returning from seeing one of the specialists.

"Noah is sick."

I suggested they look up what was wrong with him in *Doctor Spock*. They laughed.

No, they explained, what is wrong with Noah is nothing that they can cure, not right now. He has a brain problem; he is sick in the brain.

"Will he get better?" I ask.

My father looks at my mother, who looks away.

We hope so, my father says.

Someday, my mother adds.

I climb my stairs in retreat and, at the fourth step from the top, slide against the white wall. And suddenly they are there, my friends; there are three of them: one is balding with wiry hair like my father's, another is a boy-size cat with black and white markings like a penguin, and a third looks exactly like Noah. He is Noah, but normal, talking, playing with me. They are suddenly by my side and asking me what I want to do. The one who resembles my father—I don't know if I had ever seen the *Three Stooges*, but the trio, in sartorial style and tendency toward slapstick, resembles the comedy troupe—he seems like the leader, and he sits right next to me. The other two, Noah and the cat, sit one step down from us.

You can play with us, they tell me.

You can talk to me, this Noah tells me.

You can joke with us.

My mother comes and stands at the bottom of steps. She can hear me laughing. She smiles and returns to the table.

I don't understand where they came from, and I know they are imaginary, but they came suddenly, when I was told Noah was sick, and they now go with me everywhere.

You don't need that other Noah.

19.

"Meanwhile, last night, as I was trying to fall asleep, I heard Foumi crying," wrote my father the summer of 1969. "Why? She was crying for Karl, for the difficulties he would have with other children because he had an abnormal brother. I tried to comfort her, but I know she's right. Karl will have to be a remarkable kid to bear up under that load, and the most endearing thing about Karl is that he is so unremarkable. So typical, so average."

It is while I am sitting on those steps, listening to the steady drone of adult talk, the accusations, the conjecture, the hope, the dashed hope, I note the repetition of certain new words: oddism, ridirection, skizzofornia, and battle mind. These have to do, I know, with Noah's illness.

My friends and I, on the steps, exchange ideas about what these words might mean. Oddism (autism) and ridirection (retardation), I know, are about Noah, are his sickness. We talk about the sickness: Is it a cold, like the chicken pox, which I've had? No, we decide, because then they would be taking Noah's temperature and he would have to stay in bed. What he has, I conclude, is part of him. I don't know this word yet, but it is a *condition*, not a disease, not something that he caught but something he has.

And the cure, the remedy, it has to do with this battle mind. I like the hard, warlike sound of it: battle mind. My parents are discussing this, my mother objecting, my father insisting. Battle mind will know, battle mind will help.

We go to play outside, in the stones in the front yard. Let's gather all the stones we can, all the rocks with bits of mica embedded in the brown and gray, the sparkly rocks. These are better than the rest, more desirable. Collect them now, we agree, before they are all gathered by someone else who also recognizes their value. They are scattered in the back, in the ledge of landscaped yard, where my parents have carved into the hillside to make a little picnic area.

We pile the rocks in rectangular towers next to the sliding-glass door, in a patch next to my mother's flower pots. There are hundreds of them, each of them glistening and silvery in the afternoon light.

This is my rock collection, our rock collection.

We should move the rocks, we agree, move them away from the house. Here, they are vulnerable. My mother might find them; my father might throw them away. And Noah? We don't have to worry about him.

There is a place here, by the side of the house, next to a little window into my father's old office. My mother once planted some carrots back there and then shouted at me because I kept walking through the patch in my rain boots. Then she abandoned this side of the house, saying there wasn't enough sunlight. I can keep my rocks here, in a careful stack next to the white-painted shingles, where it smells like potato skins and leaves.

We have to keep things hidden, keep secrets, submerge information. Become like—what was it my friend Robe said he wanted to be when he grew up?—a spy. No, he wanted to be a detective, which is like a spy. But we will be like spies. It is important, we decide, to keep most of what we think to ourselves, to keep our ideas private and our plans hidden. My pockets, for example, always stuffed with Hot Wheels. That's stupid. Anyone can see that I have cars in my pockets. That's not how you fool people.

What you do is stuff the cars down the front of your pants, or maybe in your socks. See? That way nobody knows you have cars. You can ride the bus with them, take them to school, nobody will figure it out. Isn't that smarter?

My life can be lived in this family but also outside of it, out of the house, down on the block, but also in here, in these ideas and with these imaginary friends.

20.

For my parents, this period is an odyssey through the universe of literature and theories of developmentally disabled children, or idiots, retardates, the feebleminded, as they were then known. The most powerful voice in the nascent industry of childhood psychology, and especially on the mysterious subject of autism, is Bruno Bettelheim— "battle mind." His widely acclaimed and influential book, *The Empty Fortress: Infantile Autism and the Birth of the Self*, was published in 1967, just as my parents were coming to realize Noah was not developing typically. The book garnered glowing reviews and features in *Time*, *Newsweek*, the *New Yorker*, the *New Republic*, both the daily and Sunday *New York Times*, and propelled its author, the bespectacled, Holocaust survivor "Dr. B," onto guest appearances on the *Today* show and the *Dick Cavett Show*. Bettelheim was, in the late 1960s, the preeminent autism "expert" in the United States, and his claims to have studied with Dr. Freud himself in prewar Vienna made him seem that much more credible as America went through its prolonged couch trip.

My father, a fellow Jew whose sister Irma is in Freudian therapy, can't help but get caught up in the psychoanalytic zeitgeist of the times. Saul Bellow, Philip Roth, and Woody Allen are just three of the cultural giants who are using psychodynamic theories in their art as well as their lives. The very publications praising Bettelheim are those my father is writing for, so he is well aware of the glowing articles about Dr. B and his Orthogenic School in Chicago, the only institution in the country that is claiming not only to specialize in treating autistic children but to have an 80 percent success rate in "curing" them. Bettelheim is a compelling character, seeming to embody one of the twentieth century's defining historical events—the Holocaust—and one of its most powerful intellectual movements—Freudian psychoanalysis. To make him even more formidable, he roots his ideas about autism in the Holocaust itself, in his own experience of Buchenwald and Dachau. He claims that autistics, like his fellow concentration camp inmates, withdraw to avoid a "frightening world." "In response," Bettelheim writes of the autistic, "he withdraws to an inner redoubt in an effort to survive within a totally frustrating environment." His supporting evidence: "Maybe I can illustrate again from the concentration camps." To deny Bettelheim, to ignore him, is almost like denying the Holocaust. In *The Empty Fortress* he goes on to further disseminate perhaps the most damaging and intellectually corrupt idea ever to be foisted upon the parents of sick children: that they, in particular the mothers of these children, are to blame for their autism. "The precipitating factor in infantile autism is the parent's wish that his child should not exist," he wrote in *The Empty Fortress*. "Maternal feelings, indifferent, negative, or ambivalent, are then made to explain infantile autism." That Bettelheim had actually been a lumber salesman in prewar Vienna, not an academic psychiatrist who had, as he claimed, cured two autistic children, was not widely known at the time. Still, his fabrication of his résumé notwithstanding, that his ideas were not only taken seriously but given widespread airing and publication was not merely a matter of gullible critics and journalists. It was also symptomatic of an era during which the solution to every problem seemed like it could be found in a fifty-minute hour.

My father had been friends in Greenwich Village with several analysts, all of whom directed him to Bettelheim and to the famed Freudian child psychiatrist Margaret Mahler. New York at that point was so dominated by Freudian thought, by psychogenic theories of the mind, that Bettelheim loomed as a giant in the field to whom other psychiatrists referred their autistic patients, hoping they might secure entry into the legendary Orthogenic School on Chicago's Hyde Park. Bettelheim's books were built around vignettes, much like Freud's, little stories that illustrated extreme cases and then the remarkable therapies that cured them. Instead of offering clinical testing, baseline comparisons, scientific data, or control groups—or any science at all—Bettelheim told these wonderful anecdotes about "Joey the Mechanical Boy" or "Mitchel the Good" that were almost cartoonishly mythical in tone and quality before launching into his completely theoretical and fanciful riffs about the infant's fear of the mother's breast—at one point he cites research comparing the female nipple to a razor blade—and the suffocating damage done by improper breast-feeding that could result in "withdrawal" and "regression." The writing today seems almost hysterical and, knowing as we now do that he was an imposter, could be taken as a kind of parody if it hadn't caused so much heartbreak and damage. Richard Pollack's 1997 biography of Bettelheim, *The Creation of Dr. B*, is a thorough debunking of the Viennese charlatan that points out that Bettelheim, in blaming parents, who were "almost always confused and desperate . . . allowed the clinician to maintain his role as a powerful authority and to keep his sense of self-enhancement intact, though his progress with their child was uneven at best and sometimes nonexistent."

Yet Kanner himself in *Autistic Disturbances* had concluded that landmark paper with a paragraph beginning, "One other fact stands out prominently. In the whole group, there are very few really warmhearted fathers and mothers . . . The question arises whether or to what extent this fact has contributed to the condition of the children." He described the families as "highly intelligent" and mentioned that among the parents were numerous psychiatrists, a lawyer, a chemist, an advertising copywriter, and a freelance writer.

There were very few other accounts of autism for my parents to read. Clara Park's *The Siege*, about her autistic daughter, Jessy, came out the same year as *The Empty Fortress*. In *The Siege*, Parks wrote austerely and movingly about her daughter's delayed development and made careful observation of the methods she used to try to "educate"

Jessy. Parks is a clear, precise writer—in many ways the exact opposite of Bettelheim's jargon-driven psychobabble—whose account might have been immensely useful to more parents had they known about it. As it was, Bettelheim's book absorbed all the intellectual attention the mainstream world could muster for autism, leaving *The Siege* virtually ignored. My father heard about it a few years later from a friend who suggested it for its literary value rather than because of the subject matter. Clara Park, the mother of three healthy children, had the good sense to dismiss the psychogenic community seeking to blame her for her daughter's autism. "It would be hard indeed, in today's climate of opinion," she wrote, "for the parents of a seriously deviant first-born child not to feel they were in some way responsible." A look at her older children, she went on to write, would dispel them. "We were proud of them. We had done a good job with them. We knew it, and knew that others knew it. This knowledge and this pride sustained us as we read the formulations of the Bettelheims of the world—this, and a certain natural skepticism which had been with us even before Elly (Jessy) made us need it."

My mother is in some ways similar to Clara Park, ready to apply herself to whatever treatment might help Noah but totally unwilling to listen to Freudian accusations of parental guilt. The first child psychiatrists who agree to take on Noah as a patient insist that my parents be treated *before* they can treat Noah. Even the principal of a local school for the retarded and feebleminded tells my mother that before she can admit Noah, she and my father must agree to go into therapy. A Japanese mother in Westchester County in 1969 is looked upon, naturally, as what had come to be known as a "refrigerator mother." Her style of interaction, her stolidity and appearance of quiescence—English is, of course, her second language; she is far from phlegmatic in Japanese—make her seem to Western eyes a cold, distant woman, as many Japanese might seem at first meeting if you aren't familiar with the culture or language. My father, a writer, an intellectual, also fits the stereotype for parents of autistic children. Naturally, the experts wanted my parents in analysis. My mother's reaction was confusion, and then anger. "They weren't interested in Noah, they didn't want to help him," she says. "They wanted us to get therapy. What did this have to do with Noah? I would ask them, 'What can we do with Noah? How can we teach him?'" Like Park before her, she would argue that if she and my father were the problem, then why had their older son turned out apparently normal? "Just give us help," she would plead.

In part because of the popularity of Bettelheim and his predecessors, including Benjamin Spock and the psychoanalyst René Spitz, who went so far as to blame the mother's personality for colic and eczema, the widely held opinion was that parents were to blame for childhood disorders, ranging from upset stomachs to autism; therefore, in the view of these mental health professionals, heal the parent and the child would also recover. While my mother unequivocally rejected this notion, my father was willing to consider it. What other choice did they have? He wrote to Bettelheim to see if there might be a place for Noah at the Orthogenic School.

A few years before that, in 1964, Bernard Rimland, holder of a doctorate in psychology from Penn State, published *Infantile Autism*. Rimland, who worked with the U.S. Navy Personnel Research Laboratory in San Diego, and his wife, Gloria, had had an autistic son, Mark, in 1956. Rimland's book was a thorough, tightly sourced survey of the literature of autism as well as a précis on the current state of the science. He concluded that there was no scientific evidence to support the claim that bad parents were to blame for autism; he even had Leo Kanner, the psychiatrist who would always regret blaming the parents of the first autistic children he diagnosed, write the introduction. In *Infantile Autism*, Rimland used speculative data to suggest that autism was an organic disorder, going so far as to locate the dysfunction in a formation of nerve cells in the medulla and midbrain. Rimland's book was the scientific counterweight to Bettelheim's fantastic theories, yet it failed to find a readership outside of academia. Bettelheim dismissed Rimland's theory of organic brain damage by pointing out that, if that were the case, then how had he cured 80 percent of the autism cases at the Orthogenic School?

What was the treatment that Bettelheim claimed could cure autism? He advocated removing the child from the parents, who were, of course, responsible for their offspring's regression and withdrawal, and then placing the child in a home with counselors and therapists who would provide the accepting, supportive environment the child was so lacking. The child would be allowed to express his or her feelings and act without fear of reprimand or scolding; everything the child did, all his attempts to reach out and grow, even aggressive acts, tantrums, or biting, would be met with love, patience, and acceptance. "Our encouragement serves mainly to convince these children that they are neither alone nor in danger, in the struggle to find themselves," wrote Bettelheim in *The Empty Fortress*. "Even our pleasure at their contrariness—which comes easy because we are so happy that they do anything at all—has to be tempered, so that they do not feel committed to (or against) on our account." This allows for such curious breakthroughs as watching Laurie, one of his case studies, take a break from playing with blocks to gather some pellets of her own feces and "then (she) dropped them, in exactly the same way she had been manipulating the blocks. This sequence repeated many times . . . First Laurie would build something out of blocks, then take it apart, then move her bowels. Then she would take pieces of feces in her hand and drop them, take some blocks in her hand and drop them . . . We were greatly impressed." Other autistic cases would smear their feces and vomit, urinate, and defecate on counselors. All signs of progress, according to Bettelheim.

Bettelheim replied to my father that the school didn't consider autistic cases until the children were five or six. Then my father read *The Empty Fortress* and concluded that, instead of being a savior, Bettelheim was the enemy. "Bettelheim really sowed seeds of evil," my father told Richard Pollack in *The Creation of Dr. B*. "Intellectual evil is the worst kind, especially when it is self-aggrandizing. As his reputation grew and grew, I just came to hate the man, hate him. He was not the philosopher-poet-prince: to me he was a fucking fraud."

It is hard to quantify the damage Bettelheim did to a generation of autistic children. The cost to families like mine—who lost precious months and years because of a belief in a form of treatment that had no scientific evidence yet had begun to pervade the industry to the extent that parents of autistic children found themselves on the defensive whenever they sought treatment for their kids—the cost to us was precious, early time that we now know is crucial in terms of autism treatment. I have come to hate him as much as my father does, for just as the theories he espoused—again, based on little more than the demands of his own ego for gratification—may have cost my father a son, perhaps they also cost me a brother.

21.

Noah's autism is now a fact. He rocks for prolonged periods of time and repeats meaningless syllables, "m-m-m-m-m-m-m-m-m." He sits by himself on the white-carpeted floor of the living room, or on the striped sofa in the den, gazing intensely at his fingers as he twiddles string or a rubber band. He shows great interest only in his blanket, which he has so thoroughly chewed up, and which our mother has mended so often that you can no longer discern the Winnie-the-Pooh characters. He is prone to putting objects in his mouth, almost anything, so that my mother has to patrol regularly to make sure I have left behind nothing harmful. He chews the plastic wheels off my Hot Wheels, the heads off my Gorgon dolls, and the eyes out of stuffed animals. He blinks suddenly, and with great force, and then he raises his hand and holds it palm out against his forehead, like he is taking his own temperature. He smiles a great deal, but there are sudden flashes where his face takes on an awful cast, almost sinister, as if he is terrified. He suddenly squints, his pupils expand, then he blinks.

His facial muscles move in ways that I have never seen another child's face move; there is sinewy tension in his jaw, his neck, a sudden bulging beneath his ears. An instant of panic, a look as stricken as a victim in a horror movie, and then it has passed. He smiles.

Or he starts to strike himself, openhanded, forceful slaps against his forehead, as if he's trying to jog his memory with this exaggerated gesture.

He never looks at me. He doesn't answer when I call his name. He will never come to me; I go to him.

He wants to be left alone. He likes his crib, and the sofa in the den, and the floor of the living room. Now that he walks, he can move from room to room, but there seems no purpose to his journey. He will sit for hours by himself if my parents let him. Sometimes, he likes for me to tickle him. But then gradually, over an indiscernible period of time, he loses interest in that, stops giggling, and when I try to tickle him again, he turns away and rubs his blanket between his fingers. I don't know this at the time, but my relationship with Noah is the most one-sided one I will ever have. He seems to have lost any interest in me, and I still try to make him come out and play. I desperately want a brother.

22.

We attempt to assemble a normal life around this abnormal center. We were never likely to be a typical family anyway, if you consider my Japanese mother and Jewish father. But now we drift to the fringes, our lives swirling around an unsteady, immutable Noah whose affliction we don't understand and for which we can't find any treatment. The doctors, pediatricians, neurologists, psychiatrists, they have nothing to offer except blame. The prognosis for most of the autistic, as Rimland wrote, is "years in empty hopelessness at home or institutions." The machinery of a family is tooled to propel the children upward and outward, to grow them, teach them, and prepare them. The wishes of typical, caring parents, of course, remain, but they are refitted to the lives now emerging in their home. And the sacrifices small children require of their parents—the diminished freedoms, the financial compromises, the suspension of dreams of creative achievement—are somehow made to seem worthwhile because of the promise of the child, the future. We are hardwired to this cause, and most of us go with quiet grumbling to our tasks of supporting and nurturing. But what if the child is not requiting? How then is the family to define its mission? How often does a tired couple, sick of each other, spent from the arguing and the petty feuds of marriage and cohabitation, think of their beautiful children, of the small lives thrumming away in the next room, of the little breaths, the tiny wants, the soft voices, and realize that the family, the marriage must be worthwhile if it produced these lives? For our family, for my parents' marriage, that touchstone has been broken. "Somehow," my father writes, "the rhythm of our lives, the good fortune of our marriage, seems to have dissipated. It is hard for Foumi to believe in me and for me to believe in Foumi anymore.

Successful monogamy, of course, must be based on a faith in the union if nothing else. And how can we have faith in a marriage that has biologically backfired?"

Those who have healthy children, those parents who drop their kids off at regular schools every morning and soccer practices and music lessons in the afternoon, those brothers and sisters of developmentally typical siblings whose greatest source of tension is their sister's using up all the red crayon or their brother's borrowing and losing a favorite jacket, they take for granted their elite status.

I have two healthy daughters, and my wife and I socialize with the families of other typical children. I am amazed at the seamlessness of these lives, where the great worry is that Julie isn't reading as well as she should or that Esmee is a little behind in her subtraction. We revel in one another's company, and it is easy to forge happy acquaintances among the likewise fortunate. Having had Noah for a brother, and lived through the complications and intricacies of our family dynamic, I am amazed at how easy relationships and family friendships are when the children are all healthy. I don't believe our friends have thought about this but surely they have noticed there is not one autistic or retarded kid in the gang.

For me what is strange is that the rivalry between Noah and myself, the normal sibling struggle, has been ceded by me. Noah is the family's overriding concern, the axis around which we rotate. I don't recall even putting up a fight in this regard, but now at age six, I am brought into discussions about what to do with Noah, about what might be wrong with Noah. I have nothing really to add, but I believe my parents want to make sure I am included in what has become our family journey.

Noah doesn't participate in any of the family routines anymore. I am learning to set the table, to clear the table. I have been ordered to clean my room, to take my laundry to the hamper, to help my mother fold the laundry when it is clean. Noah, I already understand, will not have to learn these chores. I explain to friends when they come over that Noah is sick.

"What do you mean?" asks Ian.

"He's not normal. He's sick in the brain."

Ian thinks this over. We are in the den assembling Hot Wheels track, sliding pink plastic tongues into their receiving grooves. "If he's sick," Ian says, "then why isn't he in bed?"

"Because it's not sick like that," I say, looking for the right words. "He has a bad brain."

"Is he stupid?" Ian asks.

"No," I say, "he just has a brain problem."

Ian is a year older than me, a better athlete, more worldly. He has older brothers and a big dog. "I've never heard of that," Ian says. "Can you catch it? Does that mean you have it?"

"No," I tell him. "No, you can't catch it."

"You can," Ian says. "You *can* catch it. You'll get it. Your whole family will get it. Bad brains."

"No," I tell him. I'm crying now. "No."

Ian stands up and says that he wants to go home now.

When we are with friends on picnics or outings, Noah goes his own way, wandering away to play by himself on the grass or in a sandbox. He finds a leaf or a blade of grass to roll in his fingers, or he runs sand through his hands repeatedly. If another child tries to engage him in play, Noah will turn his back or stand up and trot away. Leaving Noah alone like this, we have found, is easier than trying to engage him. He has started to rail against being included, to hate being forced to sit down at a dining table or join in any activity. It feels wrong to leave him out like this, but the few times lately I've tried to involve Noah have ended badly, with his pulling my hair or scratching me.

He's developed a repertoire of defensive tactics, the hair pulling and scratching being his two main maneuvers. My mother cuts his fingernails almost daily so that he can't scratch us, but the hair pulling has become a major deterrent. Luckily, I have thick hair, but on more than one occasion I have had to retaliate by pulling his hair, which results in the two of us locked in a mutual hair tug, which can last until my mother or father breaks us apart.

Too often, his hair pulling and scratching are antecedents to violent temper tantrums. If he is coerced into an activity, he throws violent fits, first lying flat and stiff, then banging his head against the floor or slapping his hands against his head, howling and crying and shaking his head.

23.

We are at the Croton Reservoir, having a picnic with friends of ours, a Japanese family who live in White Plains. My father wants to wash Noah's hands before eating. Noah has spied some of the *onigiri* (rice balls) that my mother prepared and is upset at the delay as my father holds Noah's hands and attempts to rub them clean with a wet paper towel.

"Wait, Noah," my father says. "Wait, wait."

Noah is rocking back and forth, looking at the rice. He is struggling to get away from my father, to get the rice. He can't stand the delay and starts screaming, "doo-doo-doo-doo-doo-doo-DOO-DOO-DOO."

"Noah, you have to wait."

He is shouting louder now and collapses on the loose gravel of the picnic area, slapping his hands on the loose pebbles. His plaintive howling is impossible to ignore, and at the table next to us, a family seems frozen in shocked surprise.

I am sitting at the table, holding a barbecued drumstick. Around us, the other families similarly gathered at tables have gone still, the picnickers stopping midbite to gawk at my brother. They are all staring, and for a moment I feel ashamed, embarrassed at Noah; then I start to eat my chicken and I don't hear Noah anymore.

"Your brother is loud," says Mark, the boy I have been playing with.

My father has managed to stand Noah up, brush the pebbles off his clothes. Still howling, Noah breaks away and trots off across the gravel to the lawn and then out along the grass toward the dam.

He sits by himself in the dirt beneath a tree, his forearm held up against his forehead. Alone.

24.

I am not a smart boy. In school, in first grade, I struggle with reading, basic arithmetic. I have trouble following the routine of the day; first math, then reading, then science, then choice, then lunch. After lunch we work on different subjects: weather, history, the solar system. I can't follow when we shift from math to reading; I get numbers confused with letters, keep writing my letters backward. Mrs. Kelly tells my parents there is nothing to worry about, that I'll catch up, but my parents, spooked as they are by Noah's problems, now begin to wonder about me. I am the youngest in my class, having started kindergarten and then first grade early because my parents thought I would benefit from being out of the house, away from Noah.

25.

In the late afternoon the autumnal light is fading, just a last dash of orange where Old Post Road rises and then passes out of town in the direction, I know, of our house. I am with my father and my brother, and we stop at the local pharmacy and general store, in downtown Croton-on-Hudson. Dad is looking to buy typewriter ribbons. At the front of the store, before the counter where there are magazines and cigarettes, he pauses. Noah is his usual humming self, rocking from side to side and nodding steadily as my father holds his hand. He is asking the older woman behind the worn, soft wood counter for ribbons.

Suddenly, Noah reaches out and grabs a ball-ring key chain. He twiddles it in his fingers and attempts to put it in his mouth. My father urges him to return it; Noah puts up a struggle before surrendering the object.

The woman is leading them down an aisle, searching out the ribbons, and I wander down a different aisle, the candy aisle. I can hear my father in a stern voice telling Noah to put different items back on the shelf, to leave things alone. Hands down, my father is telling him. The woman is preoccupied with searching for the ribbons and distracted by my brother.

My imaginary friends are with me, and an idea has occurred to us. I don't know who proposed it, but it seems like we can just take all the candy we want. We can hide it all. Not in my pockets, remember, because everyone can see what's in your pockets. They bulge. But here, slide this caramel bar down the front of my pants. Like this.

And those fruit-flavor Charms, take those. Those lollipops. All of them, just shove them all down my pants. It is so easy. No one is watching. On our way back up the aisle, I take a few ballpoint pens, fancy ones with metal casings at the end. Hide those.

I hear my father's voice calling me, and I walk up to the front of the store carefully, so that nothing falls down my pant legs. I stand there quietly while he pays for the typewriter ribbons.

Later, in my room I suck down the caramel bar, which I don't really like but I eat it anyway. I hide the rest of my candy and the pens in my white desk drawer. It seems there is an unlimited supply of candy in the world . . . you just have to know how to get it.

26.

There must be a cure, a therapy, a program for Noah. My parents have made tentative forays into something called patterning, which involves attempting to make Noah crawl or creep for a few minutes, several times a day. The theory, developed by Glen Doman and Carl Delacato in the 1950s, holds that crawling on the stomach and creeping on hands and knees, activities that Noah never really did, are crucial stages of development. At first, normal children crawl homolaterally, moving their left arm and left leg in unison. Then, after a few weeks, the more efficient pattern of left arm and right leg emerges, the cross-pattern, which we continue to use as we walk and run, of course. The idea behind patterning is that the brain is programmed in steps, and cross-patterning is vital input that sets off a series of neurological changes, culminating in higher cognitive skills like talking and reading. "Patterning," my father says, "is not so much a belief that man cannot walk until he crawls as it is a conviction that man cannot even drawl until he crawls." Yet as treatment for autism, it is as unscientific in its way as Freudian psychoanalysis.

My mother, believing herself to be more scientifically inclined than my father, gravitates toward a novel multivitamin therapy.

Nobel laureate physicist Linus Pauling has been in the news lately, touting the biochemical effects of certain vitamins and minerals beyond their proven preventative uses with regard to certain deficiency diseases. In *Science* magazine, in 1968, he coins the term *orthomolecular medicine* to refer to the practice of concentrating certain substances in the body to treat diseases and even psychological disorders. In particular, he promotes vitamin C as a virtual panacea; and niacin, B_3, and E as potentially healing, and even possibly cures for cancer. My father visits Pauling at Stanford, ostensibly to convince him to cooperate for an article in *Life* magazine but actually to see if Pauling believes that vitamins might prove therapeutic for Noah. Pauling refuses to cooperate for the *Life* article, believing the publication to be "too mainstream" for him, but urges my parents to look into megavitamin therapy.

My father has been spending afternoons in the public library, looking up "autism." He reads Leo Kanner and Clara Park. He is looking for a procedure, a methodology on how to deal with Noah, and none of these papers or books tell him what to do. In fact, Bettelheim says don't do anything; it makes my father afraid even to chastise Noah, lest he harm his fragile psyche. Not even Rimland, he is discovering, has any idea about a treatment.

Desperate, my father finds a pediatrician in New York City willing to provide intensive doses of megavitamins. My parents set to work with mortar and pestle to pulverize the tablets of vitamin C, B_3, E, pantothenic acid, and niacinamide to spike Noah's orange juice. The doctor also promises newer, better vitamins: Deanor, an enzyme-producing catalyst, is thought to be a possible driver of brain-cell growth; and, coming soon, my parents are advised, "something that has been used with great success in the Soviet Union to help activate speech," B_{15}, which is supposed to oxygenate brain cells.

The therapy doesn't seem to make much difference, though for short stretches my parents are able to convince themselves that Noah's psychotic behaviors are tapering. He is looking up more, self-stimming—making repetitive gestures with his fingers, bobbing his head, jerking his shoulders back and forth—less. He's listening! Inevitably, this supposed improvement dissipates.

Noah has been deemed too disruptive for any of the local programs for retarded or Down syndrome children. And he is either too old or too young for any of the experimental programs, most of them psychotherapeutic, that exist in Westchester County. The Keon School, a little brick schoolhouse built into the side of a hill in Peekskill, is the only local school that can offer Noah a spot. The principal of the school, in thrall to prevailing thinking about alienation and withdrawal causing autism and childhood schizophrenia—the theories promoted by Bettelheim—insists that my parents go into therapy; otherwise, she argues, how can Noah get better?

My mother reluctantly agrees. At the session, as it becomes clear that the Freudian-oriented therapist has neither an inkling of Japanese society nor an interest in this "aspect" of my mother's personality, my mother asks him bluntly how he can help her if he doesn't understand where she is from, who she is? He dismisses such cultural differences, pointing out that our personalities are shaped by our infancies and childhoods, no matter where or in what culture they were spent. My father is still willing to listen to the psychobabble. If it is an organic deficit, he believes, then there is no hope. If it is emotional, psychological, then perhaps there is some therapy, some breakthrough that can be made. My mother is more realistic and soon refuses to continue, rejecting the Freudian approach as superficial.

That session, however, is enough to secure Noah admission to the Keon School. In the morning, I ride with my father to take Noah there. It is a sobering sight to see Noah among the retarded, autistic, and Down syndrome students. To my child's eye, it seems incongruent that among the rocking horses, the plunge spinners, the blocks, the Legos, and the Tonka trucks there should be adults who look as old as my father. Men with sagging faces, missing teeth, ill-fitting shirts. A boy, older than me, with brown hair and a narrow face walks up and hands me a small yellow truck. I shake my head. He insists. I take it and he starts jumping up and down, happily. Then he commences slapping his upper arms with his palms, his hands crossed at his chest. He squawks. I find myself strangely hopeful about the school; but then, just the fact that it looks like a school instead of, say, a hospital or doctor's office—Noah's usual destinations—is a cause for great optimism.

There are three classes, one for children, one for older kids, and another for retarded adults. It is, as my father writes, a "happy bedlam." Yet my father still has a hard time accepting that Noah belongs among such company, "those closed-eyed, sweetly vacuous heads. I almost cried." The school was founded by local working-class parents of developmentally disabled children, built by them brick by brick, because there were no other options for developmentally disabled children. The parent meetings are a series of desperate plans for bake sales, fund-raisers, book drives, anything to raise more money to pay the few teachers they have.

Yet this school is really a way station where very little actual learning goes on. The day is more a parody of a normal child's school routine, a kind of educational Groundhog Day, where every day starts with "circle time," a half hour of saying hello, waving, saying your name. Sitting down, keeping hands down.

During this Era of Despair, as the period was recently described by an autism professional, there was very little available to help desperate parents negotiate this difficult terrain. This was years before the Education of the Handicapped Act of 1975, which mandated that individuals be educated in the least possible "restrictive environment," and decades before the 1990 Individuals with Disabilities Act, which dictated that every child receive an individualized education based on specific needs. Resources were scarce; the state agencies entrusted with administering kids like Noah funneled most of their money into the vast state institution network, a sort of autistic gulag where the Noahs of the world were kept seventy to a ward. In the pre-Internet era, my parents were left with a grab bag of quirky therapies: patterning, multivitamins, chiropractors. They had to wing it, as did almost all parents of autistic children.

27.

It is in part because of this sense that we are stumbling, and because there is so little he has read that he could relate to as a parent, that my father, in 1969, agrees to write a story about autism for *Life* magazine. He tries writing about the state of the science—which is virtually nonexistent—about the various theories of autism, the social withdrawal, the extreme introversion. What he writes strikes him as dull and utterly unrevealing of the reality of life with Noah. He tells his editor, Berry Stainback, that he's having trouble with the piece, that he feels so close to the subject that the platitudes uttered by the supposed experts strike him as utterly phony and the expertise of the medical professionals to be totally self-serving. And the few previous books written by other parents of severely disturbed or autistic children don't palpitate with truth for him. "The parents didn't burn with enough anger," he would write later, "they were all too damned heroic for me." Because my father is angry about all the technology and all of the science that does not go into researching what the hell is wrong with Noah. "And as a parent of an autistic child, one is more ridiculous than heroic—like a sludging, sloshing infantry soldier in a nuclear age." When he tries to compose journalistic prose about Noah and autism, it feels tendentious.

"I can't do it," he tells Berry. "I'm too close."

Berry asks him if he has written anything about Noah.

"My diaries," my father says. "They're all about Noah."

"Let me see them," Berry says.

"My diaries? I've never shown them to anybody."

Berry urges my father to go through them and pull out the entries about Noah, about our family. The work is easy, my father finds, much easier than writing the usual magazine article filled with its quotes from experts and its simulated energy. This feels real and, even more important, honest, honest about autism at a time when so many psychiatrists, neurologists, and pediatricians seem to be covering up their ignorance. The story, published in October 1970, is a five-thousand-word, ten-page compilation of my father's diary entries, from Noah's birth in 1966 to August 1970. For the first time, the father of an autistic child has published in the mainstream media what it is like to be a parent of an autistic child. The story would generate the largest reader-letter response in the history of *Life* magazine.

The article lays out the hardships and small joys of our family, of life with Noah; the piece is moving in its simplicity: a date, a journal entry, another little tidbit in the gradual regression of Noah and the desperation to find out why. And finally, the grim truth: "What has been shocking to me is the fact that until I had a child like Noah, I automatically believed in the institutions of organized medicine, private philanthropy and public programs. Where there's an ill, I naively thought, there must be a way. Simply not so, I discovered. The school Noah has been attending, for example, does not have the operating capital to provide the mentally ill or mentally retarded child with the same full-time, one-on-one treatment therapy he so desperately needs to have even a slim chance of a future. As it turns out, the school is fundless, near bankruptcy.

"Even more heartbreaking still has been the three-year period it has taken us to pierce the organized-medicine institutionalized mental-health gauze curtain. Most doctors, if they were unable to prescribe any form of curative aid, did their best to deter us from seeking it. Freudian-oriented psychiatrists and psychologists, if ill equipped to deal with the problems of those not verbal, instead tried to inflict great feelings of guilt upon us all-too-vulnerable parents. Neurobiologists and pediatricians, if not having the foggiest notions about the effects of diet and nutrition, vitamins and enzymes and their biochemical workings, would always suggest such forms of therapy are practiced only by quacks. And county mental health boards, we discovered, who have charge of the moneys that might be spent helping children like Noah, usually tossed their skimpy funding away through existing channels that do not offer proper treatment for children like Noah.

"Last summer, though, we were able to make a series of breakthroughs regarding Noah . . . we heard of the operant conditioning program developed at UCLA by Dr. Ivar Lovaas . . ."

28.

Autism would turn out to be the defining battleground between two of the great philosophical movements of the twentieth century, fought during that Era of Despair. On the one side there was Freudian psychoanalysis, which claimed to offer solutions to mental health issues, yet ultimately, when confronted with autism, perhaps the most complex and debilitating of the mental illnesses, was ultimately proven to be useless.

Opposing the Freudians were the Skinnerians, the adherents of B. F. Skinner and his behaviorism, or in Skinner's case, radical behaviorism, which held that everything an organism does is a behavior, and can be shaped through a process called operant conditioning, a system of rewards and punishments designed to encourage good behavior and discourage bad. If the Freudians believed humans were defined from inside out, the Skinnerians looked at us from the outside in. "The things that can happen to us fall into three classes," wrote Skinner. "To some things we are indifferent. Other things we like—we want them to happen, and we take steps to make them happen again. Still other things we don't like—we don't want them to happen and we take steps to get rid of them or keep them from happening . . . if it's in our power to create any of the situation which a person likes or to remove any situation he doesn't like, we can control his behavior." Skinner stressed that all human beings could be conditioned to behave either in the interests of the greater good or for evil, merely by tweaking the system of what he called "reinforcements." In *Walden Two*, his utopian novel that extolled the virtues of behaviorism, he explained how children raised in this environment could be freed from greed, jealousy, and envy. Children were closely supervised and "engineered" during their early years, with that strict control gradually reduced so that by the time they were adults, they would be selfless, productive members of society, freed from so many of the negative attributes fostered by a capitalist society.

Skinner was born in Susquehanna County, Pennsylvania, to an attorney father and housewife mother. He attended Hamilton College and then received a Ph.D. in psychology from Harvard. His most influential innovation, the concept of operant conditioning, was initially applied to animals—cats, rats, pigeons—before Skinner concluded that there were possible applications for human beings as well.

It was not until the 1960s that the idea that behaviorist methods, through the teaching of what became known as "discrete trials," could be used to educate those who were struggling developmentally. The notion was a radical one, and initially dismissed by many, in particular the Freudians, as inhumane. Skinner's ideas would be applied to autistics by Charles B. Ferster at the Indiana University

Medical Center, where he would set up what he called an "automatically controlled environment" that would, in effect, "teach" autistic children to perform simple tasks, pressing a key, for example, in exchange for a reinforcer: "food, candy and trinkets." The process was easy to criticize, and the Freudians quickly accused the behaviorists of reducing human beings to robotic behavior. And many of the "automatically controlled" machines—vending machines, phonographs, a mechanical pigeon—each operated by either a coin slot or key press, had virtually no practical application or teaching objective. But Ferster's 1961 study made a crucial point using rigorously scientific methodology: autistic children's behavior "could be brought under control" through "reinforcement." It was a small victory—Ferster, using a tiny sample group, had made autistic children press a button.

Yet the application of behaviorism would form the bedrock of autism treatment. "The behavior of severely disturbed autistic children was brought under the control of an arbitrary environment by techniques of operant reinforcement," wrote Ferster and Marian DeMeyer in 1962. "It was possible to sustain substantial amounts of behavior, as well as to widen aspects of the children's behavior." What Ferster had found was an opening—"It was possible"—where before there seemed to be no possibility, no hope.

A Norwegian psychiatrist at UCLA named Ole Ivar Lovaas was to seize upon these ideas in his effort to "condition" the autistic through these "discrete trials." Why couldn't the autistic child be made to perform practical behaviors, to stop performing antisocial behaviors, or to speak, for that matter, through the same method of "operant conditioning"? Simple actions were broken down into component parts, "discrete" acts, and then the subject was urged to do these simplest of behaviors, to sit down, to sit still, to look at the therapist. For autistic children even these basics needed to be taught. If the child successfully sat down, he would be given a "reinforcer," a reward, a bit of a cookie, an M&M, a Frito. If the child continued to ignore the command, he might receive an "aversive," a scolding, a reprimand, a slap, or, most controversially, an electric shock.

Ivar Lovaas was the perfect foil to Bettelheim. Pragmatic, stolid, and Scandinavian, the holder of a Ph.D. in clinical psychology from the University of Washington, Lovaas would be scientific where Bettelheim was literary. He would demand—and offer—data instead of anecdotes, reinforcers instead of miracles, operant conditioning instead of talk therapy. Other experts had dismissed the Freudian psychopathology of autism as bunk, yet none had yet been able to offer a competing approach that seemed promising. Even Bernard Rimland, in *Infantile Autism*, could provide no substitute for the condemned Freudian approach. It was hard for parents to completely reject the Freudians as long as they were the only etiology and therapy in town. Now, here came Lovaas, ripping the Freudians, saying their nomenclature of diagnosis and pathology was "not derived from empirical analyses yielding functional relations, but rather from descriptions of patients and their environments. It was organized via analogies with other disciplines and according to the social ethics of the writer . . . During extensive research, there are not studies that pinpoint the etiology of this condition or *indicate its successful treatment*." In other words, in the twenty-odd years since autism was identified as a condition, the psychiatric establishment had not found a cause or a cure. It was time for something new. "Operant conditioning" was an actual treatment. Enough talk.

My father would hear about Lovaas through a close friend of his, the theater and movie director Daniel Petrie Sr., who had met Lovaas while shooting a TV episode of *Marcus Welby, M.D.*, that dealt with mentally disabled children. After visiting Lovaas's treatment center and watching the program there—the children so similar to Noah in their obsessiveness and stereotypy, their distance—Petrie suggested to my father that he seek out Lovaas.

A few years earlier, *Life* magazine had published a story about Lovaas's UCLA program, "Screams, Slaps and Love," written by Don Moser. My father, a regular contributor to *Life*, had missed the story when it was published because he did not then believe that Noah was autistic, but the piece had generated a huge reader response, as desperate parents wrote *Life* to see how to reach Lovaas. The article included harrowing photographs of autistic children being treated by a new therapy that alternated "methods of shocking roughness with persistent and loving attention." The thirty-eight-year-old UCLA professor Lovaas was shown in the photographs, stern faced with veiny forehead, administering electric shocks to Pamela, a girl described as having "hit a blank wall" in her treatment. During reading therapy, when Pamela would lapse into a screaming fit, Lovaas would administer an electric shock as a "last resort," teaching Pamela "new respect for the word 'no.'" The story provided Freudians and Bettelheim himself with evidence to label the behaviorist movement as inhuman. Yet for those reading closely, including Rimland, that story, once you cut through the cruel images, actually represented a possibility. Through *Life*'s reader-mail department, he was able to get in touch with hundreds of other autistic parents and use them to seed the first mailing list for his nascent National Society for Autistic Children.

For parents of the profoundly autistic, this story was the first sign of hope.

Lovaas's burgeoning reputation was enough to spur my family to take a trip to California in 1970, my father on assignment for *Life* to write a story about director Paul Mazursky, a longtime friend and future collaborator. I am terribly excited about this trip, looking forward, especially, to seeing a cactus, which I have never seen before but which has become, for some reason, a fascination of mine. We stay at the Beverly Hills Hotel, in a suite with a kitchen, so that Noah can be fed, and during the day my father goes out to see Mazursky, while my mother, Noah, and I lounge around the hotel. I am allowed to choose a toy from the hotel gift shop, a wind-up metal robot with blue legs. The real purpose of the voyage, of course, is to visit Lovaas at UCLA's Franz Hall, a futuristic eight-story building of tan rectangles overlooking a round fountain that drains in clockwise swirls down a wide hole, like a toilet flushing. Inside the building, on the eighth floor, we walk down squeaky linoleum, past the bulletin boards on which have been tacked flyers asking for volunteers for various psychological and psychiatric studies along with the sorts of notes one would expect at a university: lost cat, roommate wanted, furniture for sale. What is so seductive about this environment—the grad students in their white coats, the teams of psychologists poring over data, the one-way windows into the therapy rooms—is that this venue looks like a laboratory rather than another shrink's office. This is science, the atmosphere seems to say—a prestigious university campus no less—not the wordy hocus-pocus of Freudian psychotherapy. My mother, in particular, has been looking for this type of setting, for therapists and specialists who want to work with Noah, with the children, instead of analyzing the parents.

We watch through one-way glass as a therapist, a young, eager, blond male graduate student, treats an autistic, prompting him—"Where is the truck?" "What is the truck next to?" "Hand me the truck?"—and rewarding him with reinforcers. So that I will sit quietly, my father buys me Life Savers from a vending machine in a little conference room near the therapy room—a little real-life operant conditioning right here. It is strange viewing this through the glass, watching a boy like Noah, though higher functioning, more responsive, dutifully going through the assigned tasks with the therapist. I can't really think of more boring entertainment, but I have my Life Savers, so I suck and I watch, and even I can see that this boy, through the prompts, the trials, the reinforcers, is learning, responding, making progress. My parents look at each other, giving little nods, as if to say, This is real. For the first time, they are seeing real treatment of autistic children.

The parents of another child who they say was much like Noah tell us that operant conditioning has helped their son immensely, to the point where he is now functioning in the real world. That this entire floor of a major university's psych program is devoted to treating autistics, and the fact that there is not a hint of blame cast at the parents, makes UCLA seem like the future of autism treatment while New York and the East Coast appear mired in the Freudian past.

Lovaas is a captivating figure, with long, dirty-blond hair; large, blue eyes; and a thick beard. He has a slight accent which I don't recognize, and a booming but comforting voice. He is full of enthusiasm and quick pronouncements, utterly confident, and, even more impressive, totally at ease with Noah. Most therapists and doctors are easily deterred by Noah's unresponsiveness; Lovaas quickly hugs him and rubs his head, urging Noah to look at him, look at him. He is taking Noah's measure, of course, assessing a potential patient, but his style and interaction indicate that he is more than an ivory tower academician. He can mix it up with the kids. Yet his great appeal is his insistence on using scientific methods to measure the progress or failure of his techniques. He is working toward a method, he explains, trying to see through trial and error, through control groups and subject groups, and through careful notation of response times and frequency of prompting and reinforcement, what has succeeded and what has not worked. He has drawn young acolytes, obsessed with the then-novel psychology of behaviorism. Many of these will go on to become renowned themselves in the special-education field.

For the first time, my parents receive simple, useful instructions. From Bob Koegel, the young, eager, blond graduate student and operant conditioning therapist who will go on to found the Koegel Autism Research & Training Center at the University of Santa Barbara and help pioneer the pivotal response treatment (PRT) method of behavioral modification, they are told to urge Noah to pay attention by using simple commands—"sit down," "look at me"—and to reward him with a cookie or potato chip. He explains it as part of a system, the behavioral approach that has already proven successful with a dozen children. Lovaas explains that there is hope for Noah; he says they have worked with profoundly autistic children who are similarly low functioning. In his modern laboratory, with his techno-jargon—"fading the prompt" for withdrawing a cue, "extinguishing behavior" for putting a stop to inappropriate conduct, "primary reinforcer" for social rewards like hugging, kissing, and praise, and "secondary reinforcer" for a reward of food or juice—and his carefully tracked logs of prompts, cues, reinforcers, and performance, his scientific mission is making these children function normally and possibly even speak. Lovaas has no patience for Freudian theories of autism. His goal, he tells my parents, is to fix kids, not analyze them. Several times he is threatened with lawsuits by school districts and state agencies for taking kids out of analysis. "They think we are treating the children like Pavlovian dogs," he tells my parents. (This was precisely Bettelheim's criticism of Lovaas. Bettelheim would also claim that operant conditioning elicited the response "the experimenter wants," rather than genuine speech or purposeful behavior. "Secondly," Bettelheim writes, "it satisfies a desire to punish these recalcitrant objects: because to view them as persons would preclude any use of such procedures.") Lovaas made his greatest statement vis-à-vis Bettelheim by incorporating parents into his treatment. They were considered crucial in providing additional hours of operant conditioning at home. This was in stark contrast to Bettelheim, who, after blaming the parents, refused to let them see their children for months, and even years, once they were admitted to the Orthogenic School.

Lovaas was one of a few mavericks who, in the late 1960s and early '70s, was starting to take on the established psychotherapeutic community. Autism was then emerging as a specific field of psychiatric study, drawing to it a generation of specialists who were much more pragmatic in their approach. A new academic publication, the *Journal of Autism and Childhood Schizophrenia*, edited by Leo Kanner, appeared in January 1971, offering the first attempts to gather and disseminate scientific and behavioral approaches to autism. Among the contributors to the first issue was Eric Schopler, the psychologist and German Jewish refugee who had begun in 1966 to coordinate a network of schools and programs in North Carolina for the autistic, based on the idea that autism is an irreversible, organic disorder. He, too, disavowed the idea of blaming the parents and, in fact, also brought parents in as collaborators and leaders in the treatment of their children. Schopler's comprehensive, community-based system, known as the program for the Treatment and Education of Autistic and Related Communication-Handicapped Children (TEACCH), was centered on Schopler's earlier research suggesting that autism was based in part on difficulties with cognitive and auditory processing. He used parents, special-education teachers, speech therapists, and social workers to form a highly structured environment dedicated to creating an individualized, goal-oriented treatment program for the child. In this, TEACCH and Lovaas's Discrete Trial program have some similarities, in that each component of a task or activity is broken down to its constituent parts. Central to the TEACCH method was that the child's program be consistent from home to school to day care and back home again and that all caregivers and instructors be versed in the same methods. By 1971 the program was in place at the University of North Carolina and within a decade would involve almost all of the state's child and family services and almost every autistic child in North Carolina.

Lovaas and Schopler, despite sharing so many methods, would remain rivals throughout their careers, primarily, according to a few of Lovaas's colleagues at UCLA, because Lovaas dismissed Schopler's method as lacking any scientific proof of its efficacy. "Where's the data?" he would complain whenever Schopler published a paper on autism.

As Noah turns four, the autism community is transforming, shedding its sense of victimhood that had come from believing the medical establishment's own inflated idea of itself. South of Los Angeles, Bernard Rimland and his wife, Gloria, are running the Autism Society of America and the Autism Research Institute from their home. My family and I drive to San Diego to visit the Rimlands and their son Mark, who had gone through operant conditioning. He sits stiffly on the sofa in their den while Noah rocks back and forth on the floor in front of him. Mark is fifteen, and I have never before seen an autistic person that tall. He seems an awkward giant, quiet, clueless, vaguely dangerous, but well behaved. Mark was in diapers until he was six and couldn't speak until he was eight. Gloria and Bernie well know the hysteria and panic that having an autistic child can engender. They explain that the turning point was when they heard of operant conditioning, of Lovaas, and began to apply those behaviorist principles to Mark. But Bernie is catholic in his autism treatments. He swears by Lovaas, but also says there is great promise in multivitamin therapy. "You go with whatever works, Josh," he says to my father, "you go with whatever works." He leads us over to his pantry, where he swings open the door. "Here it is," he says.

"What?"

"The Autism Research Institute."

It is a collection of files in a closet.

Meanwhile, Noah takes a shit on their floor.

29.

We return from California with a sense of possibility. Lovaas, my parents have come to believe, represents the future of autism treatment, the great Norwegian hope.

In California, my parents now feel, Noah will have a better chance to thrive. There are practical reasons to consider the move: in the winter, keeping Noah warmly dressed is a task even more difficult than convincing a normal child to appropriately dress. Like so many American families, we look west for hope and possibly, my parents are now imagining, a new beginning. "It will be bad for Karl to be so dislocated," my father writes, "it will be good for Noah . . . I feel I must make a different choice about what is best for either child. It is a choice I do not want to make. Because either way Noah or Karl comes out a loser."

In December 1970, I take leave of my fellow first-graders at Croton Elementary School, promising to return in six months. Yellow and brown cupcakes are passed around as the teacher explains that I am leaving for Los Angeles. Initially, when the cupcakes are handed out, I am happily surprised for a moment that they have to do with me, that my parents thought to deliver them. Even six-year-olds are surprisingly sentimental when it comes to partings, so my classmates spend the morning recess trying to include me in every game and activity, and in class, as we eat our cupcakes, everyone wants to talk to me. I feel special, the impending drama of my departure seeming to lend import to these last moments together.

My father collects me from school before lunch, and I change into my gray-and-white-striped denim pantsuit—I think it makes me look like a cowboy. Watching from the sliding-glass window to the porch, I am the first to see a long, black limousine pull up our driveway and idle, the driver swinging open the door. I am proud to be riding in such a car to the airport, and I collect my red, white, and blue paisley suitcase, which I have packed with baseball and football cards, stolen candy, and a few trucks. My parents told me I could bring only this one suitcase of toys, but promised that I could put whatever I wanted in it provided I could carry it myself. They also vowed to buy me a new toy in Los Angeles. Noah is dressed in corduroy pants, a sweatshirt, and a light jacket. We don't need our winter coats, my mother told me; we will just run to the car, down the wooden steps and then down the stone stairwell to the driveway. First my father and the driver will load the trunk with the odd assortment of suitcases; Brodsky, our cat, in his wooden box, will travel with us in the car. Then we will all follow and pile into the limousine. I get to sit in the rumble seat, the fold-up seat just behind the driver. Noah sits with my parents in the back. Brodsky is on the floor beside me.

I have been in first grade only a few months and have made just a few friends in the class. Leaving them doesn't seem a terrible trial, not as exciting as the prospect of another airplane flight, the numerous gifts flight attendants bestow upon me when we fly, the new toy I am pledged, and, though I don't understand this idea, I can feel it: the sense that for the first time in a long time, we might change our luck.

My parents struggle through the airport, my mother rushing my brother and me into the terminal as my father hunches, his narrow frame surrounded by our tartan suitcases, vinyl garment bags, and baby-blue valises. This is before the era of wheeled luggage, and both my parents grapple with twice as many bags as they have hands as they keep calling for Noah and me to keep up, and I, in turn, take the responsibility of herding Noah along. I am entrusted with a bag of Fritos to coax him through the airport and onto the plane. The cabin is dark and spacious—my father has traded in a first-class ticket for our coach seats—and my brother, as if caught up in the adventure we have embarked on, behaves admirably the whole flight, steadily satiated with Fritos and cookies, screaming only when we begin our descent into Los Angeles.

We move into a five-story apartment-hotel in Westwood, near the UCLA campus, where Noah will begin the Lovaas program in earnest. My father borrows Paul Mazursky's white Mercedes for the winter; the director is shooting a movie back east. My father walks Noah and me down to the Caravel, a motel on Wilshire Boulevard near us, across the busy street from Ship's Diner. Off to the side of the Caravel lobby is a newsstand and candy store, where a lady with curly gray hair and thick, silver-frame glasses on a chain smiles at us as my father buys a paper and some peanuts. She keeps her eyes on us the whole time, I notice, so it is impossible for me to steal. Maybe things will really be different in L.A.

30.

My father drives us around our new city, down the wide avenues, the tree-lined streets. Los Angeles in the early 1970s, before the onslaught of the really bad traffic and the truly horrendous air, seemed slightly too large for its population, the clear blue sky feeling higher somehow than the gray, low-slung clouds we were used to back east. Even Wilshire Boulevard seems too wide for the cars streaming up and down it, on their way from Beverly Hills to the beach. And the weather, it is not as warm as we had imagined, but still, I relish in not wearing a jacket during the day. The cool evenings, however, require warmer clothes than we packed, so we drive to a department store, where my parents buy Noah and me matching new jackets, black vinyl windbreakers that we both immediately take to wearing everywhere. Department stores—Bullock's, May Company, Robinsons—become in my mind synonymous with California, expansive, broad-aisled, many-floored, with candy counters downstairs where we always buy bags of warm peanuts. Back in New York we never shopped in department stores, but here we stop in several times during our first few days to lay in the various housewares and linens we will need.

Noah is always in a good mood in these shops, ebullient, giggling, trotting with his blissed-out grin a few paces ahead and then circling around for more peanuts. In these vast consumer paradises, with their different floors for men, women, boys, girls, housewares, kitchenwares, jewelry, and home electronics, we vanish in the same aspiration and capitalist longing of every other family, and we seem no different, dwarfed by the merchandise, the color palettes, the choices. We are just one of many who look at all the possibilities and think, Wouldn't it be nice. There are also the escalators, which for some reason frighten me more than they do Noah. My father can pull Noah onto an escalator while I instead scramble up the stairs. The conveyer belt of metal-toothed risers that make up an escalator terrify me, the emergence of row after row of sharp, gleaming, metal stairs rising ever steadily upward only to vanish again beneath the grilled exit panel—I can't stop imagining my skin sucked from my body into the mechanized guts of this mechanical staircase. I don't know what's under there, but I can imagine the hides of similarly unlucky children, hung up and bleeding.

But Noah, with some prodding, leaps on and rides up.

It may be the one developmental area—escalator riding—where Noah is ahead of me. I am aware that this pleases me, that there is one thing Noah can do that I can't.

31.

Before I start school we take Noah to UCLA so that he can be videotaped. Lovaas wants to establish what he calls a baseline of Noah's usual pattern of behavioral responses—or lack of responses—to outside stimuli. The videotape is also intended to serve as a "before" to be contrasted with a dramatic "after."

We sit behind the two-way glass mirror and watch as he is left alone in the room for a few minutes. Noah does his usual babbling, rocking, and tiptoed jumping around. Then a student enters the room and sits there silently, making no effort to interact. Noah barely notices him. Then the student begins to try to interest Noah in certain toys: a red car, a stuffed animal, a Slinky. I am not surprised that Noah doesn't respond.

I have my Life Savers as I sit watching this videotaping, and again I feel terribly bored. Noah is just being Noah. What did they expect?

Lovaas patiently explains to my father that an autistic child who undergoes behavior modification is unlikely to end up as a normal functioning child, but that this is the first step of a ten-step ladder. The goals, he says, are to suppress Noah's self-stimulation—his senselessly repetitive motor acts, which block out perceptions of the outside world and therefore impede learning; to teach him some elementary language; to make him generally easier to live with at home by making his conduct minimally more socially acceptable.

He also reminds my father that, in addition to the rewards—the reinforcers of potato chips or candy—the treatment might call for the use of averse stimuli such as spanking, slapping, food deprivation, or electric shock. My father reluctantly signs a release.

Lovaas explains his view of the difference between behavior modification and psychogenic therapy. "Behavior therapy proceeds independent of etiology. A treatment based on etiology has to rest on very shaky grounds since we do not know exactly why these children become as they are. So in the absence of such information it seems pointless to implicate parents and make them feel guilty which is at the basis of the psychogenic approach."

My father then cracks a weak joke: "Every time somebody strikes Noah, I'm going to feel like a guilty parent."

Lovaas looks my father in the eye: "Nobody is going to bat your kid around. Don't worry about it." Then he bends over, picks up Noah, who has been prancing around his office, and begins to jiggle him playfully on his knee and laugh affectionately, burying his blond Norwegian head in Noah's giggling face.

My father and Lovaas become friends, going to dinner together and even driving off in Lovaas's Porsche to watch a closed-circuit telecast of the second Muhammad Ali–Joe Frazier fight, Ali's failed attempt, according to Lovaas, to "condition" Frazier.

32.

Just a few blocks from our hotel, Fairburn Avenue Elementary School is a white adobe building to which have been added numerous tan bungalows connected by covered walkways. We eat lunch outdoors, beneath a flat concrete roof and seated at plastic picnic tables with benches attached to them by round, steel bars. There is a peculiar smell to California school cafeterias, and it is different from anything I remember from New York; it is a slightly sour, fermented odor, like a bowl of fruit sitting in the sun. It is repellent the first time I encounter it—I am at an age where I'm particularly sensitive to smells. In fact, if I meet someone and the wrong smell is in the air, even if it doesn't emanate from him or her, I will forever associate it with that person. So it is that my first experience with Fairburn is this peculiar, fermented-fruit smell.

The second day of school, I find myself desperate to move my bowels and, on my way to recess, enter a bathroom stall, the only one with a door. I pull my pants down and sit on the toilet seat, already in the heightened state of alert that accompanies moving my bowels anywhere other than in the security of my own home, when I hear giggling coming from above me and look up to see several older boys who have managed to climb onto the toilets of the neighboring stalls so that they could look down at me. It doesn't occur to me to point out to them how bizarre their behavior is and instead feel acutely ashamed as they make fun of me.

"The new kid is shitting," they say.

"Now he's crying," they say.

Mrs. Collins, the gray-haired teacher who presides over my first-grade class, goes out of her way to make me feel welcome, and she seems to like me more than my first-grade teacher in New York did. Whereas my problem in New York seemed that I wasn't reading as well as everyone in my class, here I am fitting right in. Either I had made a great leap forward or California expects a little less of its first-graders. The sense that I am not expected to do more than I can is a great relief.

My family's life now seems to revolve almost completely around Noah. My father is writing a book about our family, launched by the success of his story about Noah in *Life*. He writes almost exclusively for *Life* nowadays, writing pieces on comedian Flip Wilson, Paul Mazursky, *Hair* producer Michael Butler, and New York mayor John Lindsay. He is also beginning his drift into writing for movies and television shows. His aborted career as a playwright makes the move an easier sidestep than it is for most writers; he soon begins work on a script with his friend Mazursky.

He is a forty-something writer, too old to be a young sensation and too politically deftless to parlay his stature as a book reviewer or magazine writer into a higher-profile literary career. Yet my father has achieved too much to succumb to the bitterness that infects so many disappointed writers. He is lucky enough or talented enough to make a living from writing and, despite his hard luck in terms of Noah's disability, remains strangely sanguine about life. From Noah, he learns to appreciate the small happinesses and to persevere in one-day-at-a-time fashion. He accepts some heartbreaking conclusions about Noah, realizing, for example, that Noah forces him, the would-be artist, to devote himself to commerce. "If one has a child like Noah, one needs money. In order to get enough money, one must have the time and the energy to work. But a child like Noah drains away one's energy, takes away one's time. There is simply no way out."

And then he adds, perhaps the harshest thing I have ever heard a father say about his son: "Sometimes I hope Noah gets sick and dies painlessly."

Later, I would read numerous books by parents of autistic children, searching in vain for a familiar feeling or emotion. And at certain points, I would find myself wondering if perhaps the author's tax returns would explain more about their lives than their prose. For just as autism was for decades mistaken to be an affliction of the socioeconomically privileged—Leo Kanner often commented on the professional success of the first cohorts' parents—books by the parents of autistic children tend to be written by those with the financial means to gloss over the monetary hardships of raising a developmentally disabled child, especially in that period before the Individuals with Disabilities Act and the Education of the Handicapped Act, which gave parents the legal clout to sue their local public school systems to provide one-on-one support so their child could be "mainstreamed," that is, attend normal classes in a typical school environment for at least some portion of the school day. In an exception to the rule, Roy

Richard Grinker, in his book *Unstrange Minds: Remapping the World of Autism*, writes a compelling story of securing for his autistic daughter Isabel adequate support for her to join a "normal" first-grade class. In a moving scene, he describes the confrontation with a room full of unsympathetic educational-system bureaucrats whose goal seems to be to deny Isabel the funding required for additional aide support. Ultimately, Grinker and family win their case, though he points out that he wonders if another child whose parents didn't have the means to mount a strong case would have won a place. Pearl S. Buck, in *The Child Who Never Grew*, goes out of her way to mention how lucky she is to have the means to afford lifetime placement for her retarded daughter Carol at the Training School at Vineland, New Jersey. Other books, including *The Siege* and Temple Grandin's own memoir of autism, *Emergence*, seem to gloss over the subject, as if the subject of autism was somehow too purely tragic to sully with talk about money. Even more extreme in its shunning of the subject is *Let Me Hear Your Voice*, the mid-1990s story of a very high-functioning autistic girl and boy who are "cured" after a few months of behavior modification. The book was pseudonymously written by Catherine Maurice, the wife of an investment banker who has the funds to hire behavioral and speech therapists to work with her daughter and son in East Hampton and at their Upper East Side apartment. (The book caused controversy when other parents of autistic children claimed that Maurice's high-functioning children were not really autistic, a claim she vehemently denies. Nonetheless, the book reads like autism porn for parents of low-functioning autistics.)

When Noah was school age, the notion that the school system might pay for intensive therapy or that he could be supported in a mainstream school was still decades away. Almost every service Noah received during those early years was paid for by my family, which was surviving on a freelance writer's modest income. The cost of switching coasts is just one of a dozen, including expensive multivitamins, chiropractors, speech therapists, tutors, and the T-shirts that Noah chews up steadily. And then there are all the hidden costs: my father can't really travel for magazine assignments because it is too hard for my mother to care for Noah by herself for extended periods; any hope my mother has to rejoin her career is lost in the steady drone of Noah-related tasks.

Yet Noah is emerging as a subject matter for my father's work, and when my mother can return to work, she will become a writer with Noah as one of her subjects. (And here I am writing my own book about Noah.) Noah becomes the main ingredient in the products of our family cottage industry.

33.

Noah gives purpose to our family, eliminates choices, forces us down narrow paths. Noah is a dream killer, reducing our family's idea of a better life to one banal state: normality.

More and more, we are becoming a unit dedicated to his care and treatment. This mission change is creeping rather than sudden. First Noah sucks up all my parents' concern, then their worry, then mind share, and finally energy as his needs so overwhelm the rest of our desires and wishes. We become steadily more fine-tuned as a support group for Noah, and our family contorts ever more to accommodate him. I often now wonder if I was aware of this shift, if I knew that our coming to California was almost entirely based on a belief that it was better for Noah, that our choice of home, furniture, clothing, was all based on Noah. I wasn't allowed HO scale army men, my mother told me, because Noah might eat them.

But am I accepting of this? I know only that I feel there is a persistent issue, like a high-pitched ringing, that I have become so accustomed to that I don't feel it anymore. I am swept up in the same hope as my parents that through this UCLA program and his new nursery school, he will improve. My parents, of course, are realists, hoping for what Lovaas called "conduct more acceptable on a minimal social level." Yet I have watched the therapy sessions, have seen the laboratory-like setting, and I am convinced that soon Noah will be cured. Otherwise, why else would we be here? The impending cure seems like a fair trade for moving to California. I will soon have a brother, a younger brother. I think we will share a room, I tell my parents. Won't that be fun?

"When Noah is trained," I ask my father when I have a fever and we are lying down in bed together, "will he be able to play with me?"

Noah, I have to admit, does not seem noticeably changed through the first few months of his therapy. We have moved to a house just a few blocks from the residential hotel, in Westwood, actually just the first floor of a stucco house that has been divided into two units. I am delighted that I can walk to school from here; my parents are pleased to be so close to UCLA. Noah seems indifferent to the new locale.

Graduate students and Psychology Department students regularly visit our home to work with Noah. He begins to represent, as one student told us, "five credits" to each of the undergrads. The students sit behind a wooden table, their halved Frito chips arranged in front of them. "Noah, look at me," says one of them, a grad student named Laura. "Look at me."

He does so and gets a Frito.

Again, "Look at me."

Another Frito.

"Clap your hands." She claps.

"Clap your hands." She claps.

Noah is looking away. Rocking back and forth, he begins to gleefully self-stim with his fingers.

"Noah. NOAH."

He focuses again.

"Clap your hands."

He has lost interest, withdrawn again into himself.

"Noah. NOAH. LOOK AT ME."

He looks.

"Good boy." She rubs his head and gives him a big smile. "Good boy."

It is slow going, even for Laura Schreibman, a protégé of Lovaas's who will go on to direct the Autism Research Program at the University of California at San Diego and author numerous papers and books about autism, including *The Science and Fiction of Autism.* A short-haired, blond woman, she is wiry and energetic and pretty. I can tell she is a little impatient with Noah, not entirely comfortable with him, but she is trained and sure of her technique. Such supreme confidence in their approach is a common trait among Lovaas's therapists. Lovaas tells his students, "We own the truth." They are true believers, and their conviction can be infectious. Teams of them are sent to our home to train my parents in operant conditioning, and my parents are eager to imitate the Lovaas method.

But my parents both struggle with the idea of aversives, the negative reinforcers that are a part of Lovaas's Discrete Trial program. The electric floor described in the *Life* article is no longer used by the Lovaas team, having given way to the so-called "shock stick," a cattle-prodlike device, which is still considered an appropriate aversive. Initially, Lovaas used the shock sticks on autistic children as young as five years old who exhibited no response to more traditional treatment. In several papers in the 1960s, he wrote about the efficacy of electric shock, drawing such stark conclusions as, "The studies show that it was possible to modify their behaviors by the use of electric shock. They learned to approach adults to avoid shock. Shock was effective in eliminating pathological behaviors, such as self-stimulation and tantrums. Affectionate and other social behaviors toward adults increased after adults had been associated with shock reduction." It is chilling to read those words today, and the studies described—"Three of the sessions are referred to as shock-relevant sessions"—make the studies seem barbaric. These are five-year-old children, after all, being subjected to painful electrical shock three times a day. Imagine watching your own child going through such a therapy. And how could any behavior that resulted from such therapy be viewed as anything but pain avoidance?

"The electric shock to a young child, the idea of doing something like that horrified me," says Bob Koegel, once a Lovaas student. "But Ivar was figuring this out as he went along. He felt he needed every tool that the behaviorists had, and those kinds of hard aversives were among them."

Laura Schreibman agrees. "People say it was like training a dog. And you know, I don't hold it against Lovaas. When I was starting out in the field, that's how it was done, and it didn't bother me. There were instances when I think it was used correctly. The contingent electric shock, I always thought I could never do that until I saw this little girl pounding her head into the tile wall of a shower. Well, she stopped." Schreibman would write several papers defending "contingent electric shock," one as late as 1976, in which she concluded, "The majority of reported side effects of electric shock were of a positive nature."

By the time Noah has entered the Lovaas program, contingent electric shock is used primarily on those children who are violently self-destructive. Laura relates a story to my parents about an autistic child who is so self-mutilating that he has chewed off his own fingers. For children who have been in physical restraints because of their self-destructive behavior, Lovaas argues, the shock sticks can coerce the child into stopping the self-injuring behavior by the administration of a low-voltage electrocution.

Still, it was easy for anyone seeking to criticize behaviorism to seize on the obvious inhumanity of electric shocks as emblematic of a flawed therapy. For my parents, this becomes a steady source of debate, as the various negative reinforcers are to be deployed with Noah, starting with slaps and pinches and extending all the way to the "shock stick." Initially, they go along with the Lovaas recommendation that all aversives be potentially allowable, including food deprivation. "A hungry child is ready to work," Lovaas explains. Yet from the beginning, there are disputes about the amount and regularity of the slaps. I can't help but wince the first time Noah is given a hard slap on the wrist by a therapist. "The trouble with most of these kids," Lovaas tells my parents, "is that they don't have any fear at all. And to begin to make them function, you must forget all etiology and implant fear in them. It's not that these kids fear too much; it's that they don't fear at all. If Noah, for example, was afraid of an electric shock, I'd use my stinger on him tomorrow. But at this point I don't think Noah is afraid of anything."

Lovaas himself might be the best hands-on therapist; he is a natural with autistic children, totally at ease with them, and able, through his own infectious personality and voluble style, to coax the kids to perform in their Discrete Trial therapies. He is remarkable to watch as he leans in close, all bushy blond hair and big grinning teeth—when I first see *Hollywood Squares*, I will realize it is the same smile as Paul Lynde's—he will hold out a piece of popcorn and say, steadily, loudly, emphatically, "Popcorn, popcorn, popcorn," until the child will say it back to him and receive not only his reward but also a thorough head patting and shoulder rubbing. They want to please him, it seems to me; they want to make him happy.

Whenever my parents have doubts about the efficacy of behaviorism, a session spent watching Ivar work with Noah reassures and reinspires. Not all his students have the same knack, however, and during this early period in the history of his program—Noah is among the first two dozen or so autistic children he has treated—they are still figuring out their teaching style as they go. Some of the therapists are better than others and among the steady rotation that comes to our house are a few undergraduate psychology students who see in Noah an easy five credits rather than a child who needs their help. They have been taught the basics, but they can be a little slap-happy, and not just with Noah. On one occasion, when I am throwing a fit in my room about not being given money to go buy candy, I get slapped by one of the students, a junior with brown hair, who mistakenly applies the aversive practice of operant conditioning to me instead of Noah.

34.

My optimism about Noah remains undiluted. He will progress, I am sure. Otherwise, why would we have journeyed so far? Why would we have changed houses? Why would I have switched schools? Since he will soon achieve something like normality, I convince my parents that we should share a room, align our two single beds in parallel with a nightstand between, as I have seen so many other children's beds on TV shows and at my friends' houses. Bunk beds would be even better, I conclude, but my mother is worried Noah will fall, should he manage to climb up to the top. This is how normal brothers sleep, I believe, side by side in their shared room. A team.

My real reason for this proposal is that I have become frightened of the dark, experiencing my first nightmares after watching a few black-and-white horror films and an episode of the *Twilight Zone* that I couldn't quite follow but found the tone and moody lighting to be so disturbing that I am having trouble sleeping. There are two sounds that I find reassuring: the late-night racket of the television in the living room when my parents are watching after I've gone to bed, an aural montage of throaty male voices, laughing females, commercial jingles, and the *click, click, click* of the changing channels. As long as I can hear those sounds I can fall fearlessly asleep; and in the morning, awakened by Noah's keening in the next room, his incessant humming and repeating, the buh-buh-buh-buh-buh-buh of his morning Noah song, I am comforted. Both sounds are the night calls of my family, and I can slumber in their atonal weave.

But when my parents aren't watching television or, even worse, when I wake in the middle of the night, I become anxious and overimagine the unnamed horrors: black-robed, large, bald-headed with pointy ears. I don't have any clear idea of their agenda, save that they want to do me harm. Who are they? Where are they from? A few years later, I will see a photograph of the actor Max Shreck in the German film *Nosferatu* and will shiver as I realize that this was the figure that haunted me, though I didn't recall being aware of this film or ever having seen images from it before.

This is the evil I feel in the evening, in the brief interlude of silence in our house, and even the embarrassing installation of a night-light in my room does nothing to diminish this hissing sense of a malevolent presence. I cannot even explain if this lurking is inside the house, in my room, or just outside the pair of windows facing the driveway. I fall asleep every night worrying about waking up in the night. And if my eyes open and it is still dark, I am frightened. Usually, the only choice I have is to lie awake until first light and then fall back asleep. I have no idea how long this takes, minutes or hours; the time passes numbly and slowly as I listen for a noise, a rustle, a faint rushing of air that I am convinced is the sound of a long tongue being drawn over dry teeth.

The simple solution, I am sure, is to sleep with Noah; for Noah, in his autism, does not seem troubled by any nightmares or imagined fears. I suppose he is brave, in his way, and as he lies in his bed, self-stimming and keening, he seems untroubled. His seeming need to sleep just four, five, or six hours a night is a burden to my parents, but I have decided that Noah's presence in the next bed will be reassuring.

My parents agree to the move and so we begin sleeping next to each other; almost immediately, my worries and fears dissolve, and Noah seems to like the arrangement. Yet I can't help but immediately notice that Noah is more than a sporadic sleeper, he is an exceedingly odd sleeper. When I wake up in the middle of the night, a feeling familiar to me mainly as a waking into a series of inexpressible anxieties, I can look over and see Noah, and, often, he is sitting straight up in bed, a corner of the blanket in his mouth, chewing it over, and then he looks over at me, and maybe he nods or just shakes his head, but he is just sitting there, like he's been there all night.

He sleeps even less than we previously estimated, I realize. Much less.

And a few minutes before dawn every day, he starts his regular humming and repetitive consonant roll calls in earnest, leaning up on one elbow as he does so.

I soon have no choice but to sleep roughly the same duration as Noah, no more than five or six hours a night, a light, thin sleep, easily pricked, that leaves me fatigued. I have traded my terror for exhaustion, a deal I am content with, but my teacher, Mrs. Collins, tells my parents I have been sleeping in class, falling asleep while digging in the sandbox. When they ask about it, I tell them that I take little naps, and what's wrong with that?

Noah is soon moved back to his own room, and I am left once again with my fears.

35.

I have new friends, Elliott and Brett down the street and Jason around the corner. A Japanese family lives in the shingled ranch across the street and down two houses. Eisuke and Shingo are their two boys, and their parents and my parents become friends. On an old bicycle—a hand-me-down from Paul Mazursky's daughter Jill—that's fitted with training wheels that growl over the pavement, I am able to range wherever I want on the unbusy block.

Our own stucco apartment is the first floor of two; a couple in their thirties lives at the top of a red-tiled staircase, which the other boys on the block and I sometimes gather on and say is our fort. I love walking to school, past the palm trees and cacti; the swishing, spitting sound of sprinkler systems switching on; the rush of an occasional passing car. Brett, from next door, a blond boy with thick lips, stops in front of my house and calls my name in the morning, and I run out to meet him. He is worldly, a child of divorce, and he tells me more during those walks to school—about human reproduction in particular—than I will learn in my first-grade classroom.

In Croton I took a bus, pushed in among my jacketed associates between hard green seats as we bounced our way to school. Here, I walk with my friends, skipping sidewalk cracks. Sometimes Brett has bubblegum or Sweet Tarts that he shares with me. One morning, and I have no idea how he has managed this, he has an entire box of glazed doughnuts, and we stuff ourselves. We tarry on our way, as boys will, stopping most mornings at a corner house where there is a trimmed hedge growing out of a strip of clotted dirt. There, we wait for another group of boys, for Jason and his older brothers, who come walking down Warner Avenue to this same intersection, and we throw dirt clods at them, the projectiles exploding in little brown starbursts against the gray pavement.

"Hand grenades," Brett shouts, and he shows me what he says is the proper way to throw a grenade: straight-armed, over the shoulder, a heaving motion.

These dirt-clod fights can go on for fifteen minutes. One morning I am struck on the side of the head by a dirt clod, the soft brown dirt making a poof as it hits me. For a moment I am playing along like I am a dead soldier, and then I realize I am hurt, and I am lying on the grass and crying.

"He's crying," says Brett.

The first instinct of boys, I discover, is to run from trouble. And the gang scampers away up the street to school, and I am left there, holding the side of my head, just above and to the front of my ear. Prone there, the grass cool against the back of my head, the lawn itchy against the back of my arms, I listen for the sounds of other boys. I don't want anyone else to see me crying, so I roll away from the street and then come to my knees, picking dirt and pebbles out of my hair.

I stumble home and open the front door, and my mother becomes hysterical when she thinks that her son has been hit in the head by a rock. I try to explain to her that it is not a stone but a dirt clod, but the difference is too hard for her to understand. When my father comes into the kitchen, she is still so upset she wants to call the police, alert the school, and complain to all the parents involved.

She says we already have one brain-damaged person in the family and her greatest worry is to end up with another.

"But I'm not brain-damaged," I point out, now realizing that my mother might make of this a more embarrassing situation than it already is. "I'm okay. I feel okay."

I should have just gone to school. Now the whole school will know that I am a crybaby, and the kids on my block will hate me.

My father runs a battery of tests on me, instructing me to count to ten, to touch my nose, and then to stand on one foot. Finally, after about a half hour spent sitting at the kitchen table with a bag of ice pressed against an emerging bump on the side of my head, my parents determine that I am well enough to head back to school.

Then there is another debate over the nature of the note that my father will write. I urge him to write that I had a headache while my mother is still insisting that there be some kind of investigation of the matter. This kind of unchecked violence, she points out, is what leads to fascism. And what if this attack was racially motivated, she adds.

Finally, I succeed in convincing them that we were just playing, that we were throwing dirt clods and I happened to get hit. But I feel better now, completely.

My father takes me to school with a vaguely worded note, and I rejoin my classroom before lunchtime.

But that night my mother goes to Brett's house and tells his mother what happened. The next morning Brett does not call for me in front of my house, and when I walk by the dirt-clod place, he is throwing them at some other boys, and when I walk past, nobody throws a thing at me.

36.

Lovaas suggests a school for Noah in Mar Vista, just a few miles in the Mercedes from our little house. Compared to Westchester County and its narrow, potholed highways sunken between stone retaining walls or squeezed into cuts through mossy green copses of trees, the wide Los Angeles freeways, elevated as they are over the single-level neighborhoods, seem like modern skyways, smooth transverses to a clean, dry, bright new world.

My father drives Noah to his new nursery school, the Westport School; even its name is futuristic and welcoming. There is an older woman there with wiry gray hair who wears simple, thick, cotton tops. Lovaas has told my parents that Alys Harris is among the best he has seen at operant conditioning. She is a natural, and he has sent his graduate students to this school to watch her work with her students.

The school is a cheery little Cape Cod–style house, set back on a lawn from a wide, residential street. By now I am used to seeing Noah take his place among his fellow autistics and retardates, but whereas at the school in New York the children were so often corralled indoors because of rainy or cold weather, here they spend before-school time and breaks and lunchtimes roaming in a spacious backyard. It lends the proceeding a different feeling, and as a young boy I can even join in and play on the jungle gym or the slides. A boy with Down syndrome, named Jimmy, seems excited when I accompany Noah, and he eagerly shows me around the yard, pointing out his favorite trucks and following me down the slide or onto the swings.

Noah actually seems jealous that I am playing with another boy in his class, and he comes over and leans his head against my shoulder and smiles, but he doesn't seem to know how to engage beyond those gestures. It is one of the very few times that Noah attempts to communicate with me in this manner, and as he gets older, these occasions will be exceedingly rare.

In class, his teacher, Alys Harris, keeps careful control. Even when she is working with one child, the others wait. Her commands—"sit down," "hands still," "no noise, no noise"—are obeyed. The children trace letters and numbers, color in shapes, work on simple puzzles. She runs the kids through a routine of simple physical activities, walking around a rope, jumping over two-by-fours laid out on the ground, carrying a die on a spoon.

Noah is at the bottom of the class.

37.

The death of our cat, Brodsky, a cranky animal not fond of children, never a friend to me, bothers my parents more than it does me. He was the good-luck charm that brought them together, the *chôchin mochi*, as the Japanese say, having accompanied my father to the MacDowell Colony. My father had intended to dump Brodsky on my mother and take off for France but instead waited for her to bring the cat back to the city with her and then soon they were married. Brodksy accompanied them to Maine, Canada, Japan, and now to California. "I think I have identified the fate of Brodsky with the destiny of Noah," my father writes. "They are both, after all, my pets—endearing helplessnesses, responsibilities without end."

Yet Brodsky's passing notwithstanding, Los Angeles feels more like a beginning than an end. Is it false hope? Desperation? Denial?

No, it is the opposite of denial. What we cannot see is that we have gone from wondering what is wrong with Noah to now pivoting our lives around whatever it is that is wrong with Noah. We are living too much of our lives through the hope for Noah, and this is a situation families of autistic children can too well understand even today—that sense of an entire family's life being distorted because of autism as the members struggle to understand the extent of the warp. I'm not conscious of where and how we are different, but by the time I am seven, I know that as a family we will never do the pro forma activities—celebrate holidays, go on day trips, eat a peaceful meal—that other families take for granted, and that we will undertake massive shifts—moving back and forth across the country—that few other families outside of the military have to endure.

For the first few years of the 1970s, we will spend each winter and spring in California, then return to New York for the summer and fall. It is a migratory existence, almost perfectly calibrated to keep me off balance in school—in third grade I will have three different teachers in three different schools—before we finally, completely and irrevocably, move to California.

I now know from watching my own daughters, who were uprooted once when my elder daughter Esmee was just four years old, how confusing such a move can be, but also how it draws the children in closer to the family unit at an age when they are already terribly bound to their parents and siblings. For my daughters, it meant that Esmee became a friend to her younger sister, Lola, at precisely the age when she might have become more outgoing, more social. In Hong Kong, where we lived before returning to New York, she had begun to spend some weekends sleeping over at her preschool classmates' homes. Moving to New York, where she had no friends, made for a hard season for her. My wife spent much of those first months in New York devising activities for her two daughters, who were out of school for the first time. Yet from that time together, our family grew closer.

I can't help but view so much of my own childhood through the sibling experience of my daughters. Their relationship—its complexities, tensions, arguments, but ultimately, deep and profound bond—helps reveal the shape of the gaps in my own relationship with Noah. My younger daughter, Lola, made our mind up for us when we were trying to decide which school she should attend, a gifted school to which she had won admission or our local school, P.S. 234, just a few blocks away. She said she wanted to go to the local school because "I want to walk to school with Esmee."

I had never considered that two siblings might enjoy attending the same school.

According to child psychiatrists, the most important age at which siblings begin to develop close bonds is when the younger brother or sister is between the ages of three and four. I've watched as Lola, now five, developed the motor skills, language, and social repertoire for her to become an increasingly desirable playmate for Esmee, now seven. In the past few years, the two have been able to share both imaginative play and simple card games and board games. They will divide up roles, mother and baby, teacher and student, shopkeeper and customer, and can entertain each other for extended periods, and through these games, and the discussions, arguments, and compromises made in playing them, they are forming a rich and complex sisterhood that my wife and I can only marvel at, and periodically intervene in when their inevitable rivalry and competition breaks into open warfare.

When we arrive in Los Angeles, I am seven and Noah is five, precisely the ages at which our brotherhood should be changing into a defining asset, a relationship that should at least yield the tangible benefit of companionship. I watch my daughters play happily at the playground—even if none of their friends make an appearance—because they have each other. They are so rarely alone at exactly the age at which I began to realize that I was increasingly by myself. They are learning to negotiate, to compromise, to communicate at the time when, in my life, I was concluding that it was best to keep my ideas and schemes to myself. They are discovering they are part of a community, a network, at the same time I was learning that I was just one boy.

My wife was the first to point out to me this simple socializing that I missed, the easy camaraderie that allows one to go lightly through peer-group interactions. What I am seeing in Esmee and Lola's relationship is the most rudimentary practice at being in a group, part of a casual clique, precisely the kind of small-talking gatherings at which I find myself persistently miserable. I don't know how to take interaction lightly, to presume I will always have company. For me, the wonder of siblinghood, as I see between my wife and her brothers and sister or between my two daughters, is the casual ease of the relationship, the frankness, the vast amounts that are unspoken that allow for easier speaking, the presumption that your brother or sister will somehow always be there, so you don't need to overload this conversation, right now. Siblings learn what to leave out.

38.

Noah is not interested in anything resembling typical play. He was never remotely interested in my behaviors, and now he seems to resent my occasional intrusion into his space. He is busy, actually, far busier than I. With the specialists and speech therapists—and now a chiropractor is making adjustments on him, too—a full litany of appointments and house-calling specialists come in to administer their various cures and remedies and therapies. And that is when he is not in the car heading to UCLA or at Franz Hall in the lab itself. His free time is precious, even to someone who seems indifferent to the passage of time, and any interruption by me must feel to him like one more demand that he focus and perform the little animal tricks—ringing a bell, pulling a chord, buzzing a buzzer—that the Lovaas team have him doing ad nauseam. And my role for the first time shifts into caretaking and occasional watching; increasingly, I will answer quick calls from my parents to check on Noah, see what Noah is doing. "Karl, is Noah in the bathroom?"

My parents are aware that my childhood is unconventional both because of my racial makeup and my brother. Yet they are hardly seeking to live by a bourgeois code anyway, and so they can tell themselves that any deviations from the typical path are as much a product of their bohemian outlook as their autistic offspring. Still, my mother increasingly worries that I am developing slowly, dimly, using the cover of Noah to hide an incipient, cretinous stupidity. As a Japanese mother, she frets that I don't grasp multiplication, have no interest in reading, and seem indifferent to schoolwork of any kind. Yet she can't monitor my putative academic flailing as closely as she would if Noah were normal, having to rely instead on periodic inspections that confirm her suspicions that her normal son is lazy.

Finally, in exasperation, she sends to Japan for mathematics textbooks and resolves to teach me at home, herself, because she fears my various public schools will leave me totally unprepared to, say, make change for a dollar or divide up a pizza. It is a reaction to the fact that Noah can't learn math, will never do his times tables, and that makes it somehow more urgent that I master them. I can't verbalize this idea at the time, but it is a feeling I have, a sense of unfairness, that Noah is rewarded for ringing a bell, pushing a buzzer, saying "buh, buh," and I am not allowed to go outside and play because I can't do my 9's yet.

My father is torn between my mother's fears and his own wishes that I enjoy a happy childhood. I, at least, am capable of such, while with Noah . . . who knows? He feels pleasure, joy, and can laugh and smile, but does he remember any of it? Can he reach back into a repository of happy sensations and turn them over to examine what it is that caused this good feeling. "This morning I took a walk with Noah in the bright sun," my father wrote, "and it felt like an eternally youthful sun, walking hand in hand with him, very father-and-son-ish, until I realized again that one of the sad things about Noah is that one can never be warmed by the sense that one is helping to store away pleasant memories in a child." (I reread that today, think of my own daughters, and gasp.)

So I am supposed to be both the repository of happy memories and the great hope for the future, the burdens of two boys compressed into one, and I am at best a typical boy, average in intelligence and athletics, and below average in character. (I soon discover that the aisle farthest from the counter at the candy store off the lobby in the Caravel Motel is virtually invisible to the gray-haired lady behind the counter. Unfortunately, that is the aisle displaying medicines, decongestants, antacids, aspirin; the only item I covet from these racks are Luden's wild cherry cough drops, and I swipe a pack every time we visit.)

39.

Bob Koegel, who worked with Noah extensively as a Lovaas student, recently told me that Noah was like "Daniel Boone, a pathfinder, a trailblazer." I was surprised by his positive assessment of Noah's role. "Noah and this group of autistic children were heading off into the unknown." Because of Noah and his contemporaries, Bob says, tens of thousands of autistic children received better behavior modification. It is comforting now to view Noah's early years as not having been wasted, his therapies as having amounted to more than lost time and graduate student credits.

Noah was proving to be a difficult case, even to the committed and hardworking undergraduate therapists at UCLA. "Noah was a tough nut," recalls Laura Schreibman. "He didn't give you a lot of feedback."

Lovaas calls a massive brown-bag staff meeting, inviting my parents to join eleven specialists and therapists and students who have worked with Noah for six months to discuss his progress. There is consensus that Noah's learning needs to be accelerated, that perhaps he requires a more innovative approach. The conclusion, as Lovaas summarizes it for my parents, is that we need to "stick a firecracker up his ass." He suggests that Noah be placed on a thirty-six-hour food- and fluid-deprivation program, so that he really craves food, to show him that communication brings rewards. "He needs to be hungry and desperate enough to do anything for food."

My parents are reluctant to go along with this program. Noah is not yet five, and thirty-six hours is a long time to go without food. My parents rule out disallowing liquids. They compromise and agree to a twenty-hour deprivation program, from dinner in the evening to the middle of the afternoon the next day.

When the big day arrives, Noah seems a little surprised that he has skipped breakfast and then my father picks him up before lunchtime at his school so that he does not have to watch the other children eat their lunch; at around three thirty, he is brought to UCLA, where the team reassembles as Meredith, one of the best therapists, begins to work him, and then . . .

Nothing. Noah is as disinterested as ever in the rewards proffered.

Lovaas convinces my parents to withhold dinner and then breakfast the next day and bring him back in the morning, "and then he will really be ready to work."

I find Noah in his bed the next morning, hacking up a yellowy, sour-smelling substance. For a second, I mistake the stomach bile for some sort of juice, grapefruit perhaps. But why would my parents give Noah juice in bed? Noah seems listless, indifferent, not suffering so much as expiring, gradually surrendering. I watch him for a moment, and then it occurs to me that he is sick. "Mom, Dad, Mom, Dad," I shout.

My father would later write that the "yellow, vomit-like mucus" reminded him immediately of the substances his father had emitted right before he died. He calls Lovaas, who sends Meredith over; she concludes that the groggy Noah is in no condition to work. My parents attempt to feed him and quickly take him to a pediatrician, who explains that Noah has upchucked bile because there was no food in his stomach for his enzymes and juices to work on. Lovaas, my mother points out, should have warned them of this possibility.

40.

The concern about Noah, the tinnitus of worry that I can never quite tune out, wrenches me out of that present before I am even aware of the concept of linear time. Think of a child growing—there can be no clearer illustration of the linearity of time—and then think of a child not growing. Does that make you more or less aware of the passage of time?

In my family's case, more. Time was frustrating, in that it was passing yet so many things that were supposed to be happening weren't happening. Noah should be walking, talking, eating. And then the Lovaas team had their schedule: saying "ah," "oh," "bah," "me," pulling this lever, ringing that bell. They did not have specific timetables, but they were aware of the passage of disappointing months. The lack of progress is perhaps the most disheartening measurement of time there is.

And there was a larger, more sinister clock that I now discover. At some point, in the distant future, we would no longer be able to keep Noah at home. Someday, we would not be a family anymore. Noah would be sent away, to an institution, an asylum, my parents tell me.

The playwright Arthur Miller, a friend of my father's, years earlier had confided to my father that he had a son with Down syndrome whom he had institutionalized. "I took one look at the baby, at the palm of his hand, and I knew. This was three years ago. The doctor said wait and see. I said, 'No way.' I knew once the child was in my house I was done for. So I put him in a nursing home straight from the hospital. You see, I had a Down syndrome cousin. Ruined the family. Brought the family down trying to care for him. Where is my son now? In the state institution not far from here. He's a healthy kid, and we visit him, but it's different—it's not as if we became attached to him from day one."

It would have been the harder way in the short term but a softer path in the long run. The initial parting would have been difficult, but with the passage of time, that longing for their son would have passed, so that, by now, Noah would mean no more to my parents than that Down syndrome boy meant to Arthur Miller, an inconvenience, a responsibility, but not a loved one whose presence one misses and then longs for. And that may have been their greatest failing.

Wait a second—wait, wait, wait. We can't send Noah away. He's my brother. However distorted our sibling bond, we still have one.

There are four of us, in this family. And there are two children, Noah and me. When my father takes us on walks and Noah sometimes slows down or even sits down on the sidewalk, my father will say, "Okay, Noah, we're going to leave you."

He is making an idle threat of course, trying to cajole Noah back onto his feet.

But I panic—I have been told, after all, that at some point we will leave Noah—and beg my father not to abandon my brother.

And Noah, my brother, he's not even aware of this countdown. They already know they won't be able to keep him at home forever. Almost every specialist they have visited has warned them: you do what you can and then you put him away. But for the first time, as I become gradually aware that the Lovaas program might not actually "cure" my brother, I can feel a greater impetus to seek a solution to the Noah problem other than institutionalization. My father has his reasons; my mother has hers. I find them unfathomable. To put Noah away? To surrender him to what I can only imagine as a soulless orphanage similar to those portrayed in movies—loveless, heartless, cold—where he will be lost. He needs parents more than a normal kid does, not less. Documentaries and news segments have been airing lately, about Letchworth Village and Willowbrook State School in New York, of the vast urine-stained, rat-infested wards; the charges drugged and untended; the accidental deaths. I have seen snippets of this footage on television, and have been in the room as my parents grew deathly quiet watching as a jerky, handheld camera moves through dark hallways; men in pajamas lie on the floor and slap themselves spasmodically in a manner that is both terrifying and totally familiar. Is this where Noah will end up?

They know; my parents are realists. By now, it is apparent, at least to them, that Noah will never be a normal boy, that he is profoundly autistic, and the prognosis for these children, even with Lovaas's revolutionary new treatments, is bleak. Lovaas has told my parents that he feels he succeeds with just one in twenty of the severely autistic. And after several months at Franz Hall, after dozens of hours of therapists living in our home, it is obvious that Noah will not be among that 5 percent. We are left hoping, then, for marginal improvements, small adjustments, a gradual creeping up to . . . what? My father observed before our cat passed away that Noah functioned at a lower level than Brodsky. So we were hoping, through Lovaas's therapy, which is sort of like animal training anyway, that Noah would eventually be domesticated in the manner of a pet: housebroken and obedient.

But Noah, despite his autism, has a definite personality, and he is stubborn, so unlike the Down syndrome and retarded boys at his school, who tend to have a sweetness because they so desperately want to be liked; Noah is indifferent to anyone's opinion of him. He simply doesn't care. If he wanted to be liked, if he yearned for praise, he would be more trainable. That is why Lovaas was tempted to use his whole quiver of aversives, hitting, food deprivation, though he had yet to use the "shock stick," wary, perhaps, of my parents' objections.

Should they allow more extreme aversives? Now my parents have to wonder, for they feel the same ineluctable onrush of time, of the future crowding us, as with each day Noah grows, becomes more burdensome, a six-year-old who is not yet fully toilet trained, who wakes up constantly because his bed is wet or he has taken a bowel movement on his rubber sheets. My parents seldom get a full night's sleep, and now, they also worry because Noah has taken to self-mutilation, banging his forehead against the floor, scratching himself, slapping his hands against his forehead. If you try to comfort him, he pulls at your hair. But no matter how many bad nights precede exhausted days, my father and mother will not allow the shock stick.

How long then? How long will we hold on to Noah? This becomes the only measure of time I understand, that this family unit, as we are now comprised, is not immutable. We are in a phase, a phase with Noah, and it will pass. It is only a matter of time.

41.

My father's book, *A Child Called Noah*, when it is published in the beginning of 1972, will immediately become the most popular and best-selling book about autism written up to that point. It is one of the first books to describe with unapologetic honesty what it's like to be the parent and family of an autistic child. The book is widely reviewed and excerpted, written about glowingly in the *New York Times*, *Time*, *Newsweek*, and the *Washington Post*. It is so simply and ingenuously written that a child can easily read it, and so it ends up being among the first books I ever read, which means that I am a character in perhaps the first adult book I ever complete. *A Child Called Noah* immediately moves Noah into that pantheon of special children who become touchstones for a generation of parents. Noah became, in a small way, famous, as photographers and writers now began to visit our home for articles about Noah and our family. It is my father's first public success, and would end up earning more through hardcover, paperback, serialization, and dramatic rights than anything else he would write. And, coming on the heels of the *Life* article on which it was based, the success of the Noah books—he would write three books about our family—would give him a little more cachet that he could parlay into Hollywood work. A writer with a reputation in the East, while still only a writer, at least had a reputation of some sort, unlike most aspiring screenwriters.

Yet the success of *A Child Called Noah*, a book, after all, with my brother's name in the title, makes apparent to those outside our family what has been obvious to me for some time: that our family is about Noah more than it is about anyone else. Noah's story, the title makes clear, is the story of our family. I am, by implication, a supporting character, a bit player who provides interesting contrast to his autistic brother but little more than that. My father would later describe my appearances in his books, my relationship to Noah and to my parents, as being like Rosencrantz's and Guildenstern's dramatic relationship to Hamlet, only without the intrigue. So by age eight I am dimly aware of being a slight disappointment even as a literary character, as a dramatic figure; otherwise, if I were more interesting, more fascinating, then wouldn't I at least rate a place in the title? "If the book is about you," says my friend Jason, "then why is it called *A Child Called 'Noah'*?" And he raises a valid point.

My father had to scramble to get me into the book, and I was, of course, disappointingly typical as a boy, my trials too familiar to any parent: I was struggling with tying my shoes, telling time, multiplication, even my shortcomings so ordinary when compared to the spectacular disappointment of my brother. To be found wanting even as a failure, that is my fate. And this is when the questions start coming, the first interviewers asking me, How does it feel to have a brother like Noah? An autistic brother?

I always tell them: I don't know what it feels like to have any other kind of brother.

But the setting down of our family's story in the Noah books is also a public mission statement: my father and mother are doing everything they can for Noah; we, as a family, are working for Noah. So we decide, finally, to make our move to Los Angeles permanent in late 1972. We move into a rented house in Pacific Palisades—a white-stucco, red-tiled Spanish house built around a courtyard. The house was once leased by Carroll O'Connor (before he became Archie Bunker)—back then Pacific Palisades was where you lived before you made it. My father can write in the room behind the garage as he works on his articles and books, and in the evenings, in the den, he watches the Watergate hearings, the long processions of dark-suited men I am told are crooks engaged in various dissemblings, the bulbous nose and slicked-back white hair of Sam Ervin—he looked to me like some sort of bird in a tweed suit—and the various billed showdowns,

Dean versus Mitchell, Haldeman versus Erlichman, that I recall as being terribly anticlimactic. I had imagined brawls on a par with Ali versus Frazier.

My father remains a slight man, wearing his collared, short-sleeve shirts and his flared corduroy trousers—the 1970s were a forgiving time for Semitic-looking intellectuals. Woody Allen was considered a sex symbol, thus allowing a generation of Jewish intelligentsia to believe they could get away with the same sartorial laxness. My father often wears a fishing hat or a checked bowler, similar to that worn by Tom Landry, perhaps to cover up his steadily expanding bald spot, which is now impossible to comb over into hiding. He still has his Boston-by-way-of-Brooklyn accent, saying Kahl instead of Karl, nevah instead of never.

If Noah has shaken him out of his lifelong indifference to commerce, the folding of *Life* magazine in late 1972 causes him to worry that he will no longer have his primary source of commerce. "The death of *Life* magazine is a blow," he writes. "I always assumed I could pick up a major parcel of my income through the magazine. And now that source is gone. I guess I will have to go local and begin thinking earnestly about writing movie scripts." My father has a gift, I realize, for never seeming desperate. Even with the folding of the magazine, and with it the disappearance of the bulk of his income, he never projects panic or worry. In fact, he still maintains a pretense of dismissiveness toward writing for money that allows him never to seem to need the work, even when he does, terribly. My mother, as wives do, will urge him to call his friends and acquaintances in New York, the editors he knows who have given him assignments in the past. "Tell them," she suggests. "Tell them you are here. They need stories from Los Angeles."

He lies awake at night, he later tells me, worrying about money, a habit he picked up from watching his father go through the humiliation of a Depression-era bankruptcy. (The shame catalyzed his family's move from Malden, Massachusetts, to Brooklyn, New York.) His career is now moving west: *Harry & Tonto*, the film he wrote with Paul Mazursky, is going into production. He is also working on another script with Mazursky, and there is the novelization of Paul's earlier film *Blume in Love*. He is reluctant to take on too many celebrity profiles, correctly deducing that you can't supplicate yourself before an actor for a magazine article one day and then pitch a film to him a month later, but after *Life* folds, fear of financial insecurity forces him to write a few.

But I never feel any sense that our family is in financial peril. He is resourceful, and now that I know something of what it is like to keep a career going as a writer, I admire his moxie.

42.

My mother is even skinnier than she was when Noah was born, now slipping below one hundred pounds. She wears her hair in a severe, black bob and keeps her clothes simple and practical so Noah can't find a free tassel or loose fold to grab. She doesn't wear jewelry, as Noah has a tendency to tear off a dangling necklace or loose bangle. At home, she's in slippers with soft soles that swish as she walks across the carpeted floor or the tiled courtyard; Japanese style, we don't wear shoes in the home. Astonishingly, here in Los Angeles, she doesn't know how to drive a car and so is dependent on my father for almost all her transportation needs. The local RTD bus system is sporadic and unreliable, but she joins the Hispanic domestics to ride the yellow buses into Pacific Palisades' little commercial district.

She doesn't even have the temporary refuge of work. She hasn't painted since I was born, and her avowed career now seems so distant as not to have been a part of her life at all. I certainly can't imagine her as a painter any more than I could imagine her as a policewoman—if it weren't for the paintings that have followed us from Croton-on-Hudson to Pacific Palisades: large, lush, complex, textural abstracts that bewilder me as a child because they look so unlike any other paintings I have ever seen. They resemble forest fires, fire bombings, managing to come across as both vivid and brooding, emotional yet not heavy. They dictate the tone of the house in the way that good art can, soothing by their presence yet also provocative; they don't yield their intention or subject easily.

They are also mocking her, reminding her of great promise unfulfilled, the gallery shows in Japan, the fellowships won at the MacDowell Colony and the Pennsylvania Academy of Fine Arts—it was her talent as a painter that, after all, got her out of Japan. She has had to forsake that as she "waits for nothing"; it is a life that has to feel wasted. Noah is seven and is not yet toilet trained, can't properly dress himself, and, as my mother says, "he can't take care of himself and we can't take care of him." She has sacrificed her best, most creative years, and for what? A boy who will never grow up.

My mother gives all she has to Noah, every day, maintaining in her stolid Japanese way a steady, patient flow of kindness, compassion, and training of the type Lovaas has prescribed, yet too often, in the evening or at night, she has nothing left, for my father or for me. She can then, in her quiet moments, bemoan the lost years. My father, at least, has his career, his escape in work; my mother has only us.

43.

We are in a new town, this lovely stretch of bluffs and cliffs running alongside the wide beaches across the Pacific Coast Highway; the village is green and luxuriant, as much with cactus and palm trees as with lawn and ivy, and to my eyes, accustomed to the East Coast, the stark, white California sun seems to flatten it all out so that the colors take a moment longer to emerge after you lay eyes on them. It is a dustiness, the accumulated sheen of weeks without rain; back east, in leafy suburbs like Croton, it pours enough to wash away any skein of pollen and settled particles. Out here, it is a drab coat that clings for months until a good soaking washes it all away. Of course, the gardeners hose it all down, soak the lawns and ivies and flower beds, the roses and hibiscus that seem perpetually in bloom, the ice plants and ferns, the desert and forest flora that coexist because of those garden hoses. They don't water the leaves and branches, and that's where that dust accumulates, a layer marking time; you can run your finger along the leaf of an oak tree and it comes away as gray as if you have just rubbed Miss Havisham's dining room table.

In this dry heat, in this new house, we are coming to terms with yet another disappointment. Before we returned to the East Coast, at the last meeting with Lovaas, there was a collective sense that he had let us down, or that Noah had let him down, or that whatever was supposed to happen for Noah—what Lovaas, and all the graduate students and hired therapists and their wonderful scientific methods, all their Discrete Trials and modern behaviorism and sleek, one-way-mirrored workshops—that whatever was supposed to happen was not happening. We have to acknowledge, we have to admit, we see, that Noah is still Noah. He has improved in some small areas, he can match a spoon with a spoon, a fork with a fork, a square with a square, he can sit still for a minute or two longer, he can slip on his own shoes and take them off, but he has not made any demonstrable progress toward speaking. Even Lovaas admits, tacitly, disappointed, that he has let my parents down.

My father says that if Noah is not making noticeable improvement in two years, then we will seek out an institution for him.

I cry when he tells me this.

We are sitting at our circular dining table, the same white Eames table we had back in Croton now set up in our southern California kitchen and still looking, to me, a little out of place amid these surroundings, the visual equivalent of a loose tooth you keep running your tongue over. I pause the first few times I walk into the kitchen at the sight of the table, confused for an instant, before finally accepting this table in this setting.

"We can't keep Noah forever," my father says.

"Why?"

We've had this conversation before. And I can already sense that we will have it many times again. It is like discussion of the federal deficit among political pundits, a subject of deep concern yet ultimately irreconcilable, insoluble, a problem that is out there, maybe in the near future, perhaps (we hope!) the distant future, or, even better, maybe there will be some miraculous solution.

"We won't be able to handle him," he says.

My mother sits beside him. She is peeling a mandarin orange.

When she cries, she tilts her head a little to the side and closes her eyes slightly. She doesn't sob, or sniffle; there is just this thin vein of tear.

Only when she talks does her deep voice betray her. "We will try, for as long as we can, we will try."

44.

In the warming sun of a California winter, a family sits around a table and dreams of stopping time. If only Noah could stay small forever, a little boy, playing as he is now in his underwear on the crabgrass just outside the kitchen, a string in his mouth, a bright smile formed around that bounty, joyous for the moment to be unburdened, to be free from demands. He is oblivious, of course, to our concerns, adrift in his own chaotic joy, unknowable, mysterious, unfathomable. Beyond reach? Perhaps. The blank heart of a family, the repository of our dreams and wishes, the source and also the cancer, the gift and the cost, the sorrow and love. Most of us, maybe all of us, embody a love story and tragic ending, and Noah does so in spades, consumed with his own chewing on old string and unquivering from the tension of those contradictions. Noah could live on death row and until he was strapped into the chair, not know his sentence.

I saw a centipede out there one morning when I was playing with my plastic army tanks—I have lately been allowed to play with army men, with military toys, with tanks and soldiers and toy guns. I don't know why my pacifist mother has relaxed her prohibition of such violent toys, yet it has happened without any discussion. In my joy, I play with the molded-plastic 1/35th-scale M-60—later I will discover the more detailed and space-efficient HO scale soldiers and models—and bend my head down low so that I can watch the tank as it moves over the brown earth, the pebbles.

A centipede is a hideous creature, its whirling antennae and elbowed legs with their unnatural bend. I was frozen for a moment by its mechanical slither over the uneven ground, more like the movement of a rubber belt over gears—a tank tread, maybe—than any animal I have ever seen. I was stung behind my right thumb, just over the bone next to the web of flesh between the thumb and my hand. It swelled up quickly, bloated and soft, like a balloon filled with maple syrup. I put a Band-Aid on it and for a few days I had trouble bending my thumb, tentatively wiggling the tip, as if it were broken instead of just filled with mild venom.

Now, as I watch my mother's tears, I suddenly get up from the table and throw open the screen door. I tell Noah to come inside. There are centipedes out there.

PART II

A BOY

45.

Fuck Noah.

I load a bong hit. I'm sitting on the porch next to an open sliding-glass door. Noah is inside the house—from where I sit it sounds like he is in the living room—chewing on furniture, twiddling a rubber band, humming in his repetitive monotone. My parents have gone out for the late afternoon and early evening, and I'm babysitting. And that means smoking dope and watching TV while Noah self-stimulates—making repetitive motions, bobbing, playing with a rubber band, nodding his head—elsewhere in the house.

I'm almost fourteen. It is autumn in Pacific Palisades, and from this black-stained wooden deck, if I strain and ignore Noah's muh-muh-muh-muh-ing, then I can hear the ocean at the bottom of the cliff across the street from our house. The rhythmic crashing of the waves against the beach is soft and gentle sounding, in contrast to the harsh and guttural engine noises from the cars speeding by on the Pacific Coast Highway. The wind has to be just right to hear the waves, inshore, the kind of breeze that blows out any possibility of an afternoon swell. I'm straining to listen, but all I can hear now is Noah inside, and he's banging the walls. I can picture his posture on the dirty yellow sofa; he is prone, on his back or propped on one elbow, masticating a corner of a blanket or couch cushion—when I would later see photographs of Yemenis with huge bunches of khat bulging from between their parted lips, they were often reclined in similar poses. With his free arm Noah is banging against the veneer paneling, the thumps starting slowly and irregularly but then gaining momentum until they are repeated rapidly, and then they stop.

Good. He's quiet. I flick the lighter, inhale, enjoy the bubbling of the water, then the smoke filling my lungs. I hold it. Exhale.

Now I close my eyes and try to hear the ocean. But Noah is keening again, sounding progressively more agitated: muh-muh-Muh-Muh-MUH-MUH-MUH. He is so fucking loud. I sigh and set the water pipe down and go into the den. Noah doesn't really like music, or at least the kind of music I listen to. He doesn't like electric guitars. Sometimes my mother will put on these old folk records—the Weavers, my father's cousin Fred Hellerman was in the group—that we listened to as children: "Michael Row the Boat Ashore," "If I Had a Hammer." This music reminds me of summer camp; it soothes Noah.

But I'm tired of hearing Noah and sick of listening to his music, so I put some Van Halen on the family stereo and go back out to the deck and sit with my back to the sliding-glass door. I mean, fuck Noah.

So I'm sort of drifting, stoned, listening to "Runnin' with the Devil" really loud, and then after the song ends, in the gap before "Eruption," I hear nothing.

That's weird.

I stand up and walk inside. He's not in the living room, and in neither of the bathrooms, which is good because when he moves his bowels and I'm babysitting, I have to wipe him, and you never really get used to wiping another person's ass. And now that Noah is hitting puberty that means there is hair involved, and confronting that after a few bong hits can really harsh my mellow. But if you don't catch him while he is on the toilet, then the cleanup of feces-stained sofa, bed, or carpet is even more work, involving, as it does, detergents, sponges, and washing machines.

But if he isn't on the toilet or in his room, then where is he?

When I go through the living room, past the front door, I notice it is slightly ajar. Could Noah have walked out? I don't remember his ever venturing outside by himself, but . . .

I quickly check my parents' room. My own room is securely latched to keep Noah out. He's not in the kitchen.

Oh fuck, Noah. I walk through the entryway and out the front door in my socks. We don't wear shoes in our house, and Noah couldn't have gone too far in just his bare feet. I was expecting to see him in repose on the lawn, maybe chewing a blade of grass or a stick the way he does when he is in the backyard. Our lawn has never looked so empty.

I check the neighbors' houses on each side. I stand in the middle of the street and look both ways. Noah is gone.

I am stoned. My parents actually pay me to take care of Noah, two dollars an hour. Extra money with which I can buy more dope and albums and model tanks and boats. Now a few scenarios race through my mind, most of them ending with me in big trouble for losing Noah. One possible outcome is that he would run into the street and get hit by a car. The other possibility is that he wanders off, is unable to recall how to come home, and when he is finally approached by someone in the neighborhood, assuming they don't recognize him, he will either attack them or be so clearly out of it in some way that the police would probably be summoned, which would mean that Noah would be okay but I would get into huge trouble with my parents and lose my easy dope money.

I go back into the house and slip on my Adidas and then trot back out into the street. Which way should I go? There is the bluff across the street from our house overlooking the ocean. When my father takes Noah for walks, they usually start along this little cliff—these are the Palisades after which our town is named. Wouldn't Noah wander that way? He would have to cross a street. Once there, I doubt he would climb down any of the trails that wind, eventually, after passing through some pretty rough terrain, to the beach. But what if he did? He does sometimes start cantering, an uneven, listing sort of gait that he keeps up for a hundred or so feet. He could trot across the street and then down one of the trails and into the brush, and if he was out there all night—the sun would be setting soon—then who knows when or if he would be found.

I run through a list of possible bad outcomes: Noah is eaten by coyotes. The police are summoned and assume Noah is on PCP, which has been in the news lately, and then taser or shoot him. Noah vanishes.

There is no scenario that doesn't result in my getting shouted at by my parents.

I cross the street to the bluffs. A few older couples are walking their dogs along the dirt path atop the cliff. Spectators in sweaters have already taken up positions on the bench at the head of one of the trails. The sun is starting to set, its late autumn descent is always a spectacular orange, the light and smog and mist interacting so that whole sections of the sky become pink, purple, violet. The colors draw a small crowd.

"Did you see a kid come by?" I ask a seated couple who have tied their dog to one of the bench legs. "Looks like me, a little shorter."

They haven't seen him.

Anyway, Noah has always been terrified of dogs.

He would stay away.

I trot back to the house and into the garage for my bicycle, which has an underinflated front tire but will still cover more ground than I can cover on foot. I coast down the driveway and onto El Medio Avenue, our street, and then turn in the opposite direction of the bluffs, looking into the front yards as I go, turning back to scan the sidewalks ahead. He has his own distinctive gait—a shuffling, foot-dragging gait—and he doesn't really bend his knees much. He's slow. I could pick him out from a group at a quarter mile.

I pedal five blocks but then realize you can't search for Noah logically. He could have turned down any side street, onto any driveway, into any backyard. Private property doesn't exist for him. He's just as likely to have wandered into someone's living room as to be on the sidewalk.

I turn my bike around to pedal back in the opposite direction, figuring I will ride around our own block.

By now, my earlier worry about rousing my parents' anger has turned into guilt. If I've lost Noah, if something terrible happens to Noah, then I will have been an awful brother. Noah doesn't know any better. He was just doing his thing, chewing on stuff, and I was supposed to be making sure that he didn't do anything to hurt himself—stick his finger in an electric socket, swallow detergent, eat a battery, or run out of the house. He can't make his way in the world, negotiate a crosswalk, know that pinecones aren't edible. The planet presents myriad obstacles for Noah. And in my stoned haze I lost track of him and now he's gone.

I need to come up with an explanation for my parents. How did I lose track of him? Why wasn't I paying closer attention? Obviously, I can't admit that I was smoking marijuana, or that I always get stoned when I take care of Noah. I'll just tell them that Noah was quiet in the living room and I went to the bathroom and when I came out, he was gone. How could I get blamed for that?

But if he really is gone, has vanished from our lives, how bad would that really be? In a way, it would solve this persistent problem: What do we do with Noah? Even when it is not uttered aloud, it is the subtext of every conversation. Noah is why we moved here from New York. He's why our house is always a mess, our furniture always dirty, the sofa velvet stiff from dried saliva. He's why our bedding is shredded in corners from where he has chewed through it, why books are missing pages because he has torn them out, why my model tanks are dented and my plastic infantrymen (which I still care about at age fourteen) are damaged by tooth marks, why our windows are always filmy with the residue of his spit. He's why we can't go on vacations, why no one can sleep late, why I can't sit down with a bag of potato chips to watch TV because if he sees me then he'll want the whole bag. Everything is always about Noah, for Noah, because of Noah. Without saying a word he dictates the terms of our lives.

So as I'm pedaling, part of me is thinking, This is amazing, Noah has solved all the problems by himself, by just walking away. My parents will be angry at me for a while, shout at me, tell me I've been irresponsible, but then, after that, wouldn't our lives actually be improved?

I turn the corner. There's the Smiths' house, then the pink house with the weird old lady who has lots of cats, the white-stucco modern house, and then the Martindales' house on the corner. Across the street is a gray-shingle house where an old couple live whom I don't know.

Noah is sitting on their lawn next to a stone walkway that runs between two rows of ferns. There is a twig in his mouth. He is frowning as he rocks back and forth. I ride up onto the sidewalk and lay my bike down.

He sees me and keeps rocking and now he's shaking his head and going, "B-b-b-b-b-b-b-b-b-b-b." Then he spits in my general direction. This gesture is usually meant to express his displeasure or to warn someone to keep away. Ignore it, and you close in at your own risk.

I step onto the lawn but stop about six feet shy of where Noah is sitting. He begins to bang his head softly with a closed fist.

"Come on Noah," I say.

"B-b-b-b-b-b-b-b."

"Let's go."

He stands up by placing both hands on the grass then assuming a position like he is about to do a push-up then bringing his knees beneath him and lifting his right leg and placing that foot on the lawn and then leveraging himself upward. He walks toward me, and now he is smiling and bending his head forward slightly so that when he comes to me, he rests his head against my shoulder and murmurs a soft "B-b-b-b-b." This is his way of showing he is grateful to have been found. I hug him and then turn to pick up my bike, and he grabs my arm, afraid I'm going to ride off and leave him.

He is shaking his head.

"I'm gonna walk," I tell him. "Don't worry. Don't worry. Good boy."

He won't let go, even as we begin walking across the street. Only when we are back in sight of our house does he release me.

At home, I change his socks and put the dirty pair in the wooden bucket we use as a laundry hamper. I wash his hands and take a wet cloth and wipe the dirt stains from around his mouth. I stand back and look him over. He looks no more disheveled than usual. I'm safe. He can't talk, can't report that he wandered away while I wasn't looking, can't tell my parents that I take out my bong whenever they go out.

When my parents return, Noah is asleep and I am lying on a bean-bag chair watching television. They ask how Noah is and I tell them he is fine.

No problem.

46.

Noah used to go shopping with us. He has always liked car rides, sitting in the back of my father's Mazda station wagon and rocking back and forth, spitting on his fingers and then rubbing them against the window. Noah marks his territory, the way a hound will piss on a fire hydrant. Often, when we're walking, he will also lick the index finger, middle, and ring finger of his right hand to mark a mailbox, a lamppost, a tree trunk. It is a filthy habit, and my mother always tries to wipe his hands with a napkin, which means that she has to walk alongside him and, each time he touches a potentially germ-laden surface, she quickly reaches out to dry his hand before he can lick his fingers again. She does it, my father tells me quietly, so that she feels better.

"You want Noah to get sick?" she asks. "When Noah's sick, he's a mess. Running stomach. You're not gonna take care of him."

But when my father and I are walking with Noah and my mother isn't around, we usually don't bother to wipe his fingers, although once in a while my father will pull out a tissue to clean him as well, not as often as my mother, but still, it's obvious he feels like he has to make some effort, despite understanding the futility of the gesture.

In the car, no one worries about keeping his hands clean, because only Noah sits in the rear compartment, so the windows are presumably laden only with his own germs. He rocks on the black carpeting, twiddling a piece of string in his fingers. "Muh-muh-muh-muh-muh." When he does his humming at this more rapid tempo, it means he's happy. My father is driving. I turn back from the front passenger seat and can see he is smiling.

"Good boy," I say.

He nods his head, as if appreciating the comment. But then he closes his eyes tightly and grimaces for an instant, as if in pain, but just as quickly he is smiling again.

I recognize that moment of tension as potential trouble. His mood, while it is now excellent, could change quickly. I decide to ignore it.

"Good boy."

We park at a Hughes supermarket in a space two rows from the automatic sliding-glass-door entrance. My father opens the back hatch while I go to get a shopping cart. Shopping was easier when Noah fit into the toddler space at the back of the cart. Now, with Noah having long overgrown that little red plastic seat, he walks behind my father pushing the cart. I walk ahead of them, scanning the aisles for items I want to convince my father to buy for me. Almost everything a boy would like—potato chips, cookies, pastries, doughnuts, soda—is a fraught matter in our house, because if Noah finds it he will eat or drink all of it. When I manage to cajole my parents into purchasing these sorts of sweet or salty snacks, as soon as we return home I have to make sure they are well hidden in the high cabinet above the stove.

Here's what I want: those cookies called Flix that are wafer-and-cream sandwiches dipped in chocolate, a family-size bag of Doritos, and a dozen or so frozen burritos—I like to eat those for breakfast. My father is paying more attention to Noah, who keeps pulling coupons, plastic bags, twisty tops, wrappers—anything loose that he can rub between his fingers—off the shelves. He can't really worry about what I'm loading in the cart. I take off down the aisle and over to the next aisle to gather white sugar-frosted doughnuts and then head one more aisle over to grab a few frozen pizzas.

When I return I find our cart abandoned. I quickly scan it to make sure all my goodies are in there and then go to look for my father and Noah. Even before I find them I know what is happening.

He is lying down, stretched out, screaming. He is banging his head with an open fist, his shiny licorice-colored hair shimmering in the white fluorescent light with each smack. It is hard to describe what his tantrums sound like because you so seldom hear screams like his. Perhaps in a war zone or an emergency ward you will hear this kind of intense shouting laced with panic. He starts with a loud "Ba-Ba-Ba-BA-BA-BA-BA-BA-BA-BA-BA-BA-BA-BA," but after just ten seconds he has raised the decibel level to well above that familiar or recognizable to humans. (The letters to represent the sound he makes would be bigger than this page.) It is raw and sounds pained. Those who hear it at first want to help, but when they see Noah sprawled, crying, just a boy, they realize they can't help.

There is my father kneeling beside him, saying, "Come on, Noah, come on, Noah." He's saying this, I know, as much for those watching as for my brother. He has to show that he is seeking a solution. If he did nothing and just waited, which is probably the most effective course, then it would look as if he didn't care, so he has no choice but to offer this weak pleading, which is drowned out in the successive waves of Noah's tantrum.

My father looks up at me and subtly rolls his eyes, as if saying, What can I do? I'm one of four people who have gathered around. The other three are trying to figure out how to negotiate their way around this scene, having rightly concluded that they want no part of it. Noah is sprawled horizontally across the rear aisle, blocking the shortest route between Produce and Dairy. Behind me, carts are starting to back up, and a few exasperated shoppers make the smart decision and detour over to the Frozen Foods aisle.

By now I'm underwhelmed by these scenes. Noah's tantrums are a familiar annoyance, and complaining or lamenting them would be like bitching about the weather. There is a vague sense of embarrassment as I stand there, because I can glimpse our family from the outside as I watch my father and my brother locked in this familiar struggle on a supermarket floor. We are all ashamed of our families. There are moments with Noah when all my family's particular irregularities—my balding, bug-eyed Jewish father, my Japanese mother, my brain-damaged brother—they all suddenly feel thrust out there for everyone to see. In those moments I wish I could be one of the crowd instead of part of the act.

My father stands up, puts his hands in his pants pocket, and readjusts keys, wallet, change, as if he is searching for something. Then he pulls out his wallet and hands me a five and tells me to go buy some nuts. I take the money, head back down the snack aisle, and grab a bag of beer nuts, but instead of paying for it, I just walk around the store for a few minutes, about how long it would take me to pay for it, and then carry it back down the aisle to where Noah is screaming. You can hear him all over the store, this shouting, these repeated syllables that are still ascending to higher decibel levels. From a distance, the sound is muffled slightly by all the groceries, by the shelves full of bread and toilet paper and bottled soda, but the size of the place also makes it echo, so throughout the store there is a ubiquitous, guttural wail accompanying the sounds of cash register drawers and shopping carts being pulled from their interlocking rows and cans being *thunk*ed down on rubber conveyer belts.

Now Noah is sitting up, which is progress, but he is still banging the top of his head and shaking it from side to side. The small crowd has dispersed. Whatever this scene is, it is weird and sad, but it must clearly be, to those watching it, a personal, family sort of tragedy . . . nothing you want a part of, trust me.

I hand my father the bag of nuts. He tears it open with his teeth, pours a few out into his hand, and extends them to Noah. "Nuts. Noah, here. Nuts."

Noah reaches up and takes the nuts and quickly shoves them into his mouth. He nods his head and demands, "Muh. MUH."

My father shakes out more. Noah gobbles them up.

"Get up," my father says. "If you want more, get up."

Noah spits, jettisoning bits of husk and wet peanut fragments that land mostly on the front of his brown T-shirt.

"Noah," my father repeats, rattling the bag of peanuts, "get up."

Noah stands up, still clearly irritable but drawn by the snack. My father gives him a few more nuts. He leads Noah back down the aisle in this manner, Noah walking as few paces as possible to win a few more peanuts and my father seeking to cajole as many steps as he can for each bribe. It takes about fifteen minutes to make it out of the market and another five to get back to the car, where my father opens the back hatch, loads Noah in, and then hands me the peanuts. When the hatch is closed, Noah's mouth opens widely and his eyes squint, as if he is outraged at this betrayal.

I'm to wait in the car with the peanuts, giving Noah a couple every few minutes while my father returns to the store to complete the shopping. I have to be careful to ration the peanuts so that they don't run out before my father returns with the groceries. How long could he take? He will rush, I know that, and will probably buy fewer items than he would have if he could shop at his leisure. But what if there is a long checkout line? That could take fifteen minutes, I estimate. If I give Noah two peanuts every fifteen seconds, that would make 8 peanuts a minute, so I will need 120 peanuts to last the whole quarter hour. How many peanuts are in a bag of beer nuts? I've never thought about that before, and the bag only describes the contents by weight: three ounces. I look into the bag and reckon there can't be more than a hundred nuts in there. I begin breaking the nuts in half to stretch out the ration and though Noah notices that he is being shortchanged, the supply is steady enough that he doesn't mount a very serious protest, spitting at me before demanding, "Muh. MUH!"

I've timed it well. Just as there are about a dozen peanuts left in the bag, my father appears rolling a cart out of the front of the supermarket. He opens the door to the backseat and begins loading the bags onto the floor, where Noah can't reach them. And though Noah complains on the way home when the nuts give out, he is apparently sated for now as he lies back on the carpet and twiddles a rubber band that he has somehow found in the rear compartment.

I view this as a most satisfactory excursion. I've made five dollars by not paying for the beer nuts and my father's forgetting to ask for any change.

Only when we get home do I discover that my father didn't purchase all the items I had loaded into the cart.

"Where are my doughnuts?" I ask.

"I didn't say you could have doughnuts," he says. "When do we ever buy doughnuts?"

I am thinking that Noah throws a fit and gets a whole bag of peanuts, one of his favorite snacks. What do I get out of the deal? I get what I manage to steal, what I pilfer through my own ingenuity.

47.

Pacific Palisades, our town, has a cruel reputation. Not in the way of Compton or South Central—there are no drive-bys or sidewalk drug sales in this white, wealthy Los Angeles suburb. It is a picturesque, sun-kissed town winding lazily along cliffs perched above the Pacific. And it really is a great place to live. For adults. Among teenagers throughout L.A., however, it is known as a socially vicious suburb, a beach town where a surfers-rule, no-fat-chix ethic is strictly enforced. (Barnaby Harris would scrawl that in huge letters on the retaining wall above Bowdoin Street.) Those who aren't blond, strong, handsome, fast, and harsh enough turn invisible or, worse, become victims of that gang of surfers and skateboarders who rule our teenage wasteland. Brewing just out of sight is a subculture of fear and kid-on-kid violence.

By fourteen I have already been beaten up twice. I've seen one gang rape. I have been robbed several times, always in petty dope deals. I have been an accessory to a purse snatching. I have participated in two burglaries. I once vandalized an elementary school library and was a lookout when another kid broke into a doctor's office. This is in a town considered one of the most exclusive communities in Los Angeles. And I am one of the good kids.

Single-parent households are the norm. And those single parents are largely absentee. Yet it is those parents who pass Proposition 13 in 1978, lowering property taxes and gutting California's public schools by stagnating teachers' wages and causing hiring freezes. At Paul Revere Junior High, which I attend, staffing shortages have forced physical-education instructors to become teachers of algebra and Spanish teachers to explain the wonders of reproduction. Courses are boring and ineptly taught. Not that it matters. We are often stoned in class. Or we just don't go to school. We unsupervised teens and preteens spend our days in a haze of marijuana smoke, Cheap Trick records, and Lonnie Toft skateboards. For those of us frozen out of the dominant crowd of Bryns, Tads, and Rommys, these years amount to a sort of social exile.

Plus, I have Noah, my retarded, autistic, just fucked-up younger brother whose disability marks our family as freaks and outsiders. At exactly the moment when I desperately want to fit in, to belong, I become acutely aware that I never will.

48.

My own morning routine requires that I ignore Noah completely. I get up, pull on shorts, T-shirt, and socks. My father has installed a latch at head height that I secure every morning so that Noah can't get into my room and chew up my stuff. If he is in the living room when I am walking through to get to the kitchen, I hardly acknowledge him. I cook my eggs on a heavy black skillet in butter, then eat them quickly out of a bowl, pretending, sometimes, that I am a soldier eating out of a helmet. I pour a glass of orange juice and drink that quickly. Noah occasionally wanders into the kitchen and dining room while I am eating breakfast, and I tell him, "Wait, wait."

I know that any surliness caused by his being denied food will take a few minutes to detonate, enough time for me to grab my notebook and skateboard and get out of the house. I usually unfold the *Los Angeles Times* and sit on the steps next to our driveway, reading *Doonesbury* and the sports section and checking the box scores while joggers trot past on their way to the cliff.

Paul Revere Junior High School is in Brentwood, the next town inland from Pacific Palisades. The bus gathers us every morning at the corner of Northfield and Bowdoin, four blocks away. I ride my skateboard—an old light-blue Bahne with Road Rider wheels—

down El Medio to cover the distance faster. It's my old deck, so I feel safe stashing it while I'm at school in an ivy embankment behind a retaining wall worn smooth by kids leaning against it every morning for the past few decades. I got the idea of stashing the skateboard from Bren Mckarron, who does the same thing with his old, wooden Logan Earthski. Skating to the bus saves about ten minutes every morning.

My parents have never told me this. But I feel that I am a disappointment to them as a student. At one point, as a third-grader, I had tested into the gifted program at my elementary school, primarily because I was reading at a higher level than my classmates. I was also the best in my class at multiplication and long division. And I still read and can calculate quickly, but I seldom read the books we are assigned or complete my math homework. I am lazy, but not because I am not challenged or find the work too easy. There is no hidden genius in my indifference to academics. I don't do well at school because I don't like hard work. By the end of elementary school, in part because of my mother's tutoring me in mathematics, my academic performance had progressed to where I was among the top performers in my sixth-grade class. By the time I reach junior high school, my arithmetic scores had landed me in the honors math. That had been a high point for me academically. I have since been steadily moving down the academic hierarchy of my junior high school, starting in seventh grade in honors math 5, the highest level for that grade, and then moving to algebra in eighth grade and finally algebra S (for slow) this year, ninth grade. I have managed to stay in the higher-level English classes, but I may have hit a wall there as well because I have not read *A Tale of Two Cities*, for which we are supposed to be writing a paper. The only class I consistently get A's in is history, and that is because it is primarily about wars, and I have already read an awful lot about war.

In addition to our academic performance, we are also graded in work habits and cooperation, ranging from E for excellent through S for satisfactory to U for unsatisfactory. Both categories are vague, with issues like tardiness and attendance and cooperation being a measure of how quiet and attentive one is. My marks in these areas have become spectacularly lousy: seven U's out of a possible fourteen. (We have six classes and a homeroom, for which there is no academic grade.) In fact, my performance has been so awful that I have been moved into what is called non-grad homeroom, the class where those of us who receive too many U's are banished. The class is so named because of the threat that, if we do not shape up, we will not be allowed to participate in the junior high graduation ceremony. The vast majority of my fellow non-grads are there because of truancy or because they were caught smoking or fighting. And most of them don't bother even showing up for homeroom, being too busy getting into real trouble. There are very few, like me, who are here because we go to class but still consistently misbehave.

My attendance is regular, and I am seldom tardy. The reason I am often remanded to the principal, vice principal, and guidance counselor, and have been condemned to non-grad, is because I am a relentless and tireless asshole to my teachers, making regular wisecracks, some of them funny—such as when I sat at my desk with the cover of *Playboy* magazine over my biology textbook, causing the teacher to storm down the aisle to discover me clandestinely doing the day's required reading—but most of them simply annoying—such as making cricket chirps or frequent, incessant, and obviously manufactured coughs or fake sneezes. All of it is calculated to annoy and disrupt my classes. Part of the reason, I know, is that I am bored, but there is also a compulsive, self-destructive streak that is manifest in these fifty-five-minute classes that I feel powerless to curtail.

My parents are both tired of having to meet with the assigned administrators about my disciplinary issues and, in some cases, have even been worn down into a state of sympathy with me. The most recent was when I convinced a fellow group of students to refrain from pledging allegiance to the flag at the start of homeroom, sending Mrs. Lester, our homeroom teacher, into a patriotic rage. I wasn't doing this out of any deeply felt political conviction but because I knew it would anger Mrs. Lester. I presented my case as a matter of personal freedom, First Amendment and all that. During a parent-teacher conference with Mrs. Lester, my father and mother defended my right to refrain from reciting the Pledge of Allegiance, my mother pointing out that as a Japanese citizen living in the United States, she didn't feel that she should compel me to pledge my allegiance to any flag, Japanese or American.

For a while Mrs. Lester ordered me to stand outside during the salute to the flag, but my transfer to non-grad ended that because the non-grad teacher, Mrs. Williams, didn't pay attention to who did or didn't salute the flag, and didn't require that we even stand for it.

I know there is discussion between my parents and the various administrators about my home life being irregular because of Noah. My father has brought this up to me, suggesting that perhaps I am causing these disturbances as a cry for attention. While I am intellectually able to grasp this simple explanation, it doesn't feel exactly right to me. I am in so many ways an outsider—half Japanese, half Jewish, a below-average athlete, introverted when it comes to my own interests in military models, fantasy role playing, and imaginary sports leagues—that it is hard to single out my autistic brother as the cause of any of my irregular behaviors. (My only mainstream interests seem to be studying sports statistics, skateboarding, and smoking marijuana.)

I am sent to see a school psychologist several times in his linoleum-floored office. He sits behind his gray steel desk. There is a flower pot on the windowsill with creeping ivy with white frosted leaves. Behind him is one of those posters of a supposedly calming landscape, a mountain creek running between sylvan meadows. We are there, I know, to seek an explanation for my compulsive "acting out," as it is called. If I were one of those kids who was just beating up other kids, the drill would be easier: warning after warning, until finally the boy is removed to another school. Any student caught smoking or in possession of marijuana is automatically expelled. But for me, a simple pain in the ass who doesn't seem a threat to other students, there is this incessant, hand-wringing-accompanied palaver.

The psychologist turns out to be more interested in Noah than in me. He has read one of my father's books, or has at least heard of them and has seen our family on *60 Minutes*. And he feels that if he can convince me that my behaviors are directly linked to my brother, then he will have made some kind of breakthrough.

"I don't know," I tell him. "Noah's my brother. I don't know what it's like *not* to have a brother like Noah."

He takes this as profound.

But despite my assurances after three sessions that I will stop disturbing classes, I never pause in my disruptive behavior, and soon I am ordered to spend my lunch hours in something called "opportunity," otherwise known as detention. I believe I am the only student who has gone from the honors section of courses to regular detention. My colleagues there are a few Mexican kids who lay their heads down and sleep during the lunch hour, a few stoners who sit and draw pictures of waves, and a few of the more precocious and attractive girls who pass notes about the stoners. And then there's me.

It would be too easy to blame Noah for all my scholastic shortcomings, for my inattentiveness in class, for my frequent arguments with teachers. Easy and, I believe, a cop out. Noah can't be regarded as the great and ultimate excuse for my own defects of character. To do so would be to deny my own personality, my own behavior. I am entirely capable of my own fuckups, no matter how eager the adults around me might be to look at my young life through the prism of my brother's disability.

49.

Our school is built on about five acres, filling a bulge on Sunset Boulevard as it hairpins past Mandeville Canyon. It was constructed in the 1950s and with its wrapping of chain-link fences surrounding bungalows laid out on tarmac paved hills, gulleys, and embankments—they paved everything back then—it resembles from the outside a minimum security prison or, I would later discover, a state mental health facility. Those paved banks, along with those at Kenter Elementary and Brentwood Elementary, would become famous as the proving ground where skateboarders, including the legendary Zephyr team of *Dogtown and Z-boys* fame, would pioneer the slides and kick-turns that would eventually result in the sport of vertical skateboarding. I recall one morning after the bus dropped us off watching two of my boyhood idols, Jay Adams and the Japanese American Shogo Kubo, shredding the banks behind the social studies building.

But during the school day, it is a grim tableau of faded, salmon-colored buildings and flat, gravel-roofed porticos supported by brown poles with corrugated drainage pipes attached by ring clamps. I shuffle from English to biology, spending the nutrition break standing among a crowd of stoners and surfers—I am not really in this clique, but I aspire somehow to join them and find their stories about small-time criminality to be fascinating. After nutrition is Algebra S, then my drama elective, where we are supposed to perform scenes, and finally lunch, when I dutifully report to "opportunity." Then comes history with Mr. Calum, a short, bespectacled man who wears brown or gray flannel suits and includes as part of our curriculum reading *Time* magazine every Tuesday. He believes in stressing current events as part of the study of history, attempting to make us understand, I suppose, that history is somehow journalism about the past. At any rate, it is a very efficient way to fill fifty-five minutes, having us read aloud passages from *Time* and then discuss them. When the magazine does cover packages about, for example, America's drug problem or a new blockbuster film, the class finds this a pleasant diversion from the Gadsden Purchase or Sutter's Mill.

This week, the cover is about America becoming a more litigious society, the cover line reading "Those **@#!! Lawyers." On page 96 there is a picture of my family standing in our backyard accompanying a two-page review and feature about *A Place for Noah*, my father's third book. I know the article is there, but most of the class isn't aware of it as the magazines are passed out and we begin reading from the front. Of course, most of the students flip through the magazine quickly, and I sit quietly. I wait for it. I wait for it.

"It's Karl!" Karen Weiss shouts.

I had known this moment was coming for at least a week. My parents gave me the option of skipping school today to avoid the awkwardness of sitting at my desk while my class reads an article about my family, but I felt that in some ways that experience was no stranger than not being there. Either way, I was in an uncomfortable and unwelcome spotlight: the kid with the retard brother or the kid ashamed of having a retard brother.

Just as embarrassing, in my view, is that in the photo, with my long hair, weedy physique, and shorts, I think I look like a girl.

And then Karen says it. "You look like a girl."

The whole class has already found the page and is looking at the photo of me and then at me. I sit there and pretend to look at the picture along with them.

Mr. Calum orders the class to return to the front of the magazine and to read in order. We page through a story about Jimmy Carter visiting South America and the cover story, about Anwar Sadat's hopes for peace in the Middle East. Mr. Calum chooses to flip past a feature on Louis Malle's *Pretty Baby*, starring Brooke Shields, and then, only when we have gone through the magazine exactly as we do every week, do we come to the story about my family, which Mr. Calum describes as being about a "touching, powerful, very important book written by Karl's father."

He looks at me, "Karl, do you want to say anything?"

I shrug.

"Does anyone want to ask Karl any questions?"

About a dozen hands are raised.

"Does Noah talk?"

"Why doesn't he talk?"

"When will he talk?"

"Was he always like this?"

"Is Noah sick?"

"Is there a cure?"

"Is Noah happy?"

"Does he cry?"

"Do you like him?"

"Was he born like this?"

"Why is your dad wearing that hat?"

50.

After school, I take a different bus route back with a friend so I can hang out at his house. Jonathan's parents are divorced and he lives with his father, who sells insurance in Santa Monica. There is a Guatemalan cleaning lady who is supposed to also keep an eye on Jonathan. She lays out a snack of potato chips and grape juice on the kitchen table, says, "Hello, Yown-a-ton," and then retreats to the den, where she irons and watches Spanish-language *telenovelas*.

I don't have my skateboard with me, so Jonathan rides his bicycle and I borrow his deck and we sidecar it down Galloway to Drummond and then wait for the light. He pedals and I catch up and we ride along Toyopa past the park to a vacant lot that connects to one of the canyons. Our town is built upon the plateaus where the various pocket canyons extending up from the ocean finally level out into buildable lots. The brush and scrub have been cleared and the dirt plowed into rectangular, ten-thousand-square-foot lots that still abut the wild canyons just beyond the sprinkled backyards.

Family cats are often taken by coyotes.

For us, for fourteen-year-old boys looking for anything untamed and feral, these canyons provide an opportunity to explore, to set off fireworks, to fire pellet guns and wrist rockets, to smoke dope, and to do whatever we want without any chance of an adult interceding.

We put the bike and skateboard behind one of the tall bunches of licorice stalks, checking to see if they are well hidden. Then we climb over a small rise speckled with ankle-high onion-smelling grass and skid down the trail into the canyon, our sneakers half sliding, half running along dirt paths and over the sandstone, granite, and mica formations that poke through the skin-colored dirt. There is a man-high hollow beneath an outcropping of pebble-studded sandstone. It is just deep enough to sit in the shade of the overhang. Jonathan pulls off his canvas backpack and unpacks a wrist rocket, a wooden pipe the length of an adult finger with a blackened screen, and a small baggie with some brown marijuana in it. Our plan was to sit here for a while and smoke and then go down to Rome's house, where his older brother has just built a quarter-pipe skateboard ramp.

The marijuana sounds dry as Jonathan crushes it to pick out the seeds. It is brown Colombian, the most readily available and inexpensive marijuana in our town. Smoked through a pipe, as we are doing now, it is harsh and dry and tastes vaguely like hay and dirt and horses. But it is bluntly effective, and after we pass the bowl back and forth a few times, reload it, and pass it again, we are both in a lazy haze. Jonathan picks up the wrist rocket, gathers up a pebble, lays it into the yoke, and pulls the surgical tubing back, firing it off with a snapping sound. The projectile hisses through the air before disappearing into a puffy clump of brush. He loads another one and fires it off.

That hissing sound is deeply satisfying.

"That sounds cool," I say.

"Dude," Jonathan says, "I wish we had some jammin' tunes."

I shrug. Jonathan is musically more sophisticated than me, already listening to Black Sabbath and Yes, while I have just discovered Led Zeppelin and still secretly believe that Kiss is the best band in the world, a deeply uncool opinion among my fellow eighth- and ninth-graders who dismiss Kiss as a kiddie band.

He sometimes quotes bits and pieces of Black Sabbath songs, verses from "Sweet Leaf" or "N.I.B."—*"Straight people don't know, what you're about / They put you down and shut you out / You gave to me a new belief / and soon the world will love you, sweet leaf"*—sound almost better to me than the songs themselves when I do finally hear them, because the songs are more complicated but the little rhymes are clear and precise and dark and always intimate that by smoking dope we are part of a great cabal of guitar rock worshipping stoners; it is the closest I ever come to feeling like part of a community outside of my family.

Jonathan hands me the wrist rocket, and I launch a projectile that hisses away, the sound now so cutting that I imagine I can see the trail of noise in the air. While I am searching for another pebble, a rock falls down in front of me with a heavy clump. I look up, trying to figure out if it fell from the cliff above us. Jonathan seems not to have noticed. I pick up another pebble.

Then another rock falls, this one into the bushes to our right.

"Did you see that?" I say.

Jonathan looks at me with red eyes and shrugs. "Falling rocks."

"Where are they coming from?"

He shrugs again and points upward.

He doesn't seem concerned.

Then another one drops, this one almost hitting Jonathan in the head. We both quickly slide back so we are against the side of the cliff and look up.

Now we hear scrambling in the bushes above us. Someone is up there.

Another rock.

"Who is it?" I say.

"I don't know." Jonathan quickly packs the pipe and the little baggie of weed into his backpack and closes it up. Then he takes back the wrist rocket and grabs a stone. He stands up and shouts. "Hey, whoever is up there, I have a wrist rocket and I'm gonna start firing."

Now an even bigger rock is tossed down, this one landing on Jonathan's foot.

"Hey," he shouts, "fuck you, man. I'm gonna—"

More rocks come raining down, and Jonathan jumps back into the lee of the sandstone cliff. We can hear more movement, a branch snapping, the zippery sound of a bush against denim. There are at least two people up there.

We feel trapped.

"What do they want?" I ask.

Jonathan shrugs and begins gathering pebbles. "Load up," he says.

What would Alexander do? I wonder. Or Napoleon or Murat or Guderian or any of the other great generals I have been reading about. I suppose some sort of flanking movement, get around and behind whoever is up there. But that would mean leaving this little bit of shelter and exposing ourselves to more rocks.

I wish I wasn't stoned.

"Fuck you," someone shouts from above us. "Pay us and we'll stop."

"We don't have any money," says Jonathan. "Who are you?"

"Who are *you*?" The voice shouts back.

"You first," Jonathan says.

"Step out," he answers, "and I'll stand up."

Jonathan pulls the wrist rocket tubing back and says to me, "Cover me."

"With what?" I say. "You have the wrist rocket."

He shrugs.

He backs into the sunlight with the tubing cocked, squinting upward.

"Who is it?" I ask.

"It's Baz," Jonathan stage-whispers to me.

"It's Jonathan the fag," shouts Baz, laughing.

I know Baz Mohegan; he's in Mr. Calum's history class with me. He looks like he's about twenty-five; he's the only ninth-grader I know who can buy beer. During lunch sometimes I listen to his stories, which involve a lot of breaking and entering and joyriding in automobiles.

"He's up there with Eric Lynch," Jonathan says. Then he shouts up to Baz, "What do you guys want?"

"Who're you with?" Baz shouts back.

"Karl."

I can hear laughter. "The girl with the retard brother?"

"Are you guys fagging off down there?" Lynch shouts.

"What do you want?" Jonathan shouts.

"We're just chucking rocks," says Baz.

"Can we come up?"

"We might chuck more rocks," Baz says. "It's fuckin' fun."

"Who doesn't like chucking rocks?" Lynch asks rhetorically.

"We gotta go home," Jonathan says.

There is silence, some sort of consultation is in progress.

"You guys have any weed?" Baz asks.

Jonathan looks at me. I shake my head and whisper no.

"Yes," he shouts back. "You want us to smoke you out?"

"Okay, come up."

We step out and then scramble up the trail, using the sandstone outcropping for support until we come to where Baz and Lynch are standing atop the cliff. They wear old Pendletons, faded denim, and two-tone Van sneakers. Both of them appear to have the beginnings of mustaches on their upper lips and already have muscular upper arms and thick chests. Baz is one of the best Little League players in the local park system, and Lynch is renowned as a good skater. They are taller than we are, and standing as they are on higher ground, they loom above us.

"What's up, dudes?" Baz nods. "You guys wasted?"

Now that we have emerged, they are all friendly smiles, as if the confrontation of a few minutes ago had happened to a different group of boys.

We nod.

"Fucking radical, man." Baz smiles. "Let's smoke."

"Where?" Jonathan says, looking around. "Right here?"

"Fuck yeah," Baz says. "Are you guys pussies?"

Of course not.

Jonathan unzips his backpack and pulls out his pipe and baggie.

"Let me check it out," Baz says.

Jonathan hands him the baggie. Baz opens it and inhales.

"Fuckin' mumbo," he observes.

Baz helps himself to a full bowl and then hits it with a lighter, inhaling and then passing it to Lynch, who, while he is inhaling, takes the lighter from Baz and sparks the bowl again. I have never seen such monstrous hits. Their exhalations seem to take about a minute each, huge billows of dope smoke that linger in the air like the residue of a fireworks show.

Then they tap out the bowl, load it again, and repeat the gesture.

While Baz is holding in a hit, he looks at me and says in a choked voice. "Fucking *Time* magazine . . . retard . . . brother . . . your dad . . . book."

He exhales and says in one long breath, "Thatwasatotallygaypictureofyouinthemagazine."

The two of them are consuming marijuana at a ridiculous pace, packing the bowl, sucking down enormous hits and exhaling.

Jonathan and I stand there, powerless to intervene as the amount of weed in the bag steadily diminishes.

Finally, Baz hands Jonathan back the pipe and then instead of returning the miniscule amount of dope in the baggie, Baz rolls it up and pockets it himself.

"Later days, Butleys," says Baz.

We watch Baz and Lynch go.

There is nothing we can do.

We don't feel like checking out Rome's older brother's quarterpipe any more and instead collect Jonathan's bike and skateboard from the spot behind the licorice plants. We ride in silence for a while, and at Galloway I part with Jonathan and walk home.

When I get to the morning bus-pickup spot, where I stash my old skateboard in the ivy, I dig around for a while but can't find it. Some kid has swiped it.

51.

After walking home, I take a few minutes to squirt Visine in my eyes and then lie down for a while in my room with my cat, TG, purring on my chest.

Noah usually eats before the rest of the family. My mother has to coax him to eat his steak and carrots before she will spoon any rice onto his plate. He likes starches—rice, bread, noodles—and will fill up on carbohydrates before he takes a bite of protein. When my mother lays down the sliced steak, he spits at her once, an expression of his disapproval.

She is used to this and stands up straight, pretending to be angry, "Why?"

"Buh-buh-buh-buh-buh-buh." He picks up a hunk of meat with his fingers.

"Use a fork," my mother says.

He spits.

"Use a fork."

He gathers the fork, stabs a piece of steak, and eats it.

After about fifteen minutes, Noah has eaten his steak and even a few carrots, and so my mother dumps a pile of rice on his plate. Noah is Japanese in his dietary preferences, and like my mother, he will find any meal without short-grain rice unsatisfactory. He eats the rice hurriedly, shoving bites into his mouth until his cheeks are bulging and then swallowing juice in great, painful-looking gulps. He finishes his juice and holds up the empty glass.

"Muh." This is one of the few words Noah can say.

My mother pours him about an inch of liquid.

He gulps it.

"Muh."

"Good boy," my mother says. She pours.

He drinks it and then goes back to shoveling rice into his mouth. My mother would later write in her autobiographical novella *A Guest from Afar* about a woman feeding her autistic son, "He could eat prodigiously, second, third, fourth and even fifth helpings—especially of rice—but eventually he would finish, rise, and try to make a hasty departure. Michiko would have to catch him with one hand as his lap emptied onto the floor, and with a cloth towel in the other hand, carefully wipe his mouth and hands, brushing away the crumbs and picking off the rice kernels still clinging to his shirt and pants. She would then have to clean up the mess, tidy up the table . . . At the same time could not allow him to get too far out of sight—or sound range—because it was after eating that he was mostly likely to have a bowel movement or need to urinate. This part of the daily routine always left Michiko completely tired."

Sill, when Noah is manageable, it is possible to imagine his staying with us forever. So he's a little unruly once in a while, prone to fits of hair pulling, pinching, biting, scratching—but families are remarkably forgiving organizations. There are plenty of abusive domestic situations, husbands beating wives, mothers hitting their sons, brothers attacking brothers, and don't those families somehow carry on for years? So in a sense, our family is just like all those other badly behaved families, only ours is more obvious and a little more one-sided. Right now, Noah has two things going for him: he is still cute and therefore easier to forgive, and he is relatively small, still a few inches shorter than my mother. When he is grown up and physically stronger than my parents, then the psychological algebra that keeps him at home will have very different values opposite the denial side of the equal sign.

The topic of finding a place for Noah has been a steady part of the family conversation. It is always discussed in a very specific context: its inevitability. Time is running out. Noah is growing. What will happen to Noah? The worry and consternation are so much a part of our psychic matrix as a family that it seems to hang over our every gathering.

He will go away, ideally into a nurturing, warm group home where he will thrive. That is our great dream, the culminating point of all our aspirations. (When I read about George and Lenny in *Of Mice and Men* and their pipe-dream farm with the rabbits, I imagine a similar sort of destination for Noah, a bucolic retreat where there would be other kids like him . . . and rabbits. Noah, of course, would be terrified of rabbits, but the idea that anyone would care enough about Noah, or kids like him, to provide them with rabbits, suggested they would be nurturing.) To that end, my parents have traveled throughout the

United States and even to Japan, seeking a place for Noah. Most of the possible group homes, facilities, foundations, and academies are deemed either too strict—in a few the staff members use aversive therapy, and in some the staff restrains the kids at night so they don't wander and injure themselves or others—or can only take clients far more advanced than Noah.

For my parents, the idea that Noah will be hit or restrained is still intolerable. Their reasoning is that as a nonverbal, Noah has no way of saying if he is being mistreated, if he has to go to the bathroom, if he is nauseous, cramped, in pain. So to restrain him is to remove his only form of communication, physical expression. The only way he can communicate that he has to go to the bathroom is to actually go to the bathroom.

There is in this, however, a slight hypocrisy. My father occasionally slaps or hits Noah and me. He used to spank me when I misbehaved, on a couple of occasions using a belt. He has similarly been impatient with Noah, though he knows there is no benefit from hitting either of us. It is his great shortcoming as a father, and out of character with his otherwise sophisticated worldview. When I've asked him about this, he says that he hits me because his father hit him, which is perhaps a causative explanation but not a logical one. Because he is aware of his own occasional impatience and frustration toward Noah, and knows that it is a failing on his part, he suspects that any others who care for Noah will fall into the same pattern.

I've never known a life without Noah, so the idea of sending him away is so abstract as to be almost fanciful, sort of like those discussions that we sometimes have about what life would be like if Noah were normal. Because I have lived my life with Noah, always in the next room or right next to me, I am perhaps the person most acclimated to Noah's noise, his presence, his personality. I take it literally for granted. My parents had lives before Noah; I didn't.

So the notion that there is another life, one without this spitting, jibbering, finger-twiddling, head-bobbing idiot riding shotgun is as fantastic as a discussion of life in zero-gravity environments: interesting, but ultimately nothing more than an intellectual exercise.

So at dinner, as my buzz recedes and I nurse a headache and sluggishly descend into the torpor of family life, the familiar discussion of a place for Noah is sort of like walking into a conversation about the weather, only one that perpetually forecasts an impending storm.

52.

My parents are out for the evening and I am watching television, *CHiPs*, and when it is over, I recall that it is Noah's bedtime. As usual, he disagrees. I persist and he spits at me.

I am patient with Noah, far more forgiving than I am with any object or any other living thing. Who else would I allow to spit at me, to scratch me, to pull my hair, to take an occasional poke at me? If I could be similarly disciplined in any other area of my life—with, say, algebra, tennis, or Charles Dickens—I would be a very different kind of person. Noah and I, despite his disability, we have our sibling rivalry. It is patently unfair, since I have so many overt advantages, but he has his own cards to play, and remember, in the competition for parental resources of time, attention, and money, he will win every race. Usually, our rivalry comes down to little more than his spitting at me or scratching me, and I have become wily at dodging saliva tracers or shaking off his claws. It is an instinct, one that my parents share: when we see Noah coming, we can detect, without even looking at him, if he seems surly or discontent. We can hear it, sense it in his pace or his body language, in how he is rocking his head, or fluttering his fingers by his ear. And we know to take quick, evasive action. First: keep your guard up. Noah is not expert at closing in and can't get to your hair to pull it if your hand is up high. Second: keep your jab extended. This puts Noah on the defensive and buys time for a juke or sidestep out of trouble.

The problem, of course, is the sneak attack, which Noah does launch from time to time. You can be lying on the beanbag chair, watching a football game, and suddenly Noah might grab a handful of your hair, gouge an eye, scratch your face. My father has been the victim of most of these attacks, which are infrequent and random, which makes them more terrifying. Noah rarely tries them with me. Anyway, I am too fast for him and am among the best in the family at identifying his moods and intentions. I can roll out of his range and be up with my jab extended faster than anyone in the family. Usually, he will just walk away.

We have, of late, settled into an unspoken truce. He knows that when I am in charge I am more lenient than my parents, more likely to hand out potato chips or cookies. And I know that he can't tell my parents that I did not practice piano for a half hour, as I am supposed to, and he will also be reliably mum about my taking bong hits out on the porch. I believe it is a happy arrangement for both of us.

But tonight, when I tell him it is time to brush his teeth, he responds by spitting at me.

As I said, I'm used to this, and often Noah's initial protest is followed by a grudging acquiescence to whatever is being asked of him. Noah is like me in that he seldom seems to do anything willingly, even those things he enjoys doing, like taking a walk with my father or riding in the car. He'll spit first and then shuffle over to put on his shoes.

This evening, however, after spitting at me, he resumes his languorous posture on the sofa; it is an almost imperial recline, crying out for toga and laurel. He has in his hand a rubber band, one of the thick-ply variety that withstand a great deal of twisting and twiddling. These are like Cuban cigars to Noah.

"Come on, Noah," I tell him. "Get up. Time to brush your teeth."

"Tuh," he says as he spits at me again.

"Noah," I add more growl to my voice. "Get up."

"Tuh."

"Listen," I warn. "Hey, listen. Get up."

He drops his head down and works intently on his rubber band.

I grab his arm to pull him into an upright position. He resists by trying to scratch my fingers, but I let go before his nails gain purchase. He flops back down.

"Noah." I point at him. "Get up. You listen, Noah. Get up."

He closes his eyes tightly and shakes his head and starts softly tapping his head with the palm of his right hand, still twiddling the rubber band with his left.

"Get up," I say sternly.

Noah then launches up from the sofa with a jerk and flips over the coffee table—this is his standard expression of anger—and runs into the middle of the living room. I assume he is going to the bathroom for his toothbrush, but instead he stops on the hardwood floor and folds his arms in front of his face so that his nose and eyes are visible above his crossed forearms—it's the pose genies sometimes strike in cartoons.

"Ba-ba-ba-ba-ba," Noah is saying. It's the start of how he says "bad boy," usually in reference to me. He learned it from teachers and my parents saying it to him. "Ba-ba-ba-ba."

"Noah, fucking *listen*," I tell him as I walk over to him. "Go brush your teeth."

I shove him on the shoulder in the direction of the bathroom. He doesn't budge.

I push him again.

This time he unfolds his arms and spits at me. His face is contorted—eyebrows angled down toward the bridge of his nose, nostrils flared, upper lip curled to the tip of the nose, lower lip and jaw thrust downward. It is an expression of rage; I have since seen warrior masks carved into a similar shape in Nepal.

I am too close, I realize at the last instant, I am within his range: he reaches out, grabs two thick handfuls of my hair.

There is no way to push him off me without hurting myself. Wherever he goes, much of my hair will follow. Instead, I reach up to try to pry his hands out of my hair, but he has clenched his fists shut tightly. I have thick hair, which is fortunate because it has been yanked many times by Noah over the years. I am lucky that Noah doesn't know that ripping out just a lock of hair would actually hurt more than pulling on huge ropes of it.

I give up working on his fingers and now hold on to each of his wrists, trying to alleviate the pressure on my hair by holding his hands against my head; he jerks back and he is now pulling so hard that I can feel the tugging as a kind of searing pain, more like a burning than a tearing.

We are locked in this position, circling each other, my holding on to his arms as he pulls on my hair, for at least ten seconds. It is a long time during which to think about how much this hurts and how long I will put up with this before I finally counterattack.

I suspect I feel his arm muscles relaxing, but then he jerks again.

I let go of his arms, which unbalances Noah and forces him to reset his feet. As he is coming forward to regain his balance, I throw a right to his chest.

"Ba-ba-ba-ba-ba—OOOOOF."

He lets go, surprised by my violence. Instead of retreating, however, Noah redoubles his attack, coming at me with claws out, seeking to scratch at my eyes. Now that I have created distance between us, keeping Noah away is a matter of throwing punches. I have longer arms and I am faster. I am, after all, the bigger brother. We are both sweaty and loaded with adrenaline. I land two more shots, one to his upper chest and another to his stomach, which finally knocks him down as he keels over on arms and legs and begins coughing. He goes silent, and I know now he feels the attendant nausea and panic that accompany getting hit squarely in the solar plexus.

I keep my distance across the living room and wait for him to regain his breath. The struggle has also fatigued me. We must have been fighting for nearly a three-minute round. He is still surprisingly quiet; I can make out his phlegmy, short breaths as he steadies himself. This is the first time I have ever hit Noah, and even though it was in self-defense, it feels like we have crossed a boundary. Previously, Noah's attacks were tolerated by me, as long as they could be fended off or weren't too damaging. Noah certainly never tested me like this before; I don't want him to do it again.

But instead of standing and resuming the attack, Noah sits back on his ass and begins bawling, rocking back and forth and hugging himself. He closes his eyes and shakes his head, and when he opens them, he is looking at me warily. When I walk over to him, he winces and uses his feet to slide himself away along the hardwood floor.

"Nuh-nuh-nuh-nuh," he is repeating to me. He doesn't want me anywhere near him.

"I'm sorry, Noah, I'm sorry. I didn't mean to hurt you."

"Nuh-nuh-nuh." He shakes his head.

I try to hug him, and he curls up tighter.

"You started it," I tell him.

Like any other younger brother who has lost a fight to an older sibling, Noah now appeals to sympathy rather than fairness. But unlike my friends' little brothers, Noah can never tell my parents what happened, and I will never talk about it until now.

He can sense how badly I feel about what has happened, and long after any lingering effects of the punch could still possibly be felt, he continues to nurse his stomach as if still in pain. I've been hit harder than that in the solar plexus. I know how long it takes to recover. Noah is dogging it at this point, but as the inflicter of the injury, I don't have the moral authority to accuse him of malingering.

Still, I feel terribly guilty, and to make up for it I offer Noah chocolate cookies.

For the first time that I can remember, he declines, as if knowing that by accepting them he would relinquish the moral high ground.

I let him go to bed without brushing his teeth.

53.

Not only does my personal and familial life revolve around Noah, but my economic life is also centered on Noah—and those like him. In addition to babysitting Noah, I also babysit for a classmate of Noah's who lives a few blocks away. Gary is taller than Noah, with a rectangular head and a thick patch of brown hair that cowlicks in the back and is scissored unevenly around his strangely angular ears. (I've noticed the autistic have badly cut hair. They just can't sit still in barber chairs, and so most parents shear them at home.) Gary is higher functioning than Noah, and if left alone, he will actually play with toys instead of stimming. He is obsessed by the Hasbro toy Lite-Brite and enjoys making repetitive patterns of the translucent plastic pegs, vertical lines of reds, greens, yellows, or horizontal rows. He never makes angular patterns or any of the pictures that come with the instruction manual. Once, over Gary's vehement protests, I arranged the pegs into an airplane while Gary paced behind me flapping his arms, repeating, "Lite-Brite, Lite-Brite, Lite-Brite, he's not making Lite-Brite. He's not making Lite-Brite." As soon as I finished the airplane and showed it to him, he quickly pulled the pegs out, putting each color away in its respective storage cup and then closing up the box. "No more Lite-Brite. No more. No more." Now, whenever I come to babysit, he is careful not to play with his Lite-Brite—he's worried I will commandeer it—instead he draws patterns on his Etch a Sketch.

I've given up trying to engage Gary, since he doesn't really want me playing with any of his toys and it's boring watching him make repetitive patterns on his Etch a Sketch. And also, he smells. He has grown too big for his mother to bathe him easily, so he goes more than a week between scrubbings.

Instead, I watch television in the living room, and when Gary's mom comes home, she gives me twenty dollars.

54.

Sometimes, after school, I earn a few dollars helping out at the Palisades Day Care Center run by my mother. This after-school program, called by Gary "second school," is in a Presbyterian Church in Brentwood. There are four other kids there besides Noah and Gary, and most days there are two teachers to care for them. The school was founded by my mother to address a cruel irony afflicting the Noahs of the world: that the very children who need the most schooling—the autistic, the developmentally disabled, the retarded—are given the least, with programs that start later in the day and end earlier and have more days off than regular school programs.

The project was four years in the making and occupied what small portion of my mother's energy she didn't allocate directly to Noah. The idea was simple: parents know better than special-education professionals what will work for developmentally disabled children. The professionals tended to apply theories; parents were all about practice. Several early efforts had failed as my parents teamed up with evangelical educators or careerists who saw in the Noahs of the world a ticket to academic or professional success. The special-education field attracted, I had already concluded, the best and worst kinds of adults, those who were strangely drawn to the fucked-up and dysfunctional because their own egos told them they could work a miracle. When it became obvious that Noah could absorb a dozen miracles before manifesting any loaves or fishes, these types would lose interest. Or there were those who professed to want to help these kids but were frightened of getting too close, of literally getting their hands dirty.

And then there are the best, those who are unafraid, who engage them, who can make Noah or Gary or any of the other kids actually sit down and sort blocks or trace letters or make circles and, most important, not overreact when they are spit at or scratched. Reva, Katie,

Alys, there are a few women at the day care center and at Noah's regular school who deserve medals for their patience.

This was the mission statement of the day care center:

The developmentally disabled child is also usually an educationally disadvantaged child. Because of his malady he requires more education than the normal child; instead, ironically, more often he receives less—the victim of a foreshortened school day. This places an additional burden on both the child and his parents. The child, without peers, has long afternoons to fill; the parent has the fruitless task of serving as custodian to this vacuum. The child, lacking social graces, cannot even play with siblings; may even further sense his own alienation. The parent, without the grace of respite, often feels too keenly his own bondage; reaches too quickly his own breaking point. To service the need of both the developmentally disabled child and his beleaguered parent the Palisades Day Care Center for Developmentally Disabled Children has been formed. The center proposes to provide an extended day of supervised training and activity for children suffering from Down syndrome, brain damage, autism, and other severe neurological impairments. A nonprofit corporation, the Palisades Day Care Center for Developmentally Disabled Children represents a unique parent-conceived, community-supported, child-oriented pilot day-care program. A parent-professional advisory board will guide the center; every member of the board of directors will serve without salary.

There had been numerous obstacles. At first, the local Episcopal church indicated it would provide a venue. Then at a meeting of the board, my mother was told shortly before the school's opening that the church would provide space only between three fifteen and five fifteen on weekdays. No holidays, no Saturdays, no summer vacation. Furthermore, she was told by the principal of the church's school for normal children that he did not want his normal children "even to have to look at these handicapped children."

I remember my mother being in tears at hearing this. And my father having to sit down again and call local churches and community organizations to see if any of them had a suitable classroom and outdoor space. My parents had to do hours of paperwork—filling out tax-exempt forms and applying for insurance waivers, fire-safety inspections, zoning board approvals, health department licenses. The two of them would sit around our dining table in the dim sconce light of our dining room and pore over the forms and documents. My mother wrote letters to our congressman and to Governor Jerry Brown when the process bogged down. It looked like awfully boring work, but it distracted them sufficiently so that I was free to watch all the television I wanted.

I would look over at Noah, sitting on the sofa, chewing on a piece of string, and think there is some upside to having a crazy little brother.

55.

I used to go with my mother to the day care center at its first site, in a Family Services building in Santa Monica. Besides Noah and Gary there were Carlos, a chubby Mexican kid who sometimes wore a helmet; Barry, a tall, blond kid who walked with a listing shuffle; Cindy, a little blond girl who would occasionally cut herself with whatever sharp objects she could commandeer; and Michael, a cute boy with Down syndrome who tried to pinch me whenever I walked by.

It was easier to interact with the higher-functioning autistics, and

Gary was probably the highest functioning of the whole gang. There was a fenced-in lawn by the back door of the adobe building, and Gary and I would play catch back there. He clearly enjoyed playing with a "normal" child and I liked feeling useful while my mother was inside talking to the teachers or the director of Children's Services. There were always thorny issues: one of the kids had peed in the hallway; another had injured himself on the swings; a third had tried to pull the hair of someone heading in to use the Community Room for an AA meeting. At one point, the director requested that a screen be put up so that the rest of the clients at the center wouldn't see Noah and his classmates. As if autism were an infectious disease.

My mother would get so angry with the director that she could barely speak with her. Finally, my father went to see the president of Family Services, a Freudian, it turned out, who still believed that the parents were somehow responsible for their children's disorder.

But I didn't mind goofing off for a few minutes, playing catch with Gary and tag with Cindy and Michael.

In fact, I was becoming so popular with the kids that one afternoon when I broke off a catch game with Gary to chase Cindy around the lawn, Gary kept following me, "Karl catch. Karl catch. Karl catch," and when I didn't immediately turn, he became agitated, repeating himself, "Karl, KARL, KARL CATCH. KARL CATCH."

I turned to Gary and in a stern voice said, "Not now, Gary."

Gary froze, dropped the ball, and folded his arms over his head. He never played catch with me again.

The day care center moved to the Presbyterian church in Brentwood with the same roster of clients. When one of the best teachers, Katie, moved away, my parents found themselves shorthanded. Sometimes my mother would fill in, sometimes my father would, and finally, in desperation, my parents turned to me.

This makes sense. From experience, I know more about dealing with the developmentally disabled than almost anyone else, professional or not. But I am not a teacher, and with me in charge there is little chance that any of these kids will advance, though, to be honest, most of them were written off by their schools years ago. For their parents, the day care center provides a few crucial hours of additional relief, and forestalls the inevitable decision about institutionalizing their child.

And since Noah is among the most difficult kids in the program, and I can usually manage him at least to a standoff, it seems I should make a suitable stopgap assistant teacher—and earn a few dollars while I am at it. (Initially, my pay was in toys or record albums, but at some point I calculate that what I was receiving came to less than a dollar an hour, so I insist on some sort of actual wage.) My salary is below minimum wage and off the books, which is another benefit from my parents' point of view. The amount of paperwork my father has to complete to deal with issues like payroll is a source of steady argument between my parents. "Every two weeks I prepare a payroll," my father says, "just like a Republican. And all the forms I have to fill out will make me one."

The job is a grind and requires that my father pick me up from Paul Revere and drive me to the day care center. I usually eat a snack in the car, a bag of chips and a can of soda, because to eat this stuff around the other kids would be like eating gazelle entrails in a cage of hungry lions.

The classroom is on the second floor of a tan granite and brick building behind the large, modern church and attached to it by long, open-air, flat-roofed hallways—similar, actually, to my junior high school. There are several other rooms the church makes available to the community for the usual benevolent purposes: AA meetings, Boy Scouts, veterans groups. There is a gymnasium with a basketball court where we can take the kids if it is too cold outside and no YMCA basketball team is practicing. Most days we use the fenced-in yard, which has a sandbox, swings, climbing bars, and cartoonish ducks and horses on giant springs.

The room has several tall lockers in which much of the school's paperwork and the kids' medications are kept. Beneath the windows, which face an alley and some trees, are low shelves on which are arranged the cast-off toys donated by friends of my parents. These are usually the games and stuffed animals outgrown by normal children, and they tend to be of very limited interest to the autistics and the retarded. I picked over them when I first visited and found almost nothing that wasn't either broken or depressingly worn-out.

Based on the detritus left behind by the previous tenant, I determine that this had been a preschool classroom. The electrical outlets are already sealed off with plastic covers. And there is a pile of plastic furniture too small for anyone but toddlers to use. A band of cardboard Muppets marches atop a chalkboard on which we have written birthdays, schedules, and medication reminders. Beneath that is a laminated sheet on which each child is supposed to mark whether or not he is present, when he has had his snack, and if he has washed his hands. There is very little to interest an overstimulated teenager like myself. It is a slow afternoon, as boring in its way as my own school.

The other teacher is an African American woman named Reva, who takes the bus an hour each way to come to the day care center. Her commitment to this job strikes me as being almost as strange as the kids we are supervising. She is a charmless, asexual woman with thick forearms and a solid lower body. Her hair is a kinky Afro that she wears unbraided so that it extends from her head like a motorcycle helmet made of wire. She is taciturn, steady, and indomitably patient. She can sit and wait for Carlos to stack his blue blocks for five minutes, if necessary, without just giving up and reaching over and doing it for him. If Noah is stimming and flapping in his metal frame chair, she will say simply, "Shh-shh-shh," until he stops and lays his hands down on the table and is ready to sort his triangles and squares. It is a wonder to watch, and my great shortcoming as an off-the-books substitute teacher is that I see my role as being primarily to keep the kids from injuring themselves and taking them to the bathroom when it is necessary. Reva takes Cindy to the bathroom, and the boys aren't too much trouble. I just stand outside the stall and pray they don't have a bowel movement. Only Gary stands up while he urinates, but he uses a stall because he is obsessed with privacy. This poses a problem because one of Gary's strange proclivities is to plug up drains, sinks, toilets, anything that involves water going through a pipe.

On my first afternoon as an off-the-books substitute teacher, I tell Reva I have to go to the bathroom and then wander down the hall, checking to see if the doors to any of the other Community Rooms are unlocked. I don't know what I am looking for, but when I come to the offices for a local Gardening Club and find the door open, I quickly slip inside and then rifle the desk drawers, poke through the file boxes, and try to jimmy open the stainless steel cabinet doors. I am sure there is money in there, but to get it requires that I bring some sort of crowbar or hammer with a nail remover.

I make a mental note and then go to the bathroom before returning to the classroom.

56.

When we take the kids down to the little playground, they walk single file, Carlos and Gary up on their toes, Noah in his flat-footed shuffle, Cindy in her trot, Michael in his pigeon-toed waddle, Barry listing so far to port that his helmet is scraping against the brick wall. Reva leads the way, carrying a plastic bag with apple juice and graham crackers that she will dole out on the round picnic table next to the sandbox.

I bring up the rear. At the end of the hallway is the bright, late afternoon light. From behind, with Carlos and Gary in their helmets, this looks like a football team coming back onto the field after a disastrous first half.

"No swing for Barry. No swing for Barry. No swing for Barry," Gary keeps repeating. Barry has had numerous mishaps on the swing, sliding off in midflight and bruising his back and behind. Reva has taken to blaring out, "No swing for Barry," at the start of every trip to the yard, and that statement has come to symbolize the start of the kids' yard time.

Barry, of course, immediately heads for the swing.

Gary starts jumping up and down, flapping his arms, sounding the alert. "No swing for Barry. NOSWINGFORBARRY."

"Barry," I say firmly. "Stop. Stop."

I walk over and take his hand and usher him back to the table. He looks up at me, nodding his head as if in agreement, but I know better than that. He is biding his time.

Noah wanders to the sandbox, where he will sit down for a while, running the sand through his fingers and rubbing the grains between his palms. The sand ends up everywhere, in his shoes, pockets, underwear.

Cindy usually trots around the perimeter of the playground, bobbing her head as she goes. Michael is the only one who tries any form of social play, sometimes trying to interest Noah, Carlos, or Barry in a plastic horse or Matchbox car he has brought down with him.

Noah sometimes will take the plastic horse and give it an exploratory chew, whereupon Michael will grab the horse back and Noah might spit at him.

The rest of the kids have no interest in this sort of interactive play, so I am often left playing with Michael, who, besides his pinching, is a sweet kid who just wants to play.

"This is m-m-m-m-my horse," he says in his slightly slurred speech. "His name is, um, um . . ."

He pauses and looks down at the black plastic horse with the brown saddle and bridle. "His n-n-n—"

"NOSWINGFORBARRY."

I look up to see that Barry has climbed back on the swing and is about to launch himself when Reva takes him by the hand and removes him.

After a few minutes, the kids start to mill around the table, sensing that snacks are imminent.

"Who wants juice?" Reva asks. "Who wants crackers?"

There is a parking lot on the other side of the chain-link fence, and whenever I see adults walking to their cars, they are always gazing over at this crowd; there is something anachronistic about this crowd of boys and girls playing in a yard clearly meant for much younger children.

Reva pours juice into paper cups and then hands out a rectangle of graham cracker to each kid. They all drink their juice in quick, steady gulps and hold out their cups for more. Their second serving is smaller, just two inches in the bottom of the cup. They gulp it and extend their cups. Now they get just one inch. They gulp that. This goes on until they are drinking just drops of juice.

"No more," Reva says, then she waves her hands horizontally. "Finished."

They all start to eat their crackers; a few, like Barry and Carlos, stay close by while they eat. Noah wanders back to the sandbox. Michael eats just a few bites and offers the rest to Carlos, who stuffs the cracker in his mouth before Reva can stop him.

"Okay, yard is over," Reva commands.

The class is gathered into the same irregular line as before. Per my mother's instructions, we are to first go to the bathroom, where everyone is to wash his hands before returning to the class. Carlos, Barry, and Michael put up their usual resistance, while Noah is particularly stubborn. Like me, he is so tired of my mother's endless orders to wash our hands that he resents having to do it anywhere else. Today, he goes through the motions of washing his hands—holding his hands under the tap, pretending to use the soap dispenser—without actually turning on the water. I catch him glancing sidelong at me while he is going through this pantomime. I laugh and Noah smiles.

"Okay, Noah," I say.

Meanwhile, Gary has plugged the toilet with a roll of toilet paper.

The rest of the afternoon is sort of a wind-down. Once a week a woman named April comes and passes around maracas, tambourines, sticks, and drums, and the kids sit around and make noise, accompanying cassettes of children's music or Beatles songs. Gary likes the honking and whistling noises in "Yellow Submarine."

Other afternoons a physical therapist visits, an older woman who wears white button-up shirts, blue cotton or khaki slacks, and white plimsolls. She has black hair graying at the edges and a long face; she sort of looks like President Andrew Jackson, if Andrew Jackson were a gym teacher. She helps the kids through a series of what are called "integration exercises" intended to increase sensory awareness. One by one the kids are stretched over huge balance balls, massaged by a handheld, wooden wheeled device, pushed around on roller boards—carpeted plywood squares mounted on furniture wheels. As the three of us work the kids through this session, it looks a little like we are manning some weird assembly line manufacturing developmentally disabled children.

At the end of the forty-minute session the kids are squeezed between heavy gym mats like big, gray burritos. We lean on the mats to put a little extra pressure on them, so they feel more tightly encased. They all like being in the mats, even Noah settles down to a quiet, happy gurgle while he's in there. I understand. At home, I sometimes like crawling under the beanbag chair and then piling pillows and other stuff on top. I even once asked my mother to sit down on it while I was under there, but then she thought I was being strange and refused. Something about being squeezed by an object instead of a person is appealing and comforting, a steady tension that is so different from the awkward hug of a person, where there is the flush contact from the front and the broken, uneven feel of a hand here, an arm there, on the back.

Only Gary hates the mats. The one time we tried to roll him up in it, he protested, saying that it wasn't his bedtime.

"No nap for Gary. No nap for Gary," he insisted. "I have a note."

Reva and I looked at each other. What was he talking about?

"Noooooooo," he began screaming, so we let him out of the mat, and he took a seat by the blackboard, repeating "No nap for Gary. No nap for Gary."

It turned out that Gary was exempted from his nap times at his own school because of a note written by his mother.

The only thing was, Gary was now twelve years old, and he hadn't been required to take a nap in school since he was five. His mother had written that note all those years ago and he never forgot it.

So no nap for Gary.

57.

They are L.A. taxis, blue or white or even orange, but never yellow like in New York, and the only time I ever really see taxis in Los Angeles is when they are picking up or dropping off kids at the day care center or Noah's school. I associate them with the developmentally disabled. The drivers sit in the front seats, smoking and reading their newspapers, and when they see their fares emerging, the best drivers, the regular ones, make sure to get out of the car and open the door, not really out of respect for the customer, but out of courtesy to whoever it is that is loading the kid into the car. Once Carlos or Barry is buckled and the door closed and locked, the driver is given a voucher that is prepaid by Westside Regional Center. Reva rides with Carlos back to

East L.A., where she catches a bus from Carlos's house, which isn't far from her own neighborhood.

Most days my father comes and picks up Noah, Gary, and me to drive us back to the Palisades. Gary sits in front in the passenger seat. Noah sits beside me in the back. No one likes traffic, but if you are sharing the backseat of a Japanese compact car with an irritated autistic adolescent, you dread it. Noah dislikes being stuck in heavy traffic, because it is the opposite of moving, which he enjoys. At some point in the drive, if we are caught at enough red lights or clogged intersections or gummed-up onramps, he will reach across and scratch or pinch or try to grab a handful of hair. If he doesn't quickly calm down or we can't find any open road, then he will keep on reaching out and probing and gouging. Often I am forced to hold both of his arms and restrain him, rather than let him pull my hair. He then tries to bite me, but I'm adept at leveraging his arms around in such a way that he can't reach my arms.

Meanwhile, Gary turns to my father at every red light to try to convince him that the light is "Broken, broken, broken," until the light turns green, when he says, "Go, go, go."

58.

One Friday night, my friends Jonathan and Hollis and I ride the bus into Brentwood, where we ride skateboards outside of Jerry's liquor store until it turns dark enough for us to ask youngish-looking shoppers on their way in to buy us a sixer of Mickey's Big Mouth. When a barely legal buyer finally takes pity on us, extorting from us five extra dollars as he does so, we get our beer and skate over to the dirt loam next to a wire-mesh country club fence where we drink the beer and smoke more of that raspy Colombian dope. We then skate over to the Presbyterian church.

We are three kids in OP shorts, Mexican parkas, zip-up windbreakers, long hair almost shoulder length—on skateboards, our silhouettes are horizontal lines with a lot of hair and sleeves protruding at jagged angles as we pump. I'm the only one who appears in any way out of the ordinary for the place and times—I have straight black Japanese hair. The commuters driving along San Vicente or Bundy pay no more attention to us than they would to one of the palm trees lining the road.

I know the church well from working at the day care center. Here, in the shade of this willow tree, is where we hop the fence. We can get to the second floor walkway by climbing on top of the water fountain, reaching up to the bottom of the handrails that line the walkway, and swinging over. From there, it's just a quick trot down the hall to the Gardening Club and that locker-cabinet full of who knows how much money.

We're stoned and a little drunk. We are giggling and frightened at the same time. The night is cool, as it often is on L.A.'s Westside in the spring, and there is that faint burned-incense smell of eucalyptus in the air. The parking lot beside the church is empty. And the back of the church, as I had figured out from all my careful reconnaissance, is an easy target.

"Leave the boards down there," I whisper-shout to Jonathan after I have swung to the second floor.

"Dude?"

"We're coming back this way and we only need one," I tell him. "Hand me up mine and leave the rest."

We all scramble and then walk quietly along the hall.

"Here." I try the handle, and the door of the Gardening Club opens.

The room picks up atmospheric light from a lamp mounted in the corner of the parking lot outside. The weak yellow glow is unbroken by any blinds. The seedlings in their little rough-textured cardboard cups are all arranged in uneven rows on a school table next to the window, presumably to get whatever sun they can.

"Should we turn on the light?" Jonathan asks.

"No."

He and Hollis come into the room and look around. Plants. Bags of fertilizer. Gardening implements.

"Fucking shovels and dirt," Hollis says, then he sees the locker-cabinet. "Ah."

"Yeah I looked through a window and surprised what I saw / Fairy boots were dancin' with a dwarf, / All right now!" Jonathan sings.

"What the fuck is that?"

"Sabbath, dude," Jonathan says.

Hollis is the most experienced criminal among us—he became a legend when he was arrested in sixth grade for having stolen a neighbor's Mustang. Other than his predilection for petty crime, he doesn't really have any other winning attributes and virtually never speaks. He would later enjoy a second measure of local fame when another friend shot off three fingers of Hollis's left hand in what was ruled an accidental discharge of a firearm.

Now that he has sized up the locked cabinet, he takes over our little caper. It is a flimsy cylinder lock with a metal lip braced against the inside of the opposite door. He pulls once, twice, and seems to be thinking about ripping the door open, but he stops and then comes back and gets my skateboard. That was my idea, using the skateboard as a sort of crowbar to pry it open. He fixes the tail in the crack between the doors and rips it open with a loud but very short groan.

In the shadowy recesses, we can see files and what look like packages of seeds. In fact, as Hollis goes through the cabinet, pulling out the packets and tossing them over his head, Jonathan and I are catching them and reading the envelopes with the colorful photographs on them.

"Camellias. Callas. Fuchsias. Poppies," I announce.

"I'm keeping those," Jonathan says and takes the poppy seeds.

We all crowd around the cabinet. Hollis tosses the papers out in a flurry, then the files.

"Open every envelope," I tell them.

We begin ripping them open. It's a boring list of projects, parks, permissions, applications, objections, proposals. It seems this room is responsible for much of the beautifying of public spaces in Brentwood.

"Ah-ha." Hollis is holding a small, copper-gray, folded-metal lock-box, more like a tool chest. He shakes it, and we can hear the rattling of change. "Let's go."

For some reason, we run at top speed down the covered walkway to the point at which we climbed up. We jump back down, grab the other skateboards, and run to the back of the building. Then Hollis hands me his deck and climbs the fence and waits on the other side as Jonathan and I toss over our skateboards and the box.

We skate down the alley back to Bundy, Hollis holding the lock-box next to him like it's a lunch box.

"Dude." I stop him. "You can't just carry that thing around like that. It looks totally snaked."

Hollis shrugs and stuffs it under his parka. "Let's go."

The plan is to head back to Jonathan's house, where we can use his father's tools in the garage to pry it open.

On the bus, we can't stop speculating about what is in the box.

"Dude, hundreds."

"Thousands!"

"I'm buying a new Lonnie Toft 9, Road Rider 6's."

"New stereo."

"Weed."

We yank the cord indicating our stop and get off at Sunset and Galloway and then skate up Galloway. We skate down the driveway, past the kitchen window, and then Jonathan goes in through his back door to get some project he can plausibly tell his father we're working on in the garage.

We wait in the dark.

Jonathan returns with a wrought-iron bird feeder, of all things, something he made in seventh-grade metal shop.

His father actually believes we are gathering in his garage on a Friday night to work on a bird feeder?

Jonathan shrugs.

There is something brilliant about the way Hollis bypasses the padlock and instead attacks the rear hinges of the box. I would have spent a half hour trying to somehow cut the lock with a bolt cutter or something. Instead, Hollis just turns the box around, studies the hinges for a second, and then selects a stout little screwdriver with enough leverage and pushes it in the gap next to the hinge and between the box and box top. Then he finds a crowbar that seems almost as big as he is, and sets the lockbox on the floor of the garage with the screwdriver wedged into it, shoves the crowbar into the space between the screwdriver and the lockbox, and then stands on top of the crowbar. For a moment nothing happens, and then there is a popping noise and a series of ricochets as the screwdriver shoots around the garage, fortunately missing all of us.

"Jesus fuck," I say.

Hollis is unperturbed.

The top of the box has been pried open about two inches. Hollis takes the crowbar, shoves it into that opening, and wrenches it another two inches. He shakes the contents of the box onto the floor.

We net four dollars each.

59.

My parents start talking more and more about Noah moving some day to a group home, or a residential program. The dark word, seldom spoken, is *Camarillo*, a California state hospital for the developmentally disabled, a Hogarthian institution currently much in the news because of a series of deaths involving clients and indifferent staff. Parents of kids who've been placed there, some younger than Noah, report their children were beaten, starved, drugged. But one by one, we can see the parents of Noah's classmates putting their kids into residential programs because they have aged out of programs or their schools can no longer handle them.

The day looms, my parents feel, when Noah will be asked to leave his school. He's manageable now, at eleven, twelve, but how's it going to be when he's, say, sixteen, seventeen? He's just an inch shorter than my five-foot-tall mother now. When he has six inches on her, how is she going to manage him at home? How is my father, for that matter, who is just five feet eight or so himself? The day is coming closer. It has to be, so it becomes more a topic of conversation, or, when it's unspoken, a topic of nonconversation, what we are *not* talking about.

"But the problem of Noah always remains and now seems larger than ever," my father wrote. "The fact of the matter is that one day I will no longer be able to control him physically . . . Every parent, of the normal and the abnormal, can give only so many years to an offspring. Eventually, even Noah has to be on his own. The day will soon come when I simply must pass him on."

But where can he pass him on?

I look at Noah now and can't imagine his living anywhere else. He's still my little brother, with his mop of badly cut hair (same color and shape as mine)—my mom barbers my hair just after she cuts my brother's—his delicate, small nose (it looks almost exactly like the shape you get when you take a piece of clay and push it into the gap formed between closing the tips of your thumb, index, ring, and pointer fingers), his round eyes, his bony jawline. He is beautiful, fawnlike: even his slightly bowlegged walk is like a fawn's first steps.

I don't ignore the topic, but it has been there so long that I don't have to pay attention to it. I believe, anyway, that Noah will never leave us. And that is how it should be. He should always be there, down the hall, humming away in his room. He should always be there, making his mess in the kitchen, wandering around the house with his rubber bands, sitting on the floor between two sofas flapping his fingers next to his ears. Despite his infrequent interaction with the rest of us, he manages to be ubiquitous, his humming and keening like the static on a radio station slightly out of range and out of tune. And it becomes a comfort after a while, this noise, this Noah, having him there. No, not a comfort, that's wrong. A familiarity.

The price I pay is social. I no longer have friends come over. In elementary school we often played at my house, but then something changed. Did I become more self-conscious, or did Noah become more obtrusive? It was a combination. Noah is just so there all the time, and requires so much explanation, tilting the house toward him just by sitting there and being nuts, that it becomes easier to just go to my friends' houses.

I'm at that age when I'm not always sure who my friends are anyway, so it doesn't help to have them ogling my little brother and listening to my natural history museum–like explanations of the autistic boy exhibit. I just want to get along, fit in, be normal.

60.

I still like Kiss, and my hobbies are eclectic and anachronistic for my age group. I am still, at fourteen, obsessed with military models, with Dungeons & Dragons, with my own versions of what will later become known as fantasy sports leagues. I make these up myself by using statistics I gather from the back of old baseball cards as well as completely imaginary players whom I've created and a few real players I've heard of who never made it in college or even at some local high schools. I mix and match different players onto different teams and then pit my created rosters against each other, rolling dice to determine the result of each at bat or play. It is laborious and takes hours to work through an entire game. I fill reams of pages with stats and results that then have to be copied neatly into standings and charts, which I try to update weekly. When I tell my parents I am in my room doing homework, this is what I am actually working on.

Or even more complicated, I have maps and military campaign charts, with little rectangular unit counters that represent armies, divisions, and fleets, and I have redrawn our house, reimagining it as a combination of Napoleonic Europe and the World War II global battlefield. There are imaginary empires—Karl, Noah, Foumi, Greenfeld (Josh), TG, Painting, Assyria, Israel—and they are constantly making and breaking alliances and embarking on wars of conquest. Karl began, strangely enough, as a colony of Noah, much like the United States began as a colony of the British Empire. It took not one but three wars of independence for Karl to break the cruel reign of the Noah tyranny, and in the last war, the counteroffensive went all the way from Karl (my room) into Noah (his room), ending forever the threat posed by Noah to Karl.

Karl has characteristics of the United States, but with Germany's army, and I mean literally Germany's army, complete with generals named Guderian, Model, Rommel, and von Manstein. Greenfeld is Russia, a vast, inhospitable country (my parents' bedroom) that Karl is constantly invading but never subduing. Foumi's territory correlates to the kitchen and is an ally of Greenfeld but is ultimately not a warlike nation. TG is Karl's great ally and most resembles World War II–era England—tough, doughty, overextended, with its huge territory of the den and some of the living room. Noah, after starting out as eighteenth-century England, ends up more like modern France—neutral or at worst a liability if you find yourself in the same alliance. Painting is an archipelago nation in our backyard that is a version of Imperial Japan transposed to Japan's modern economic clout and aesthetic.

The regular state of this imaginary world is war, protracted, resource-depleting conflict, in which civilian populations are subjected to brutal carpet bombing from Karl's B-17's and B-29's or Painting's Kawashini Tigers (my invention) or Greenfeld's Bear bombers (a variation on the actual Russian Bear strategic bomber). I fight imaginary battles in my head, deploy armies, launch aircraft carriers, concoct diplomatic incidents, and break treaties. I keep careful counts of relative fleet strength—Karl has twelve aircraft carriers, Painting has twenty-one, Greenfeld has six, TG has four, and Noah two. Those areas outside our house are considered oceans—the Pacific is our backyard, the Atlantic our front, and the side driveway is the Indian Ocean. I tally bomber production, tank output, divisional muster. I know how many new soldiers each country is capable of producing in a given month, and hence how many they can afford to lose in massive tank and infantry engagements that rival Kursk and Normandy in their intensity and size. These are nations that don't think twice about throwing the flower of their youth—and much, much more—into the maw of modern battle. Countries exist entirely to feed and support armored divisions and carrier battle groups.

This map of our house exists primarily in my mind and soon doesn't correlate any more to our actual home—though I can still tell you what exists in my own imaginary geopolitical conflict zone at any spot in the house. It is a densely packed fantasy environment of battlefields, factories, rebel strongholds, defensive redoubts, island bases, trench works, forward artillery positions, air bases, dry docks, sub pens, minefields, and command posts.

Soon, the amount of calculation and archiving required exceeds what I can keep track of internally, and I have to start writing down massive ledgers of tanks produced and lost, of submarines at sea and those being refitted, of divisions at full strength. This is in the era before computers, and much of the back office of my fantasy life has to be noted down in hard copy.

It is what I think about when I am at home. I can tune out everything, sit in the same room with Noah, even fend off a few exploratory pinches, and still be laying out the battle order of a panzer army as Karl prepares for yet another invasion of Greenfeld. It is, I would later realize, a form of mental self-stimulation, an exercise designed to allow me to check out in the middle of dinner or even when I'm talking to my parents. It becomes so easy to space out and consider possible new aircraft-carrier designs for the Imperial Painting Navy—Painting always has the best aircraft carriers, ornate, impeccably and individually designed aircraft carriers, some which have no superstructure at all, like Japan's carriers in World War II—that I make a rule that I can't play this mind game at school, only at home or walking to and from school or riding the bus. It is a treat I save for myself when I am at home, where I need something to divert me mentally from the war going on in my family.

I have never mentioned it to another person until now.

61.

My father wrote about Noah's typical day on October 26, 1978: "He's usually up before Karl's alarm goes off at 6:30. But we try our best to ignore his morning sounds. And sometimes he does actually sleep past Karl's awakening. We get up at 7:45, toilet, dress, and breakfast him; prepare his sack lunch; and get him ready to leave the house by 9:00, at which time either I or Gary's mother—with whom I carpool—drive him to school. His school runs from 9:30 to 2:30. He is then taxied over to our day care center. I pick him up there at 5:15 and he's home at 5:30. Then he usually has a tantrum, dinner, and lounges around eating his shirts, our sheets, towels, anything he can get his mouth on. I give him his bath around 9:00 and he goes to bed about 10:30. It's a pretty full day for him and he doesn't get much reading done."

62.

My own days are lived around Noah. We pass through each other or around each other, as brothers must, I suppose, and there is, for the most part, a recognition that we can do nothing for each other. I wish I were one of those who could say that I see in my brother a great gift, a blessing, for what he has taught me, for how much he has revealed to me about giving. But what I give, I believe, I have given because I had no choice. So what do I really learn?

I try my best, when I'm home, to stay out of his way. And in some sense, I am lucky, for my parents, as much as they worry and hand wring about my academic failures, they can't spend nearly as much time monitoring my daily negligence in terms of homework and school assignments as they do attempting to get Noah to sort blocks or match pictures of bunnies.

But every few months, my mother suspects something is amiss—it's not difficult detective work: my report cards are filled with C's and D's—and when she investigates she discovers that if I have been working at all I've been working on my nonsense fantasy projects. It is after one of these investigations that a new academic regime is imposed. French lessons, math lessons, all this in addition to my piano lessons. Just as Noah is shuttled from school to day care, I will now begin a series of after-school classes intended to buttress the lousy education I am receiving at Paul Revere Junior High. My Japanese mother was brought up in a school system in which she was doing the work I'm now supposed to be doing in the ninth grade when she was ten years old. (Keep in mind, I've been doing the same work now for three years, since I've gone from honors pre-algebra to algebra S over the course of my junior high career.) If I don't learn math, she believes, I will be doomed.

She is wired in to a network of Japanese housewives who exchange and share information about this decadent society in which they now find themselves. There are numerous quaint by-products of this network—a Japanese man in a refrigerated panel truck drives to our house twice a week and sells cuts of sashimi that he has purchased from the harbor that morning, literally boat fresh. He has arranged the inside of his truck to be an ingenious little traveling store, with an aisle down the middle between glass cases of glistening *maguro*, *hamachi*, *toro*, *hirame*, and *uni*. And above the refrigerators, on shelves, are Japanese snacks, sauces, and pickles, all secured in place behind wires. He's sort of like the ice-cream man for expatriate Japanese who miss their native flavors.

It is through this network, however, that my mother also discovers the cram school. Oh, this is the cruelest fate of being half Japanese, having to attend this noisy little *juku* in the Sawtelle District of West Los Angeles: a rectangular room with old, splintery wooden desks, filled with forty-seven chattering Japanese kids, doing algebra, and nothing but algebra, for three hours a day, three days a week. On Monday, Wednesday, and Friday, I am picked up at school and driven to a Japanese school where three bungalows are arranged in an L around a concrete school yard. I didn't even know such places existed in the United States, little schools for Japanese expats—the families of salarymen sent overseas by their global Japanese companies—they are like a Japanese version of those colonial schools the English set up in Burma or Malaya, second-rate epigones of the great schools back home, intended to ensure that the children of exiles are indoctrinated in the ways of the tribe, lest they go native during their youth in the West and face the Japanese university entrance examinations totally unprepared.

The primary method of ensuring these young Japanese retain their Japaneseness, or at least the preferred approach here, are mimeographed sheets of algebra, all kinds of algebra, from quadratic equations all the way to three-dimensional graph equations that I have never seen before. When I first enter the room, my Jewish father walking in behind me, I shake hands with the fat Japanese tutor who sits behind the desk and dispenses these endless supplies of equations.

"Hello," he says. *"Konichiwa."*

He unleashes a stream of Japanese, very little of which I can follow.

"I, I, I don't really—" I turn back to my father. "You can't make me stay here."

"He doesn't speak Japanese," my father says to the tutor. "Neither do I."

"Hmmm," the tutor says. "I am Okada-sensei. Here is your math."

He hands me eight sheets of a dozen equations each.

"Sit anywhere," he explains. "If question. Ask."

My father takes his leave.

I take my equations to a desk in the back and then return to the front of the room with a few pencils that I sharpen. I look through the sheets. Most of this work is far too difficult for me, so I return to the front of the class and explain to Okada-sensei that I don't understand this kind of math.

He frowns, takes back four of the sheets, and hands me four new sheets. "Easier."

I sit back down and look around. Every kid in the room is Japanese, most of them two or three years younger than me. There are a few boys and girls my age, and they seem to go through their math easily enough, chatting as they grind through equations harder than any I've ever seen. A gaggle of much younger children is basically allowed to chase one another around the room, pausing every few minutes to do a few of the kind of simple algebraic equations that I am doing as they stuff Pokys into their mouths.

Every half hour or so, Okada-sensei stops the class and begins scratching long series of numbers, letters, and symbols on the board, solving, methodical step after methodical step, an equation that includes symbols and operations that I have never seen before, until, after five minutes of such scratching on the board, which happens while the class behind him remains in high din, he comes to an answer like $X=\sqrt{3}X\Sigma$ with numbers all around the Σ. I don't know what provokes these outbursts of public equation solving or who exactly is supposed to benefit, but it is the total extent of instruction that is given in this cram school. At first, I tried to ask Okada-sensei for help if I couldn't solve an equation, and he would pull out a blank sheet and solve it in front of me so quickly that I could never follow his steps, or, when I returned to my desk and tried to duplicate the process, I found I couldn't make out his handwriting.

So I just sit there, hour after hour, and do these equations. Any sheets I don't finish I am supposed to bring home with me. There is no way to complete it all, the dozens of equations, the hundreds of ways to solve for X, and in the case of two and three variable equations, Y and A as well. Naturally, I fall behind, taking with me the dozens of problems I can't complete and then failing to return them two days later, and then additional equations are thrown on top, which I can't finish, so that I take those home. I am very soon drowning in equations; a couple of mimeographed sheets quickly turn into dozens, and at eight to ten equations a sheet, that means I'm behind by more than a hundred equations, and it keeps adding up, every other day, another few sheets. Linear, quadratic, and simultaneous equations (even logarithms!) bulging with polynomials, inverses, integers, ratios, and proportions. An insurmountable pile of problems.

One afternoon, I smoke a bowl of weed with a few friends just after school lets out and before my father picks me up to take me to the cram school. Which means I am facing the dozens of equations through the gauzy paranoia and general muddleheadedness induced by crappy, low-grade THC. It's hard enough for me to look at polynomials when I'm sober, but when stoned, as I am now, getting a handle on the factorization or even the basic assumptions or required estimations becomes an impossible and exhausting mental quagmire. And this noisy classroom only adds to my sense of isolation and confusion.

I have no friends here. I am invisible here. No other student has even spoken to me since I began attending. I am discriminated against here even more thoroughly than I have ever been at my own, mostly Caucasian, junior high school. As a half Caucasian I stick out here just as much as I stand out for being half Japanese at my own school, yet

I don't speak the same language as the rest of these squawking, noisy kids. The racket makes it impossible to concentrate.

I'm thirsty. I get a drink of water and grab a few sheets of scratch paper from a pile on the desk. These scratch paper sheets are the recycled blank sides of old problem sheets, practice tests, even, I discover, old answer sheets. I quickly scan the equations—these are the same as I am working on now. And the answers are provided right there. What a lucky score! I return to the desk and gather more scratch paper, a half-inch thick stack, and return to my seat and shove the pile of paper into my notebook.

When I get home I go through the answer sheets, locating numerous correlations to the equations I've been given. Unlike my junior high school, the cram school doesn't care if you show your work—they want answers. And here I have the answers!

During our rides to the cram school, my father admits to me that he sympathizes with my plight. He knows how awful it is to have to go to cram school three days a week instead of hanging out with my friends. He feels sorry for me but says there is nothing he can do about it, my mother has determined that I have to do this and she is resolute. And this is in addition to my weekly French classes, piano lessons, and soccer practice. My days are being taken away from me, systematically, I am sure, by my mother, who worries constantly that her putatively normal son is also turning out to be an idiot. "Foumi is convinced that Karl is a wrongo," my father wrote, "another bad apple in our genetic bushel."

Am I expected, in some way, to offset Noah by being an exemplary boy? Our only area of competition, perhaps, is in fecklessness, and by the time I am a teenager I am giving Noah a run for his money. "It's an irony I've always feared," lamented my father. "Karl turning out to be the problem." The misplaced sibling rivalry is low-hanging fruit for an analyst, and it is a theory that I am very familiar with, though knowledge of the idea does nothing to change my behavior or study habits. The mystery to me is why my teachers and parents remain convinced that beneath my laziness and insubordination is some sort of intelligence that they can yet discover. At no point in my academic career have I showed any flash of brilliance at *anything*, yet there is this persistent talk that I have potential, that there is some sort of mathematical tiger in me waiting to be unleashed.

But all this algebra, of course, just bounces off me like 76-millimeter incendiary ordnance off a Tiger tank. I have devised several modifications of the old German Tiger and King Tiger, bringing those tanks, which are really the first modern, main battle tanks, into my own imaginary household conflicts. My King Tiger Mark 78 has a 120-millimeter automatic cannon *and* a 20-milimeter automatic coaxial cannon next to the turret gun, in addition to hull-mounted and cupola-mounted 7.62 antipersonnel machine guns. It also has a more rounded and sloped turret and can be produced in numbers greater even than the Greenfeld T-75 main battle tank. Noah, my mother shouting at me to do my homework, my father's periodic growls about my dishonesty, my teachers, the principal, everyone shouting and complaining, expecting something of me—very little of it gets through.

"She had caught Karl lying about doing his math assignments," my father wrote in 1978, "he was way behind . . . I picked up Karl at his French lesson and was appropriately angry with him, keeping up the mad until I got home. And at dinner I let loose something I never should have said. I was chewing him out for lying to us about doing his math when it just suddenly slipped out. 'Sometimes you make me glad Noah is the way he is.' "

I don't feel bad that I lie about my schoolwork, lie to my parents about everything, lie to anyone if it will buy me time to skateboard, smoke dope, fantasize. I just don't think much about the dissembling.

Ah, but now I will get caught up in my algebra homework because I have the answers to at least a half-dozen sheets of equations. This is one of those rare gifts, like when my father surprised me with a box of fireworks before the Fourth of July, a whole deluxe set of Red Devils, screamers, flowers, smoke bombs. That sort of unexpected happiness is not a big part of my life—if I didn't set up a tree myself and then launch a steady campaign, I would never even receive any Christmas gifts in this family. But these answers to the insurmountable pile of algebra equations carry with them that sense of pure, simple joy. I will be free.

When my father drives me back to the cram school the next week, I am almost eager to attend. Before each class I am to hand Okada-sensei my completed sheets, and he marks them quickly, scanning down the answers with his red pen and marking with an X those I have erred in solving. Those have to be redone. I hand him my pile of sheets, almost all the back equations I owe, and stand as he begins marking.

Wrong. Wrong. Wrong. Wrong.

Those answer sheets, apparently, are all wrong. They have either been planted there by the teacher or . . . what else could they be? Of course, they were planted there, probably by Okada-sensei himself.

Okada-sensei looks at me. He doesn't betray any smug satisfaction at having trapped me. Perhaps this is some sort of moral lesson that I am being taught: maybe the cram school is intended as more than a factory for linear and quadratic equations, maybe it is also a hothouse for inculcating values and morals. I don't have a clue.

I will never catch up.

63.

What is awful is that everyone knows about Noah, about my family. Noah has become, probably, the most famous autistic child in America. My father's books receive steady streams of attention. His own success as a screenwriter and Academy Award nominee lends the story an added and helpful dusting of glitter. The *Los Angeles Times*, *Time*, *Life*, the *New York Times*, *Esquire*, *Rolling Stone*, Noah is steadily discussed and photographed and, by extension, our family's story has become one of the public accounts of autism. My seventh-grade health report about Noah ends up on the *New York Times* Op-Ed page and a poem I wrote about him is reproduced in a piece John Gregory Dunne writes for *Esquire*. Television crews make appearances in our home, the *Today* show, and then Dan Rather and the crew for *60 Minutes*. Dan Rather is a strapping, charming man who speaks in an easygoing drawl and talks to me about soccer and baseball. He was a soccer player himself, he explains, back in Texas, and his interview with me is conducted on the floor of our den, both of us sitting cross-legged.

He is here, of course, because of my brother. I would later read of families that hid their autistic child, of poor parents in Africa or India who tied their children to bedposts or chained them to stakes in the backyard. I'm not saying I approve of that, but I understand the impulse. Hide Noah. If I had that option, wouldn't I?

Instead, we have this television crew living in our house, filming our breakfast, lunch, me playing with my friends, my parents feeding Noah, my mother doing her operant-conditioning lessons with him. Noah is on his best behavior the entire three days, having only one tantrum the second day.

Every teenager is ashamed of his family, of course, but why do I have to deal with this extra, unwanted scrutiny brought on by having an autistic brother, the spitting, hair-pulling, screaming, tantruming younger brother who doesn't allow me to pretend, for an instant, that we are a normal family. As if having a Japanese mother and Jewish father is not enough, I also have to share with the world my autistic younger brother. The publicity about my father's books, the *Time* magazine articles, the *60 Minutes* segment, they ensure that every one of my classmates knows. I become locally famous in my school for nothing more than having a retard brother.

In fact, that is an unwanted consequence of my parents' agenda. They want to increase awareness of the obstacles faced by the developmentally disabled and their families. There aren't sufficient programs for kids like Noah. There are no alternatives, few schools, insufficient research. And there are so many fallacies and myths about these kids. This is all about, at its core, finding a place for Noah.

"Are you jealous of Noah?" Dan Rather asks me.

"I don't know," I tell him.

"But do you feel he gets more attention than you?"

"Well, yeah, but he needs it."

"What will happen to Noah?"

"I don't know."

"Can he stay here?"

"He has to," I say. "This is the best place for him."

I've never been jealous of Noah, or I've never thought that I was. But I am resentful that even though he can't say a word, he still manages to say more about our family than the rest of us combined.

64.

Let me go. I just need time. A few hours here. A whole afternoon there. Out of the house. Away from Noah. On my skateboard, Lonnie Toft 8½" with wheel wells, Sims Snakes, Trackers, the whole afternoon ahead of me. Who cares if I am a month behind in my equations, haven't practiced piano or completed my French homework? When I skate down my driveway, leaving Noah and my parents behind, I can forget every obligation. A test tomorrow? A paper on *A Tale of Two Cities* due? I can live in bliss despite the impending doom. My parents always discover my failures and shortcomings, they discover the myriad areas in which I am fucking up, yet I live on in optimistic denial that there is ever a price to pay.

Noah teaches me to live for today. Haven't I been told, for as long as I can remember, that Noah's days at home are numbered? He won't be with us forever. So we all live in the moment, my parents and me, so why should I have to worry about tomorrow, next week, when life with Noah is minute by minute, day by day? My parents are making it up as they go along, trying this multivitamin therapy, that sign language program, hiring and firing teachers and aides for the day care center, visiting this possible group home or institution. All so they can buy another year . . . or day. "Fight as hard you can, then give up," a friend of my father's once told him. But what does that really mean but that the fight is already over and we lost. So why, I sometimes wonder, don't we just wave the white flag now?

"Last night at dinner, Karl and I had one of those father-and-son altercations. I had sharply criticized him for his refusal to eat with chopsticks or to accept any rice on his plate," my father wrote in 1979. "And suddenly he was shouting: 'I hate this stupid family. You and Foumi are idiots. Wasting your lives because of Noah. Picking on me because of Noah. You should have put Noah in an institution years ago. He's going to wind up in one anyway. You're both fools and take it out on me.'

"And it is true that while I was asking Karl to eat his rice with chopsticks, Noah was clutching at various foods with his hands. But I did think Karl understood that there is no other place for Noah we know of at the moment. Foumi, of course, was soon in tears."

Noah may be autistic, but he still knows how to look smug when I am being yelled at. He sits there, stuffing himself with rice—and nods his head delicately, making the enigmatic half smile he can make when he is happy but knows he has to be careful not to gloat.

There is a remarkable consistency to Noah's fine behavior whenever I am on the receiving end of parental disapproval. If I am being shouted at for some transgression, then Noah can be relied on to be at his giggly, smiling best. Noah in that state is easy to love, he becomes gentle, melodic; the right word, I guess, is *soft*, which he knows and I know he isn't, really.

That is how he buys more time, of course, convincing all of us that it's sustainable, for a few more hours, a few more days. He becomes cuddly and squeaky; he will even spit less and shit in the toilet instead of in his bed. And you forget, we all forget. It's human nature; it isn't denial, it's hope. I guess, with my misbehavior and my failure, I buy you more time, Noah. I make you seem not so bad by comparison.

My war games, my fantasy life, they tide me over. A massive invasion along an eight-foot line extending from the bathroom all the way to Odessa, 296 divisions, including 45 panzer and panzer grenadier divisions, 28,000 tanks, 13,000 aircraft, the largest assembly of military manpower and equipment in the history of our family, under the command of Field Marshal Murat (I always had a fondness for Napoleon's fine cavalry general), all hurtled against Greenfeld in an attempt to break the will of that vast, Bolshevik, Jewish empire. Operation Winter Lion will be the grand land war of our house, the great duel between antagonistic and oppositional societies to determine who will rule the family. The campaign takes weeks for me to prepare, a long, mental tallying of munitions and equipment, of final touches applied to new tank designs and the replacement of old Super Saber aircraft with newer Phantoms. I lie in my room for hours, scheming and imagining this campaign. Wars, in my house, are as inevitable as the weather, and I end up launching one every few months.

They always end in bitter stalemate, however, as the warring states find in conflict a kind of equilibrium. They are, after all, not so much nations as mustering grounds for armies.

I need other escapes, and so when I can, I ride away from home on my skateboard. My mother will be busy with my brother, showing him how to line up blocks in the same pattern, or how to connect two dots, rewarding him with raisins or potato chips when he succeeds. He has been working on a version of this behavior modification for eight years, and if he is making progress, it is infintessimal at best.

And for all the hours and days my mother puts in, Noah will regress if he misses a day.

Noah is lazy, as indolent as I am; he will shirk as readily as me. I recognize this and have given up trying to motivate him. This aversion to any hard work, on my part as well as Noah's, drives my mother crazy.

65.

These are the years my friends and I accelerate our experimentation with drugs. For most of us, this exploration is at first tentative, a few joints, pipe loads, some beer, maybe some Southern Comfort stolen from our parents' liquor cabinets. And then there are those who more aggressively investigate illicit substances, a few associates of mine who seem to have an absolute knack for finding, procuring, and ingesting drugs that, at the age of fourteen, I have yet to hear spoken of out loud. We embrace marijuana eagerly, promising, as it does, an initiation into a subculture that seems to extend everywhere, from album covers to *Skateboarder* magazine to FM radio stations.

My friend Jonathan, the goofy foot skateboarder with blond hair, the boy given to quoting Black Sabbath lyrics, takes me one afternoon to see another friend, Giancarlo, whose older sister, Jeannie, is famous locally, though for what, exactly, I am never quite sure. Giancarlo is one of those boys who seems to go from playing with toy soldiers to injecting Demerol over the course of one summer. When we were friends in elementary school, he was as obsessed with HO-scale army men as I was (and am, in fact, still). We would ride bikes to the hobby shop together to select boxes of Airfix 1/72-scale soldiers and Minitank 1/85-scale tanks and then set them up in his backyard, making engine and cannon fire noises as we did so.

His older sister, Jeannie, a physically precocious brunette who seemed to date guys in their twenties when she was thirteen, didn't pay much attention except to make fun of us for still listening to Elton John. She liked, if I recall, Peter Frampton and then began telling us about Led Zeppelin. I didn't see Giancarlo much over the summer before junior high school, and we drifted out of our friendship as happens easily at that age. Now, in ninth grade, he has become a local legend for his drug use and, according to Jonathan, his procurement of a firearm.

His parents, of course, are never home.

The top half of the front door is open and Cheap Trick is blaring from the living room stereo. Giancarlo waves at us as we come in and sit down on the leather sofa, our skateboards leaning against the couch.

He is shirtless, with his unevenly cut brown hair hanging down to his shoulders. It is strange how someone you were friends with just three years ago can suddenly seem like a completely different person. Giancarlo now has that aura of teenage cool that can make a local kid seem practically like a rock star. He no longer acknowledges our old friendship, our formerly shared mutual fondness for army men; his mystique is built on his hard-core drug use. I have heard the stories, breathlessly relayed by Jonathan, about Giancarlo scoring liquid Valium, about Demerol, Mandrax, quaaludes. Jonathan says he has taken some of these pills at Giancarlo's, and among the stoner kids more inclined to straight up criminality—Bryn, Tad, Baz, Perry, those guys—there is grudging respect for Giancarlo and awareness that he is, in his own way, more hard-core than any of them, no matter how many times they joyride their parents' Mercedes.

Giancarlo was expelled from Paul Revere Junior High School over a year ago, after his locker was raided and he was found to be in possession of narcotics. He now putatively attends a junior high in Santa Monica. His mother is a local Realtor, and quite successful; she is so rarely at home that her house has become a frequent hangout for local kids looking to get high. (About a year from now, Hollis, who aided in the break-in at the Presbyterian church, will have his fingers shot off in this very house. That will pretty much end the party.)

"Dude," Giancarlo says, "are you ready to meet Dr. Demerol?"

I don't know what he's talking about.

Jonathan is sitting and bobbing on the sofa and I realize that he will go along with anything that Giancarlo proposes. "Let's get ripped."

I shrug.

We follow Giancarlo into his room.

"What are you little burnouts doing?" his sister asks as we file past.

"Shut the fuck up," Giancarlo says.

"You are such little fuckups," Jeanine says. She is smoking ultra-long cigarettes. "Hey, Gianni, give me a 'lude?"

"Five bucks," he says, holding out his palm. "Dream on. I don't have any."

"We're gonna get ripped," whispers Jonathan.

"What does he have?" I ask.

Jonathan shrugs. "I don't know. But Gianni always knows."

Gianni's room is perhaps the messiest physical space I have ever seen. His bed is filthy, and there are bagel crumbs on his sheets. There is a stereo in the corner, and numerous albums spread out, with jackets and sleeves mixed up and the vinyl platters sitting on the carpet. His clothes are piled in the corner and on a folding chair that sits before a desk where there is a huge, multichamber bong. Giancarlo's mother allows marijuana smoking.

He pulls out a vial of clear liquid. What are we supposed to do with that?

Then a syringe.

"No way," I say.

Jonathan is visibly excited by the rig.

I am fourteen and watch the two of them tie off and skin pop liquid Demerol. "It tastes like glue," says Jonathan. "I can taste it, in my throat."

I am too frightened to try it, but I have never seen anything so interesting in my life.

A few days later, everyone on the school bus watches as Jonathan's father beats him with a dog leash because he has found Jonathan's stash and has come to the bus stop to confront him. The next year, Jonathan will be sent by his father to a boarding school in Oregon.

After the shooting, Giancarlo will be sent to a military academy in Arizona.

Noah manages to stay uninstitutionalized for longer than they do.

66.

"It seems a lot of people would like to take a crack at curing Noah. But no one wants to take care of Noah," writes my father in the summer of 1979. "There is still no place I know that we can entrust him to confidently. Noah is also, I fear, a dark cloud forever looming before Karl, the reason for Karl's tendency to be pessimistic and negative. Karl knows too much about life and its cutting edges. He knows more about life than many of his teachers do."

That summer, we begin a more intense drive to find a place for Noah. Previously that summer, in July, my father had written, "Last night as we were going to bed, Foumi began to cry. And hit me with some facts: She is deathly tired. We cannot go on with Noah too much longer. We must seriously seek to find a place for him. The place has to be in visiting distance, close enough so that we can monitor the situation . . . Noah is acting more aggressive. He has evolved into the most fearful of all species to deal with: a teenager. Normal or special, it seems, there is simply no way of dealing with them."

On a hot spring morning we climb into my father's Mazda station wagon, while Noah is at the day care center, and drive out to the San Fernando Valley to visit the Behavior Modification Institute, a residential facility where a former classmate of Noah's, Barry from the Westport School and the day care center, has been making progress. Their regime of behavior modification calls for rewards for good behavior and "aversives," pinches, slaps, or sprays of cold water, for negative behavior. This regime seems brutally simple but is rife, my parents believe, with potential for abuse. It is a variation of the same operant-conditioning programs we first encountered with Ivar Lovaas at UCLA nearly a decade ago, only ratcheted up; made, if anything, more intense.

The San Fernando Valley is a different world from Pacific Palisades, hotter, smoggier, and my mother has always worried that Noah wouldn't be comfortable in the climate. The tan stucco house with Spanish tile roofing sits up a slight rise on a quiet street. There is a three-car garage and a huge, fenced-in backyard. The house is divided into residential and schoolroom areas that exude the same barren feeling as every special-education classroom, or, for that matter, regular classroom I encounter. These spaces are somehow made even sadder by the halfhearted and doomed-to-failure attempts to brighten them with a cute cartoon or poster of an athlete. No one is fooled.

There seem to be an abundance of teachers' aides working one-on-one with the residents, applying the behavior mod techniques that have been successful with their previous clients. I don't like the woman who runs the place—she wears hoop earrings and an elaborate hairstyle that suggests she doesn't get into close contact with the kids. She explains to us that the kids stop having tantrums because of contracts they draw up with them. They are told, for example, that if they keep quiet for thirty minutes, they are rewarded with a cookie or a potato chip. My mother points out, correctly, that Noah has no sense of time.

I've been to a half dozen of these group homes; they are always hot and far away, and poorly furnished with the cheapest, flat-springed couches that state funding can buy. I don't know what my parents are expecting, or, actually, what my mother wants. My father is more willing to compromise, to overlook the inevitable shortcomings of a place like this and think that maybe, perhaps, this could be a place for Noah. My mother sees the flaws, the fact that staffing at night is reduced to just one person, that the behavior mod system is overzealously applied—they should, for example, be allowed to drink all the water they want—and that in the valley in the summer the temperature goes well above 100 degrees and this house has no air-conditioning.

But it is reassuring to see Barry from the day care center, the boy who wasn't allowed on the swing, working in a one-on-one session and sitting quietly, sorting different letters into egg cartons. Barry was perhaps as low functioning as Noah, similarly nonverbal, slightly more violent, and here he is, seemingly mellowed and teachable. (Though my mother points out correctly that Barry was doing the same assortment exercises at the day care center.) His mother says that so far Behavior Modication Institute (BMI) is working out for Barry, that she has been told he has adjusted and is sleeping through the night.

While my parents talk to the director and the program administrator, I sit on one of the soft sofas, careful to check first for feces stains or fresh saliva, and try to imagine Noah in a place like this. I can't help but pity him because I know that I would dread having to live in a home like this, surrounded by crazies. I mean, just because Noah is crazy doesn't mean that he prefers their company. Why wouldn't he prefer being surrounded by putatively normal folks, by a family, just like anyone else? This has always been my father's central thesis about Noah, that he feels happiness or sadness more acutely than the rest of us, rather than, as some psychiatrists have theorized, less intensely. And it is obvious if you spend a minute with him that he *feels*. And because he can't talk, he is a prisoner of whatever discomfort he is suffering until it passes. He can't even say if he has a headache. Doesn't know to ask for aspirin.

We have kept him at home entirely because of this view that it is a happier place for Noah, which means we have been doing a kind of service for Noah. "Our family has to endure as a monument to him," my father has said. Now my parents feel they can't go on much longer. Noah is taller than my mother and practically marvels at how small she is. It is only a matter of time before he outgrows my father. It is becoming harder for them to ward off his occasional attacks, to fend off his scratches. They haven't had a full night's sleep in a decade, always getting up at least once to wipe Noah after a bowel movement or clean up his mess. They are worn down.

Still, I can't imagine Noah in a place like this, and in the car on the way back, riding up the San Diego Freeway over the Santa Monica Mountains back to the Westside, I voice the obvious, that the place sucks, it's depressing.

My parents are silent. Then my father offers that he is pleased that BMI doesn't administer any sedatives. To some extent, we have become numb because of the sheer volume of these residences we have seen. They are never stately mansions perched on cliffs overlooking the ocean or Georgian plantations amid lush fields, they are always cheap little houses, the kind real families don't buy, in marginal neighborhoods; they are institutional and feel that way. They can never feel as warm as even our flea-ridden, chewed-up little house. My parents know all this and yet they are calculating all the time, how much longer can they go on? A month? A few months?

67.

My mother would later write about the decision to institutionalize a developmentally disabled child in *A Guest from Afar*, "In the end, living with a severely handicapped child could destroy everything. Caring for Ken, day in and day out, had already ravaged their lives; they were badly in need of a break—or respite." She added that they were thinking of their own physical health, the well-being of their marriage.

I don't know anything about matrimonial survival, but I know that my parents are frequently in the kitchen arguing, about Noah, about the day care center, about me. They close the slat doors that do nothing to muffle their voices, and I can hear them whisper-shouting as they talk about what to do, who is to blame. Yellow light spills out and seems to carry with it their accusations and arguments. Noah sits on the sofa, chewing the cushions, twiddling his fingers just above his ears, as if he likes the dry sound of his fingers rubbing against each other.

My mother's concerns are Noah's diet, that he avoid sugars and oily foods, and that he take his multivitamins every morning. Perhaps he is allergic to wheat? She urges him to eat more vegetables. She sews his pants herself; because he cannot operate a zipper or belt, she stitches elastic bands into the waists so that they can be easily removed. His shirts are all chewed up, and she stitches extra bands of coarse cotton into the neckline, to deter him. (This doesn't work. He goes through about a dozen new T-shirts a month.) She hunches over an old Singer machine she received as a wedding present from her father—his original intention was to give the newlyweds a house in Japan, which my father stupidly refused. The machine makes a stuttering, thumping noise as she runs the needle over Noah's clothes. She is relentless in pursuing these projects for Noah, sewing his clothes, working with him on his behavior modification exercises, following him around the house to make sure he hasn't spit out his vitamins.

One night, as my parents are arguing about Noah, my mother blaming my father for not turning on the heater while Noah took a bath, and then the argument spiraling from there into his not monitoring my homework, his indifference to my academic shortcomings, and how he didn't make sure that Noah was warmly dressed when he took him for a walk in the evening.

"You're crazy," he says dismissively.

She has followed him into the hall, standing in front of their bedroom.

"You never listen," she shouts.

"If you're this crazy, I can't listen."

"You are making him sick," my mother says.

"Fuck you."

My mother does not use profanities, and her English sometimes breaks down when she is upset. When she is thus speechless, she often cries, quietly sobbing, and she says that she doesn't know how she can handle it anymore, that she works so hard, with Noah, with the day care center, and that my father and I don't seem to care.

"You worry about nothing," my father says. "You spend your energy worrying about unimportant issues. Who cares how he's dressed?"

"If Noah gets sick, who is the one who takes care of him?" she says. "I have to. You have your office. You can work."

"Leave me alone," he says. "You're crazy, you know that?"

She stops crying for a moment, and then rears back with her right hand and swings, landing a hard blow. From where I am standing, behind her left shoulder, I can see the whole thing. My father's head recoiling and then bashing into the doorway.

He holds his hand up to his forehead, and when he pulls his fingers away, they are smeared with blood. The redness frightens him, and he backs up and sits down on their mattress.

"Oh my God," he says.

"You hit him," I shout.

"No," she says immediately. "He bumped into the door."

"But you hit him," I say. "That's why he bumped his head—"

She refuses to admit that she socked him. Meanwhile, my father is seated, holding his hand up to his forehead and then studying his fingers.

"I'm sorry," my mother says.

"For hitting me?"

She is quiet.

My father stands up and walks to the oval mirror in the bathroom. There are two parallel, bloody gashes in his right temple.

My mother follows him into the bathroom and digs through the top drawer in the cabinet beneath the sink, seeking a small tin of medicated balm, which she opens and attempts to dab onto his forehead.

My father theatrically recoils, as if she might hit him again.

"You hit him," I say again, surprised at my mother's violence. It is the first time I have ever seen my parents resort to physical violence with each other. My father has hit me, plenty of times, and my brother as well, but they have never struck each other. And he is bleeding.

"Should I call the police?" I wonder aloud.

"Let me see," my mother is saying to my father.

My father bends down slightly to show her the wound. He feels vindicated, whatever the cause of the argument, my mother is now clearly in the wrong for having resorted to violence, for having drawn blood.

"It's nothing," she says, adding, quietly, "I'm sorry."

He takes the medicated rub and a Band-Aid, and then picks up his glasses from the sink and storms out of the bathroom, through the living room, and out of the front door. We can hear his car ignition start and then he backs out of the driveway and is gone.

"Why did you hit him?" I say.

"I didn't," she says.

"Yes, you did," I tell her. "I was standing right there. Why is he bleeding if you didn't hit him?"

"He bumped his head," she says. "On the wall."

"But that's because you hit him."

"Then why is he bleeding on the other side," she asks. "If I hit him, then he should be bleeding on the same side."

"So you did hit him," I say.

She shrugs. "No, he bumped his head."

"For no reason?"

"He overreacted," she explains.

"—to your hitting him," I say.

She can't admit that she took a swing at my father. She maintains that the wound was self-inflicted, or that he was overreacting to something, but what exactly he was reacting to she won't specify.

When my father does come back the next day, he wears the Band-Aid over the wound and we never talk about what happened.

68.

The house devolves into a steady state of conflict, the first truly global conflict in the history of the house. Karl faces a second front now in the Pacific, as Painting aircraft carriers mount a sneak attack on forward Hawaiian bases in the backyard. The Painting fleet is a technological marvel, as if the Imperial Japanese Navy had continued on through Japan's great economic boom of the late twentieth century to reflect the design and technological virtuosity of that era. The aircraft carriers and battle cruisers, named, like their real-world counterparts, for sacred Japanese locales, the *Akagi*, *Kaga*, *Hyriu*, *Soryu*, *Shinano*, are far superior to Karl's outmoded and undergunned fleet. Karl's resources, after all, have been spent in the great war against Greenfeld and fighting on two vast fronts soon overwhelms even the finest war machine in the family.

The great offensive in Greenfeld bogs down along a line extending from Stalingrad through the closet to the Channel, the name I have given to the dirt patch that runs along the side of our house. The rapid early offensive, the great promise of those early armored thrusts into Greenfeld territory, turned out to have been merely the overture to yet another long, protracted conflict. The master bedroom is the second-largest room in our house, and the vastness of the territory overwhelms even the largest armored force in the history of the family. Finally, after months of retreating, the Greenfeld forces make a stand at Greenfeldgrad, a vast, medieval castle town atop a huge hill nestled into the bend of a river—the battle that ensues is a hybrid of the German stand at Monte Cassino Abbey on the Italian peninsula and the siege of Stalingrad. Karl troops, elite panzer grenadier units, have to fight their way up the treacherous, fortified mountain honeycombed with extensive dugouts and pillboxes from which the Greenfeld troops can pick off the invaders. The issue is finally forced when a fleet of Karl aircraft carriers and battle cruisers sails upriver from the Channel and bombards the castle, after which a great armored thrust encircles the city. However, in a great act of patriotism that further inspires the Greenfeld troops, the city refuses to surrender. Greenfeld submarines, meanwhile, force the Karl fleet to withdraw from the river, allowing Greenfeld to resupply the besieged castle town by air.

With this unreduced stronghold to the rear, the Karl offensive has to pause, vulnerable, exposed on the great, frozen plains past Greenfeldgrad, and dig in until sufficient forces can be brought up to destroy this great redoubt. The failure of the offensive has caused a shake-up in the Karl general staff, the relieving of command of Field Marshal Murat, who will be replaced by Field Marshal Guderian. Additionally, for the first time, the possibility of a truce with Greenfeld is considered, though any diplomatic solution would require the concession by Greenfeld of significant territory.

Meanwhile, the campaign map is constantly reshaped and reshuffled in my mind, I know where most of the twenty-two Karl armies are deployed, as well as the six carrier battle groups, each with two aircraft carriers. I can sit in the living room, while my brother chews on his collar and my parents lament their wasted lives, and think of phony military campaigns.

69.

My parents do feel their lives slipping away from them, their dreams of becoming writers, painters, artists are being compromised and destroyed, by us, by Noah; never mind that life destroys such dreams anyway, with or without an autistic child, but how can my mother and father ever remove themselves from their specific lives for long enough to figure out how much is Noah's fault and what is economic reality? My father takes on television projects for which he has no real aptitude or interest; rewrites of TV movies, never-to-be-shot pilots, all for the money. My mother, meanwhile, has poured her energy into the day care center, and it has been over a decade since she even thought about painting. Now she has begun writing in Japanese and dreams of becoming a writer.

And Noah dreams, I guess, of a bowl full of rubber bands.

For my parents, the possibility of BMI, of that being a place for Noah, is becoming so tantalizing that they are able to ignore the downsides. They need a respite of some kind, and exigency has a way of making even the barely tolerable seem richly promising.

We are staggering as a family, out of step, making negligible progress. Families must feel that they are going forward as a unit, that together they are headed into a brighter future. It is the conceit that keeps the whole operation going. The children will continue to mature, to grow, to eventually take their place in society. The parents will pursue their careers or projects, will tend to those children, will achieve important financial and social milestones, the members of the family theoretically and symbiotically benefiting. Never mind that the reality is often—mostly?—disordered. We like the illusion that we are better off together than apart.

In this family, I realize, this is impossible. Each of us is lurching in his own direction, frustrated at how there is so little to derive from the unit. My parents are resentful, blaming each other for their squandered creative lives. I am also heaped with blame, for not being a good student, for spending too much money, for lying, for dreaming. Additionally, I am too often made aware of my father's thwarted dreams. He wouldn't be writing the sequel to *Oh, God!*, arguing with the star, George Burns, if we didn't need the money. He says he would be writing plays and novels and sonnets if it weren't for Noah and me. If he didn't see the burden of caring for us extending indefinitely into the future.

I tell him, well, if he is writing for the money, why doesn't he just write the kind of movies that make a lot of money, instead of these pictures—*Harry & Tonto*, *Oh, God! Book II*, the TV movie *Lovey*—that nobody really wants to see, I mean, why can't he write an *Animal House* or something that will make millions, if it's all just for the money anyway? In my ninth-grade English class, after we are done searching for the symbolism in *A Tale of Two Cities*—the broken wine cask spilling its blood-colored contents on the cobblestoned streets and the prerevolutionary proletarians fighting to lap it up, get it?—we are given scripts of *Lovey*. For some reason CBS has printed scripts for English classes throughout L.A., so here we are, reading my father's writing in class. I don't know why this is considered a logical follow-up to *A Tale of Two Cities*, but we read the teleplay aloud in class, the story of a special-education teacher, Mary MacCracken, reaching out to a low-functioning, developmentally disabled, nonverbal girl. There's a little Anne Sullivan and Helen Keller in the story, but I find the whole subject, of retarded kids and their teachers, of special schools and the struggle for communication, to be familiar and banal. Why do I have to read about this in school when I am living it at home? My father has published books about our family; now there are TV movies about retards that my father is writing, and the teacher is telling the class, as if I should be proud, that "Karl's father is the writer." And now my mother is writing her own books about special education. Her first is a nonfiction account comparing American and Japanese programs for developmentally disabled children. Her second will include the novellas *Passover* and *A Guest from Afar*; the former will become a best seller and win the Akutagawa Prize, Japan's most prestigious literary award.

It's like we are a family industry churning out content about fucked-up kids.

70.

But despite my father's professional success—all achieved while he complains that he never wanted to write "this crap"—there lingers the sense that as a family we are failing. It is a stench that now hangs over our gatherings for meals. I want to be as far away as I can, yet I am always roped in to care for Noah, to babysit, to mind him, to keep an eye on him while he is sitting in his little egg-shaped wicker swing suspended from a beam in the carport. From behind, it looks a little like the rear gun turret of a B-17 Flying Fortress.

Sometimes I feel that our entire purpose as a family is to keep Noah out of an institution. We exist to be a place for Noah. But is that really a justification for a family?

My father sometimes talks to me about divorce. He mentions it lightly, as if trying out the idea. I know it is fantasy because the unfairness of either of my parents leaving the other with Noah precludes the possibility. But he likes the sound of it, turning the words over in his mouth, the sense of possibility it brings. He wouldn't have to write TV movies, he could instead work on the quality projects that keep drifting tantalizingly out of reach.

The fights between my parents are so frequent that Noah and I barely pay any attention to them.

In the midst of one such argument, my father comes out from the kitchen, folding open the slat doors and standing in the square of yellow light.

"Karl, can you brush Noah's teeth?"

I am mapping out a battle, laying out the defensive formations for the vast and endangered salient that now bulges out past Greenfeldgrad. A massive pincer counterattack could turn the tide of the whole campaign. But we will never retreat, Karl has vowed; we will hold the line.

"Karl," he shouts.

"What?"

"Brush Noah's teeth."

"No."

"Karl, come on, you've got to help out."

I sigh.

Noah is lounging on the floor of his bedroom, leaning on one elbow. He has taken off his pants—who knows why. He's uncomfortable? It's hot? He just sometimes likes to take off his pants? At home, it's fine. When we're in the supermarket or taking a walk, it can be embarrassing.

He spits at me, a little reminder that I am in his territory.

"Okay, come on, Noah," I say. "You have to brush your teeth."

He nods his head. "M-m-m-m-muh-muh."

"Mommy is busy, in the kitchen."

He rises in stages, awkwardly, climbing onto his knees, then one foot, then standing. He's actually in a good mood, flashing that big, catlike grin that is so often accompanied by a tilt of his head. He walks toward me, touches his head to my forehead, and then leads me out of his room into the bathroom.

He makes a sign language gesture for a drink—a fist tilted thumb out toward his mouth—and then nods at me. He's thirsty. I fill a paper cup and hand it to him. He drinks. "Mo-MO," he demands.

I fill another cup but before handing it to him, I rinse his toothbrush and apply some Colgate. He shakes his head. Makes the drink sign. He wants the water.

"First brush," I say.

Finally, he opens his mouth slightly, enough for me to jam in the toothbrush.

"Now brush," I tell him.

He chews the toothbrush for a moment. Then he begins to move it around his mouth lazily, not really brushing but sort of running the bristles lightly over his teeth.

"Do more," I say. "Do better."

He spits again, without much velocity, and then removes the toothbrush and holds it out to me.

"I'm not gonna do it," I tell him.

He nods his head once, emphatically.

It's faster if I do it myself, but we're supposed to have him make an effort. "You want water?"

He nods.

"Then brush."

He puts the brush back into his mouth and moves it around enough for me to declare "good job" and hand him the water.

He takes a sip, spits out the toothpaste, and then drinks the water. Then he holds the paper cup out, and I refill it.

My parents don't let him drink as much water as he wants before he goes to bed because that increases the chance of an accident. Lately, he hasn't been wetting his bed very much, but he seems to go through phases and he still sleeps with a rubber pad over his mattress.

I always let him drink water; I don't change him when he wakes in the middle of the night.

"Go pee," I tell him.

He pulls down his underwear and sits on the toilet. "Muh-muh-muh-muh-muh-muh," he is humming to himself and rocking as he pisses. He is smiling and pleased, nodding at me. Noah, a year and a half younger than me, already has pubic hair. I have yet to sprout any. This precocious puberty has alarmed my parents. They have long believed that it will be easier to place Noah in one of the better institutions if he is still young and cute, as he is now. The more he becomes like a man, another feeble-minded adult like the thousands who cram the wards at state hospitals like Camarillo, then the harder it will be to find a place for Noah.

He is still physically attractive, retaining the last vestiges of androgynous youth in his delicate features; his nose is softer and more delicately shaped than mine, his eyes more rounded, his chin defined above a narrow, shapely, long neck. And as he smiles at me, yanking up his briefs, the idea that we would ever put Noah away seems gratuitous and unnecessary. He is my adorable brother, and we do share some semblance of a sibling bond.

Though we are an ineffectual combination, we are still, at times, a team. United as the disenfranchised members of our household. Order takers, as feckless as we are, rather than order givers. But Noah can shirk without repercussions. It is never his chore to prepare me for bed. He helps by clearing the dinner table, yet his job—carrying dishes to the sink—is far simpler than mine—washing pots and pans and loading the dishwasher. And there is no possibility for our jobs to be rotated.

There is, of course, no one to blame.

I wash Noah's hands and lead him back to his room. I hand him his cotton pajama pants and the chewed-up flannel top. He climbs into bed. "Goo-goo-goo-goo-goo," he is saying as he smiles. "Goo-goo-goo."

He sits up and rocks back and forth.

"Good night," I say.

"Goo-goo-goo nigh," he says.

I hug him. That might be the only two-syllable phrase he will utter this year.

71.

In my room at night, I apply oil paints to various models and figurines. I have a magnifying glass and ultra-fine 1/64" bristle-width camel-hair brushes that allow me to paint the corneas and irises of lead Dungeons & Dragons figurines or the gunwales on a Tamiya Water Line Series destroyer. I like to take a bong hit, blow it out the window, and then sit and assemble and paint my little armies, sometimes narrating my imaginary campaigns as I work.

I can't really listen to any music on my little Sanyo stereo because then I wouldn't be able to hear the approach of my parents, if one of them chooses to check on me. If I do detect their footfalls in the hallway, I can swivel in my chair to where I have laid out a sheet of algebra, one of the hated mimeographs of equations that I now owe in insurmountable numbers.

What I am doing, I later realize, is warding off adolescence. The first flickers of puberty bring with them confused longings. New social skills are suddenly required. The conversation in my junior high school has shifted from Kareem Abdul-Jabbar, the center for the Los Angeles Lakers, to Teresa Jordan, this totally hot girl in my health class. Socially, I haven't figured out how the landscape has changed, but I am acutely aware that it has. A few of the guys are evolving flawlessly. One week they're collecting baseball cards, and the next they seem to be driving Mustangs and dating Teresas. Instead, I've retreated into a refined hyper-geekdom. I get deeply, almost disturbingly (to my parents) into very specific aspects of military modeling and discover Japan, or at least its sophisticated plastic model culture.

I'm particularly enamored of the nautical ones manufactured by Tamiya. This Shizuoka-based firm, and to a lesser extent its competitor Hasegawa, produce plastic kits far superior to the American versions. U.S. companies such as Revell, Heller, and Monogram make clunky plastic parts that need filing upon removal from their sprues and molded castings that resemble gobs of melted cheese. Tamiya's models, on the other hand, are exemplary—pristine, perfect little gunwales, torpedoes, and conning towers. The parts trees came shrink-wrapped and are rendered with such precision you can see the bolts on a battleship's antiaircraft cannon. And as a fourteen-year-old desperately trying to stall the onset of puberty, I need to see those bolts.

Just as important as the quality and precision of the models is the subject matter. Tamiya and Hasegawa are the only companies that make scale models of Japanese Imperial Navy vessels. The American companies are squeezing out endless reproductions of the aircraft carrier *Enterprise* and the battleship *Missouri*: model kits as cookie-cutterish as the ships they represent. American naval vessels seemed mass-produced—Yorktown-class carriers, Iowa-class battleships, Portland-class cruisers. Credit Henry Ford for the assembly lines that won the war. But blame him for the blandness of the fleet. What was the difference between the *Enterprise* and the *Yorktown*? The *Iowa* and the *Missouri*? None that I could see from the Revell kits they sold at my local hobby shop.

But Japanese aircraft carriers and battleships are idiosyncratic, unique, individually laid down in Yokosuka and Shikoku shipyards and fitted with quirky characteristics. Superstructures set too far aft. Smokestacks emanating from the ship's hull. With their jeweler's attention to detail and scholar's obsessive historical accuracy, the Tamiya Water Line models somehow evoke the mystery of these lost ships and a world where technological marvels like an aircraft carrier are still individual, handmade creations.

Though I was born in Japan, these plastic kits and the ships they represent are among my first independently-arrived-at impressions of that country. What kind of nation could produce these strange-looking ships? And then, just a few decades later, distribute these wondrous plastic replicas? It has stayed with me ever since as my internal, almost subconscious response to the notion that Japan is a copycat nation: no other country, before or since, ever made aircraft carriers that looked like the *Akagi* or *Shokaku* or *Hiryu*. At the same time, only Japan ever made toys as wondrously byzantine as the model kits of those ships.

I am torn between the lure of drugs and petty crime of adolescence and the toys and military models of my childhood. "I have always thought an interest in toy soldiers is a sign of a rejected child," my father wrote. "And now Karl is a kid lost in military affairs." It is my retreat, my own self-stimulation. I can divert myself in this rich, private life of my own creation and invention; it is an intersection of history, myth, and fantasy, everything but the quotidian reality of the faltering machinery of our family. My mother complains that I am becoming too old for toys, and, of course, she is correct, for a normal boy in a normal family. But my armies, my fleets, make the present endurable.

I cannot share this with my teenage associates, because they will view my diversion as immature, childlike. We are supposed to care about skateboarding, surfing, metal, girls, smoking dope, quaaludes. And when I am away from home, with my friends, I can subsume myself in that scene, in that culture of guitar rock and thirty-dollar halves of brown Colombian dope. But at home? I am left with my armies.

72.

Noah rages, turns over the living room table, yanks on the cat's tail, pulls my hair, shits on the carpet. He is shirtless, screaming, bashing his fist against his own forehead, scratching his own arms. He looks in pain, angry, demented, hurt, pitiful, but also detestable. There is something so ugly about dementia that you have to turn away. When you encounter a madman on the street, you pass him by, step around him, and never think of him again. When the madman is in your home, is your brother, you are engaged.

As an adult, I will know how a putatively normal family works.

I will have two daughters. Thankfully, neither will be developmentally disabled. I will discover that their progress, from turning over to crawling to walking, from talking to reading to writing, will also be the measure of progress for our family, perhaps the most important gauge. They grow taller and my wife and I can't help but notice and feel a certain pride. They master subtraction and cartwheels and we can believe, perhaps subconsciously, our family as a machine for living is validated. It works.

What happens with Noah is that one of the key metrics by which a family determines its success or failure—no, wait, that's too drastic, the measure of where a family has gone—is broken. So we feel as if we are going nowhere and so we are, collectively, consciously or unconsciously, a failure, as a unit, a team. We are not an efficient machine.

And that is a terrible conclusion for a family to draw about itself. If we're not better together, then why are we together? This is the issue my mother and father struggle with constantly. They can't help but judge their own progress as a family. And when it is found wanting, as it must in the case of Noah, then what choice do they have but to perhaps examine more closely the other metric, their allegedly normal son. They so desperately want me to be normal, to carry the banner for their hopes and aspirations. That is why they overzealously encourage my algebra, French, writing, and piano, none of which I have any aptitude for or interest in. That is why they constantly worry that I am a discipline problem at school, that I am smoking dope, that I am, as my father writes, a "bad apple." (How can a fourteen-year-old be a "bad apple"?) But they can't help themselves, they see in me the only hope for a future for our family. How can they see themselves reflected in Noah? They have no choice but to overburden me with their desire for a sense of purpose, and I fail them in every way.

Is my underperformance related to these demands? It is not conscious; no one tells me that I must succeed, excel, but there is always a sense of worry, of doubt, a vetting of my academic skills, my facility with equations, my conjugation of French verbs, even my ability to write an engaging story. (I must write a composition a week for my father. The subject is of my own choosing. But it must meet his specifications, not just grammatically but also conceptually. I don't know any other kids in my neighborhood whose parents are ordering them to write essays every week, or ever for that matter.) The attention is not constant, it is instead targeted. Days go by when Noah absorbs all the parental focus, and then suddenly, in an early evening while I am settling in to dream my epic battles—a ten-division armor thrust through the center of the Russo-Greenfeld lines, the tank division drawn from the most elite units in the Karl Army, a carrier sortie through the Indian Ocean (the paved driveway leading to the carport) with the target being the destruction of Painting port facilities around the plum tree—my parents will demand to see my schoolwork or my father will go through my compositions, striking through those passages he deems too childish, shaking his head at my juvenilia.

My mother, educated in the rigorous Japanese school system, is always worried that her older son is an idiot. She complains that I am lost in fantasy, adrift in my military models, my rock music; she studies my Kiss albums, notes the leather uniforms, the bandoliers, the Nazi lettering, and insists they are fascists. I don't believe they are Nazis, or political in any way that I can recognize, but to her they represent the vacuous stupidity of her son and confirm for her that I am drifting into a life of cretinous American consumerism. She has never really become Americanized, my mother, still clinging to basic Japanese values of diligence, honesty, and stolidity that drive her until she is in tears, until she can't take Noah's violence and my own laziness anymore. Nothing in her background prepared her to confront an American teenager, especially one failing at school and stoned much of the time.

I burn, cotton mouthed from cheap dope on long afternoons and evenings while my parents either worry over Noah or lament my academic fecklessness. When I'm stoned, Noah seems harmless, his humming and self-stimming the ambient sounds of our house. I can look at him and pet our cat and think, This is all okay, you know? We can sort of stay like this, in the den, Noah on the floor, the cat on my lap, the three of us diverted—Noah by a piece of string, TG by my stroking him, and me by marijuana and my fantasy life. Can we stop time?

73.

His peers are dropping away. The boys in Noah's Westport class, at the day care center, they are disappearing into group homes, state institutions, residential facilities. The boys are growing, becoming men, and it is first the single mothers who surrender to the inevitable and concede they cannot care for their sons any longer. Or the administrators at the Westport School will inform the family that they have gone "as far we can" with Willie or Barry or Carlos. And Noah's time is coming, he is just inches shorter, a year younger than the boys whose parents are being told it is time to go.

For those higher-functioning autistics, like Gary, the boy who I babysit down the street, there are programs, facilities, even vocational schools where he can learn a trade. He is verbal, nonviolent, toilet trained, and compared to Noah a civilized pleasure. I regard Gary and his family with envy. If Noah were like Gary, we could keep him at home forever. We would not be living with the sense that the family, as constituted, will be coming to an end. My mother's goal all along—with the behavior modification, the sign language, the picture boards, the operant conditioning, the hours of programming, the vitamin therapy, the allergy tests—was to somehow get Noah to the point where he can communicate. And now, after surrendering a decade of her life to this cause, even she has conceded that whatever progress Noah is making—if there is any at all—is made at such a pace that he may never be able to communicate sufficiently so as to obviate his tantrums. These spasms of violence and aggression, coming more frequently now, as often as three times a day, are overwhelming for her.

Noah and I have been growing apart for some time now. Perhaps if he spoke, if he could communicate, there would be some bond. But as it is, my arguments for keeping him home—and that is always my position—are based on our family's established belief that we are the best place for Noah. Any other view would be apostasy. But how much of my stated position is just a reciting of the family liturgy?

But the situation has transcended faith for my parents and become a matter of physical survival. My father is fifty, my mother just a few years younger. They are losing their strength at precisely the instant that Noah is finding his. "Foumi is tired, overwhelmed with day care duties, confused as to what to do about Noah . . . She worries about everything down to the tiniest detail, asking 'what then?' the way a child keeps asking 'why?' There is no solution to Noah and she cannot accept that. She wants me to act when there is no action to take . . . Getting Noah out of the house is the only way our marriage can last. I guess I will apply for a placement for Noah at BMI."

My parents inquire about placement and seek to secure funding through our local Regional Center for the Developmentally Disabled. BMI is all we have, and my father views it as stopgap, a chance for respite. He says that he wants to try a few months, that perhaps he and my mother can regain their strength, their sanity, if Noah is gone for a while. But they are still undecided, debating, arguing, struggling to determine if this really is the best place for Noah.

74.

My father is driving Noah to school one morning, and I go along for the ride. It is a warm day, late spring, the morning sun powerful enough to burn off the haze even down near the beach where we live. As we drive inland on the Santa Monica Freeway, you can see the layer of smog over downtown and feel the bad air in the back of your throat.

"Ma-ma-ma-ma-ma, ma-ma-ma-ma," Noah is sitting in the backseat, rocking backward and forward, smiling. He is in a good mood, seeming to enjoy my company. I'm looking forward to the end of the school year, but I'm not even sure Noah is aware of the end of the semester or term or however they mark academic time at Westport.

The building is the squat little brick house in Mar Vista, set back on a lawn bisected by a pink paved pathway leading to a two-step stone porch and a white door. There is a macramé sign over the door spelling out the school's name, and inside the living room, dining room, and den have been converted into four classrooms, with the regular wooden doors replaced by institutional doors with push bars instead of doorknobs. Along the walls, the supplies, toys, and training materials are neatly stacked and shelved, ready for their daily deployment. At the rear, through opened double doors with quarter-paned windows, the morning sun streams in from the east. Outside, we can see the grass yard with jungle gym, swing set, seesaw, and sandbox. In the shade of a willow tree at the rear of the lot, a little playhouse with a miniature window is kept padlocked.

The other children are playing in the yard, and Noah walks in his side-to-side gait out the back door, across the gray-painted wooden porch, to join them. Or perhaps join them is the wrong word, to wander among them, to bounce, to jump, to rock, to nod, to spit, to look for a twig to roll between his thumb and forefinger. Last summer I remember a black girl named Latanya, retarded but verbal and far higher functioning than Noah, who would come and find Noah every morning and lead him by the hand to a red wagon that she would pull around the yard. He would smile as he rode; all he had to do was wave, and he would have seemed almost presidential. She was a beautiful girl, with her kinky hair tied back into twin, beribboned pigtails, almond-shaped eyes with black-green irises at the center of stark whites, a long nose with perfectly round nostrils like miniature jet-engine cowls, and puckered, pert lips. When she called out, "Noah! Noah!" he would go to her and touch her hand. It was the first time Noah had ever responded to another student, his teacher Adele Morton told us. His first girlfriend, my father joked at the time, and it elicited in me surprising pleasure to see Noah so contented. At the same time, I was jealous. Why should my autistic brother have a girlfriend before I did?

His docility was his gift to Latanya, his love offering, the only thing, really, he could give her. "Noah, Noah," she called out. "Come play with me, Noah."

By the end of the summer she was gone. Noah, of course, could never say if he missed her.

Today, Noah walks between the swings and the jungle gym. He likes the swings, to gently rock back and forth, the gravitational assist given to his self-stimming—what else is swinging anyway, but a more accepted form of self-stimulation? The other boys and girls are a mixed group of autistic, retarded, and Down syndrome children; the Down syndrome and retarded kids are, of course, far more social than the autistic. They show one another toys, push each other on swings, can even collaborate in the sandbox. The parents stand on the porch, drinking coffee from Styrofoam cups, watching their children, taking the exact same interest in the proceedings as parents anywhere would. These are the only individuals who know what it takes, what the kids need, what it does to a family: the professionals, the experts, the psychiatrists, the counselors, the therapists, even the teachers, they can all go home at night; the parents, the families, we never leave our Noahs behind.

My father takes a moment with these parents, but then wants to leave, to get to his office, to work for the few free hours that he has. But while we are standing on the porch, a mother watching her physically precocious autistic child swing apelike through the jungle gym observes, "Somewhere in the jungle, there must be a monkey with brains."

Noah's school day consists of regular behavior modification. His two teachers over the years at Westport, Alys Harris and Adele Morton, are two of the best at training and teaching these kids, surpassing the professionals churned out by the branded and richly funded programs. Alys Harris was never even state certified. She learned behavior mod or operant conditioning through pure trial and error; twenty years of working with the developmentally disabled had shown her that patient, constant monitoring and reinforcement and regular prodding—her only aversive was verbal, never a slap or a pinch—was the only method that showed any results, not matter how infinitesimal. She was one woman working with four children, and she could work with only one at a time. Yet she made steady progress as her boys sorted shapes, connected dots to form letters, stepped over a rope stretched out on the ground or through an obstacle course made of blocks. They re-created patterns she drew, matched the sequences of blocks she laid out, placed the dolls of the family into the house-shaped box. Slowly, laboriously, she urged them to say, "My, my, my, my" until finally, even Noah would repeat, "Muh, muh, muh, muh." She knew to break every motion, every act, every utterance down to its most basic component. Noah wouldn't imitate anything. If you wanted him to make a line, you had to start by showing him how to hold a crayon, and if you wanted him to hold a crayon you had to first show him how to pick it up. Alys would pick up a crayon.

"Now you," she would say.

Nothing.

She would pick up the crayon again.

"Now you."

Nothing.

She would then place Noah's hand over the crayon, wrap his fingers around it.

She would pick up her own crayon.

"Now you."

And Noah would pick up his crayon. This sequence repeated for each part of each movement of the appointed task. It was slow, boring, difficult work, and this lovely woman with white frizzy hair and wire-frame glasses and a gentle smile could outwait even the indifference of these autistic boys. She was firm, steady, yet never brittle with impatience. My mother once described Alys Harris as the best technician of operant conditioning, as behavior modification was then known, that she had ever seen. What was more amazing to me was the fact that when she was working with one of the boys, the rest would actually sit quietly instead of bouncing around the room or banging their hands against the table. It was inspiring to think that Noah could sit still for these thirty-minute stretches.

Yet at the end of these school years, when we would visit the school for the official review of what Noah had been doing, it was always disheartening to see just how little progress had been made. He could step over a rope. He could stack a few blocks. He was drawing lines from point A to point B. He could trace his name along a dotted line. For the last few years, these tasks had kept repeating as if we were all doomed to some kind of developmentally disabled purgatory. The teachers and staff of the school, even the best of them, I suspected, must feel the same sense of futility as they considered what they were actually achieving. Oh, some children progressed, and that's part of what I found so heartbreaking. The retarded boys and girls, they weren't stricken by the layer of indifference, of antisocial static, that made it so hard for the autistic boys to make progress. They were desperate to please, to learn, to socialize. They were frustrated at times by their own disability, but they wanted to learn. Noah never really seemed to want to learn. He wasn't even slightly interested in the prospect.

So today, as I watch Adele Morton, the successor to Alys Harris, who recently retired but passed along so much of what she knew, I am impressed again at how she coaches and herds her gang into cooperation and a semblance of orderly classroom behavior. The boys sit at their little tables—Noah and a few of his cohort having already outgrown the furniture—their hands twittering and flickering and slapping the laminated wood. Adele speaks sternly, "Hands still."

The boys continue their self-stimming. It is established that the boys can't learn if they are stimming; their hands and bodies must be settled, their eyes directed, their heads steady, their bodies rigid. For an instant, it seems that Adele calms the room like a hypnotist. And then the boys are at it again, stimming, fluttering, twitting.

"Hands still," she orders.

I know that I am remiss at home in that I don't police Noah's self-stimming, that I don't participate in his operant conditioning, in his behavior modification, but I can't be a prison guard with my own brother. No one expects me to take on that role, but I know the prevailing ideology—that this is the only way autistic kids can learn to communicate. It offers hope, at least for some, for the higher-functioning kids, for that lucky Gary down the street who can talk—even if it's babble—and play with his Lite-Brite.

But after seven years at Westport, what have we really achieved? And they aren't going to keep him here forever. He is practically man-size, with pubic hair, and here in the next classroom are four-year-old autistic boys as delicate as toothpick sculptures. Noah could snap one of them in half. Perhaps Noah's celebrity helps, his star turn on *60 Minutes*, my father's books; could his fame buy him a year or two? Everyone in southern California is susceptible to star power, as limited as Noah's might be.

But even I have to concede that this is going nowhere, that Noah's progress has slowed down to almost imperceptible. I occasionally read other books about the developmentally disabled. There was the best-selling *A Circle of Children* and also the memoir *The Siege*; in each of them the beginning was familiar—the struggle to break through to the seemingly closed-off child—yet by the middle of each book I am jealous. These kids are talking, are learning, are somehow becoming part of the family. They are drawing wonderful pictures, playing music. Noah is still shitting in his pants. He seems to excel only at autism. Why of all the gifts does he have that instead of, say, being able to replay a Mozart sonata after just one listen?

75.

What does Noah know? What does he think? For those meeting him for the first time, he inspires the belief that there is an intelligent being just under the rocking, twisting, twittering surface; he is like a TV whose vertical hold is lost, the picture in there somewhere between the static and the broken black bars skipping down, if you can just find the knob, twist it, he will come into focus. We know, of course, that there is no such control. But for those unfamiliar with the autistic, there is the belief they can reach him, can heal him. They want to try out their pyramid power and their crystals and their copper bracelets; they troop through our house, usually friends of my parents whom we put up with because we have known them for so long, and they all want to heal, as my mother says, but they never want to help.

But they all comment that inside Noah, there is a beautiful being. It helps that he retains his good looks, his delicate features. "Of course I know Noah," wrote my father's friend John Gregory Dunne in *Quintana & Friends*. "If I had to pick an adjective to describe him, it would be beautiful. He played in the sand, crooning to himself, and except for the monotony of the croon and the fact that he acknowledged no greeting—not in itself uncommon in a small child—there was no indication he was suffering with what Josh calls, with terrifying detachment, 'genetic rot.'" John went on to describe our family as having "a second life of which I was only dimly aware, a community of parents whose only bond was the wreckage of their brain-damaged children. To institutionalize or not to institutionalize, that was the question that haunted them." John, who would generously donate his fee for writing that column for *Esquire* to my parents' day care center, was among the more realistic of our friends. Others would imagine that they, or someone they knew, could unlock Noah. I watch a Native American healer, the girlfriend of an actor, rub some sort of muddy-colored herbs against his chest; I've had to remove a copper bracelet after Noah was so cuffed by another friend of my parents. My parents tolerate these feckless attempts at healing, as long as they require no time or energy on their part.

I am depressingly realistic; if I once dreamed that Noah could be trained to talk, I've swung violently in the other direction, to where I no longer see any possible progress.

I have ceased to wonder at what goes on in his mind, at how he perceives the world. "Men differ from other animals in that they are the most imitative," wrote Aristotle, "and their first learning is produced through imitation." I don't remember Noah ever imitating, or even being interested in what the rest of us are doing. Does he see colors as colors or shapes as shapes? Does he hear sounds as we do? Does he smell as we do? I don't know any of it. He likes certain songs, or at least he doesn't leave the room when they are playing. He has no interest in television, less in books unless he is tearing pages from them. His sole talent, if he has one, is to locate rubber bands or pieces of string no matter where they are hidden—in drawers, beneath sofas, behind bookcases. As he twists his rubber bands and strings, wraps them around his fingers, twiddles them between his thumb and pointer, they become his autistic rosary.

He is compulsive about order, insisting that doors be shut, that tabletops be pristine, that papers be gathered from wherever they are and tossed into wastebaskets. We have learned to keep important documents safely locked away or hidden where Noah can't trash them. He doesn't like clutter, to the point where if he finds your sock on the floor he will deliver it to you and nod slightly, as if reprimanding you.

Yet he is not compulsive about cleanliness, only order. He doesn't mind if his anus is unwiped, but he insists that all toilets be flushed as soon as he has moved his bowels.

76.

He is receding, and now we must consider the inevitability of his departure. Soon, I have concluded, I will no longer have my brother. He will be gone, the decision made to institutionalize. My parents vibrate with the guilt of putting Noah away; I shudder with the guilt of why him and not me? I am logical, I know why. Just as the raccoons that tore up our shingled roof had to be caged and trucked away just for being raccoons, so Noah will be sent away just for being Noah. He has never once acted out of character or contrary to what I know to be his nature. And for that he is being punished?

As if he knows that he is on the verge of expulsion, Noah mellows out. He attacks less frequently, he smiles more, he is gentle. It is as if he is saying, Give me one more chance. "Karl has been arguing against Noah's leaving the house," my father writes, "claiming that Noah has been behaving well lately. And it's true that he has. But Noah has to be leaving us one day and it is time to make the break. I'm getting older, and without being morbid about it, one day he will have to live on without me."

My parents essentially talk to themselves, justifying their already-made decision to each other, while I listen and resign myself to the inevitable.

The mystery to me is why I care. Why do I want Noah at home?

77.

In the evenings we take walks, my father, brother, and me, along the cliff that runs down Asilomar, the ocean on one side and the Cape Cod–style houses across the street on the other. The top of the bluffs are rises of hard-packed earth studded with mica and granite that extend seaward in promontories shaped like lions' paws. There are green- and olive-colored horsetail and thistle bushes, and the smell of licorice, and stalky mustard plants, and occasionally the sweeter smell of honeysuckle. We have been walking these cliffs for as long as we have lived here, at least five years, and it's where my father and I talk most freely, with Noah trailing along behind us, catching up when he sees a dog, even in the distance—it seems Noah can spot a dog at close to a mile away.

I know what my father is doing; he is preparing me for Noah's departure. We argue, my father and I, about everything: my schoolwork, my laziness, my stealing, my dishonesty. What is stopping me, he wonders, from dispatching my assignments, learning my polynomials, and writing my paper on Tolstoy's *Master and Servant*, which we are reading in English. Why, for a nominally intelligent boy like me, it should just be a matter of applying myself. Yet I flounder, continually, and in an uninteresting manner.

"If I behave better," I ask my father, "can we keep Noah at home?"

He says that Noah's eventual departure has nothing to do with me. That Noah and I are two completely separate issues and that I should never, ever feel as if I am responsible for Noah. "What we are doing is for him and for us," he tells me. "It's not your fault, you understand that?"

I do. I think I do.

But a few weeks later, when I return home stoned, drunk, puking on myself as I sit defecating into the toilet, crying to my parents that

I will never go to college, that I am a failure, I feel I have let down not only my parents but Noah, too. I tell them that I remember being at my friend Mike's house, drinking beer and then rum with his older sister and her boyfriend and taking a few bong hits. I don't remember how I got home or when. I blacked out and came to on the toilet seat with my mother and father shouting at me, wondering where I had been and what had happened. They shower me off, put me in pajamas, and then lay me down in my bed. While my parents have suspected for a while that I have been smoking marijuana, this was the first time they have caught me, and it confirms for my mother all her worst suspicions about her allegedly normal son. Boys in Japan are not coming home drunk at age fourteen, she says. (Later, I will discover that she is wrong about this.) They are not smoking dope or going to school stoned, either. She further insists they don't spend their lives assembling military models or playing Dungeons & Dragons or listening to rock music or skateboarding. This family isn't functioning, she bemoans; this family is lost. She cries that she is a failure, as a mother she doesn't understand where she went wrong, to have one son like Noah and another like me.

When she regains her composure, she forces me to sign a contract stating that I will never drink or smoke again until I turn eighteen, and that I promise to do one hour of math, one hour of French, one hour of essay writing, and one hour of piano a day, every day, until I am of voting age. I also must promise to put away my military toys, to stop playing Dungeons & Dragons, to forgo listening to rock albums, and to stop skateboarding. It is a preposterously stringent document, one whose demands I know I can't keep even as I am signing it.

My parents later find out I have a pellet gun I've been using to shoot at birds and squirrels; they never discover my career in larceny. Is my teenage misbehavior somehow related to Noah's disability? Of course not. Millions of fourteen-year-olds without autistic siblings are getting stoned and listening to Cheap Trick albums. To blame

Noah for my own shortcomings would be to give him too much credit. I am my own person, Noah or not. I have to hold on to that; otherwise, what am I but a reflection of his disability? Yet in the speeches that I now must endure from my parents, the subtext is always that they have enough to worry about with Noah, how dare I add to it?

Noah, meanwhile, seems thrilled to be out of the harsh parental glare. He rocks back and forth on his sofa, chews on his T-shirt, and as he walks by the dining room where I sit during prolonged interrogations by my parents, he is smugly smiling at me. As if to make a belated case that he is the better son, his behavior has become almost impeccable; for a few days, he becomes one of those sweet, nonviolent, developmentally disabled kids, eager to please, helpful when my mother is clearing the table, eagerly sorting his shapes and identifying matching images, gently laying his forehead against my father's and mother's when he greets them. It is an act, it has to be, and I sometimes feel like telling him to knock it off, but then I also know that this stretch of good behavior is perhaps Noah's last argument to stay home. It won't work, of course, I'm sure of that. Noah's improvements, in behavior, in language, they are always followed by rapid regressions.

But the mood in our home has shifted. Remarkably, my parents are now talking about sending me away. Whether this would be in concurrence with Noah's departure I am not sure. "Noah has been lovely," my father writes. "At this point I think I can hold on to him longer than I can hold on to Karl. The atmosphere of our family evidently is wrong for Karl."

Wait a second, I'm thinking. I go from arguing that Noah shouldn't be sent away to suddenly arguing that *I* shouldn't be sent away? The implication being that I've been the problem all along? Of course, I would be shipped off to Choate or Andover or another prep school back east. The brochures are now arriving almost daily, and my father is starting to work his connections—he calls Choate alumnus playwright Edward Albee, to see if strings might be pulled. I don't want to be sent to New England, no matter how theoretically better for my future it would be. Why I want to stay here isn't clear, but I'm convinced that here must be better than there. I quickly figure out that by now, early summer, it is too late for me to possibly be admitted for the upcoming September term, even with Albee's lobbying. The argument is academic. My father threatens me, insisting that he will not let me further harm my mother. "I will destroy you first," he warns. After some arguing, he calls the parents of those boys whom I was smoking and drinking with to tell them what their children have been up to, and so, as a bonus, I start the summer before high school with a reputation as a snitch. (Mike's mother never bothered to call back. My friends Erich's and Max's parents confront their kids who then, temporarily, break off their friendship with me.)

And Noah, of course, offers no brotherly support when it looks like I might be forced to leave home. I buy him a few months, and what do I get in return? Nothing.

78.

I am enrolled in a private summer school, four and a half hours a day of algebra. Making lines of numbers balance on either side of an equal sign has become my daily penance for being a teenage wastrel. Every day that summer, I get up at six thirty to ride the Santa Monica bus to Euclid Avenue—how the Gateway Math School managed to rent space on such an appropriately named street is a coincidence that strikes my parents as funny but doesn't register with me.

I am spending the last summer of the 1970s, the summer before I begin Palisades High School, when by rights I should be at the beach every day, smoking dope with my buddies and surfing, in a stuffy second-floor classroom doing more fucking algebra. I feel like I have spent the decade trying to solve for fucking X, so it is actually an appropriate way for me to celebrate the end of a pretty shitty decade. Why should I suddenly have fun when the nation as a whole didn't exactly have a blast?

I'm stupid and lazy. I want to get stoned, play Dungeons & Dragons and listen to Zeppelin. I want to be normal, to be a regular kid, to be part of a typical family.

Noah.

79.

In my algebra school, while listening to the chalk scratching against the blackboard as Mark, the teacher, runs through the basics of polynomials, I reengage in my fantasy life. I see the battles more clearly in my mind than ever. Over the rolling, running farmlands, I can picture the smoke rising in ribbons from a city of rubble a few miles ahead of me. Strung out on a road winding through the approaches to the city, the gray and green tanks are stalled, waiting for sappers to sweep the road ahead for mines. To my left, a column of infantry goes from farmhouse to farmhouse, checking for snipers. The smell—what is the smell?—it is smoke, of course, and burning wheat. I don't know the odor of corpses, I really know nothing of death, but I try to imagine it; for I know that war must be above all about death, about millions of deaths. It is a shame, of course, to imagine a meticulously painted 1/72nd-scale paratrooper, for example, just winding up another corpse. As for civilians, they don't really exist in this world of constant war. We live to fight. We are a warrior society. The women will make baby boys who will grow up to take up arms.

The armor column advances, finally, the treads clanking over the grinding wheels, the track making a clicking noise as it engages with the teeth of the guide wheels, the throaty whir of the diesel engines. A few dozen tanks running on scavenged petrol are making a desperate attempt to break through Greenfeld lines.

The Karl lines break at Greenfeldgrad, Army Group Center collapses, those lovingly described and catalogued tank armies falling prey to fuel shortages, partisans, and the massive waves of Greenfeld reinforcements that eventually reduce and finally force into capitulation the most advanced products of Karl factories and the flower of Karl youth. The retreat of other armies from Greenfeld is as ordered as such an operation can be; armor and equipment are abandoned, and the columns are harassed constantly by Greenfeld aircraft, but Karl is a far more pragmatic commander than, say, Hitler. There is no order given forbidding retreat. Karl knows he will need his army to fight another day. Yet any hopes of a quick victory, a favorable treaty, are dashed, and now the goal will be to fight the Greenfeld hordes to a stalemate on Greenfeld territory, perhaps along a natural defensive line of rocky cliffs running from the bathroom along the Oder River. Yes, despite our setbacks, the loss of 450,000 men in the Greenfeld winter, the surrender of Army Group Center, the loss of the Greenfeldgrad salient, Karl will persevere. Karl has lost the campaign, but not the war, not yet.

And deep inside Karl territory, in a series of bunkers built in a mountain redoubt, a top-secret project is under way to develop weapons more destructive than have ever been deployed in these conflicts. Terrible weapons—harnessing the power of atoms, neutrons, molecules, bombs capable of destroying an entire city, and that can turn an entire room into a wasteland—are now being developed and refined by Karl scientists. The project will soon produce a bomb ready for deployment; it is only a matter of time, if Karl's military woes continue and his armies and fleets are kept in retreat, before this terrible, destructive bomb will be used.

80.

Noah's reprieve is brief. I knew he could not maintain his run of exemplary behavior, no more than I could live up to the ridiculous promises my mother extracted from me after I was busted. We revert back to our mean. I am mean and lazy; Noah is mean and lazy. But miraculously, I have secured an A in algebra. My parents are so pleased with me that they buy me new toys, fancy N-gauge railway sets, even though my mother is opposed to my continued childishness. It is probably my first academic success outside of history, in which I have always excelled, and my parents like to think that it augurs well for high school. Perhaps instead of being a disruptive stoner, I will turn into the disciplined student for whom my mother yearns.

Noah, on the other hand, will never turn into such a student.

He has taken to angry rages, to sullen behavior, his face taking on what my father calls a psychotic cast. It is impending puberty, of course, the same hormonal confusion that is causing me to spew venom at my parents, to offend their liberal sensitivities by vowing to buy a handgun as soon as I am of legal age. (They refuse to return my pellet gun.) Noah doesn't express his teenage angst the same way, but it is there, is real. He has the same confusing rush of hormones, the same awkward growth spurts as I am having. He is physically more precocious than me, in pituitary terms he has erased the eighteen-month gap between us. He has the beginnings of facial hair, hirsute legs, a lowering of voice, while I won't really need to shave until college.

Noah has taken on an almost reptilian disdain for my parents, for everything. He wants to be left alone, to self-stim in peace. But he is becoming aware of his newfound strength, his developing musculature. He is bigger than my mother, and possibly stronger than my father. He knows that it is only a matter of time before he can push them around, and so he is constantly testing, checking to see if his moment of supremacy has arrived. Perhaps he misinterprets his continued stay at home as a permanent state of affairs.

It is a miscalculation. The day is fast approaching. My parents make another visit to the Behavior Modification Institute; they continue to monitor the progress of Noah's former classmate Barry; they talk to Barry's mother, who says that she is very pleased with the residence. They have doubts, but they also worry that if they miss this opportunity, then Noah might not get another spot. It is the best residential placement they have found, and who knows what the next place might look like?

They have known this day was coming, almost from the first rounds of seeking a diagnosis, a clue, as to what was wrong with Noah. Even then, doctors, psychiatrists, other parents, friends warned them, told them to get rid of him.

But you see, my mother and father love Noah as any parents love their son. Had they felt for him less, been able to cut their losses as ruthlessly as their friends recommended—"You have to put him in a place and just forget about him," said the novelist and publisher Sol Stein—then this moment would never have come. For my mother especially, for tiny, wiry, stubborn Foumiko, breaking down her love of Noah was as impossible as trying to divide a prime number. It is just there, in all its indivisible and impractical glory, in the way she would sew his pants, prepare his *onigiri* rice ball lunches, fix his favorite *gyoza* dumplings for dinner, sit with him at his wooden table and try to coax a word out of him, with pictures, with positive reinforcements. "Good boy," she would say, handing him a raisin. "That's right. Good boy."

I swear to you, if you watch her those afternoons, the hours she puts in, the effort she makes, you will marvel at the patience of human beings. If I ever in my life worked as hard on anything as she did on

Noah, I would have been a great success. Watching her, I get some idea of what parental love is, of the burden of it, of what it requires, of the demands. I also realize that if she loves Noah that much, then she must also love me. And that is reassuring.

I learn, too, as I see the labor, gauge the weight of the burden, that I do not want children. Who wants ever to make such a sacrifice?

They are in this together and, it looks like, forever. They can't put Noah just anywhere, and that is why this opportunity, to place him in BMI, in a supposedly state-of-the-art institution that is implementing the latest thinking in behaviorism, the principles developed by Ivar Lovaas at UCLA and now refined to pseudoscience in this Northridge house. A little discipline might be just the thing for Noah, my parents reluctantly conclude. And so the decision is made.

81.

Now that I have children of my own I have some idea of how hard it is to part with a child. The first time I left my oldest daughter at her preschool and walked down the veranda hall away from her at the church up on Borret Road in Hong Kong, I felt like crying—and that was leaving her there for a few hours in the morning. In the documentary film *Without Apology*, Susan Hamovitch recalls riding with her family to deposit her autistic brother Alan at Letchworth Village in the 1960s. He was an eight-year-old boy, consigned to live with eighty other mentally retarded and autistic children in a "cottage" supervised by five staffers. When I saw that film, I thought immediately about my parents and our drive out to BMI the day we brought Noah to his first institution. He was thirteen years old, still a boy, and while the residence to which we were delivering him was theoretically far better run than a state institution, it was for my parents the worst day of their lives. Noah is their son, no matter how dysfunctional or autistic or retarded. He is their son, and when they look at him, they feel some version of the affection and fondness that I feel for my daughters—or that you feel for your children. And to have to deposit your child in a residence, an institution, a place where he will be cared for, fed, perhaps educated and trained—but not loved, for love is not something you can hire someone to give, no matter how generous your budget for staffing—is for most parents, for normal parents, a tragic mission. It is like you are driving your son to jail.

That is how it had always been framed to me, and to add to the shittiness of the drive, the whole journey out to the BMI is logistically fraught as Noah immediately begins pinching and scratching me, forcing my father to pull over at the supermarket; we all leave Noah alone in the car for a few minutes while my mother peels mandarin oranges and slides him slices through the open window. Noah eventually becomes curious about where we are and calms down enough so that my father can move him to the front passenger seat. We resume the drive, with my mother giving him slices of tangerine, rationing them so they last as long as possible, and my father warily regarding him sidelong as we inch our way over the mountain pass and into the valley.

This is the day we have been preparing for, and I have thought this through so many times that I believe I have had every idea and feeling possible about Noah and his institutionalization. But now that we are on our way, I am surprised by my own emotional response. My mother is already crying, quietly, beside me in the backseat, peeling the tangerines for Noah.

When we arrive, we are shown the room—four beds, three along one wall and the other in the corner, two windows with vinyl drapes—Noah will share with three other boys. My parents sign some paperwork and show the staff how to use the rice cooker they are donating so that Noah can still eat his favorite food. My mother has sewn labels into all his clothes, prepared a huge sack of *gyoza* dumplings for Noah, and then they are given an additional stack of forms to sign, including one that allows for the use of aversives, but not muscle squeezing or pinching, which my parents oppose.

This ranch house feels barren to me, the cheap slip-covered furniture failing in any way to conjure the warmth of a real home. And Noah's schedule and routine, as it is laid out to us, seems impossibly strict. He will be living by the clock and fed according to how he behaves; his every activity and meal will be dictated by his responses to set commands, by his sitting still, his eye contact, his use of signs, his use of words. Food is the primary reinforcement (reward), and Noah will not be snacking if he doesn't accede to staff commands. He will, they have promised, still receive his regular meals and all the water he can drink, but I know how miserable I would be if my caloric intake were in any way based on my behavior.

The staff has been indoctrinated—in Behavior Modification They Trust—and they believe their one-size-fits solution will apply no matter the "client." But I can't see Noah as just another client, and I know that he is as unlikely as I am to respond to disciplined programs. We are similar in our unwillingness to conform to any strict regimes, and I can see by the schedule, the spartan furniture, and the undecorated classrooms that this is a life of regulation and limits. Noah will infrequently leave this hot little house. His schedule calls for one walk a day; the range of his world will be this house and this sad little neighborhood. If Noah has dreams and aspirations, or if we want Noah to have them, then where is the runway for them to take flight? Not here.

I take my father aside and tell him, "It's no good here. It's too strict."

I want to bring him home.

And part of my mother and father want to bring Noah home, too.

I was not present when the decision was made, I tell them, I did not agree to this. But even if I do have a vote, then I lose two to one.

It's not forever, my father believes, as if he has packed his son off to a military academy for some discipline. But he knows, he already knows, that this feels wrong.

My mother is crying.

Noah bounces on the soft leather sofa, indifferent, and then reclines on his elbow. He doesn't know this is forever, he doesn't even know he is staying here tonight.

We leave Noah sitting there. He waves to us, a weak, indifferent, limp-wrested gesture. Good-bye, like he doesn't care.

Driving away feels like a crime.

82.

A boy sits by himself.

PART III

A BROTHER

83.

It never feels real, this Noah-less interlude. From the very first days Noah is at BMI, I can feel his presence as if he were right outside the door, waiting to return.

On one of his weekend visits home, while my mother is bathing Noah in our little white-linoleum-floored bathroom, she notices a series of bruises on his body. She calls the parent of another child in placement there who reports discovering similar bruises. Noah is moody, unhappy, and my mother is convinced he is trying to tell us that something terrible is happening to him. He rocks back and forth, shaking his head, closing his eyes, murmuring "Nuh-nuh-nuh-nuh-nuh-nuh-nuh-nuh," as if willing us to understand that he doesn't want to go back to BMI. My father calls the administrative director of BMI, voicing his alarm at the bruises, and he is assured that the matter will be investigated. That's a flat reassurance, but my parents, exhausted after just two days with Noah, try to stay optimistic, despite knowing, already, that Noah can't stay there. When the weekend is over, he is unhappy about the prospect of returning, screaming as he holds his forearm against his forehead, like a Munch painting of a distressed southern belle. We all wrench him into the car, load him down with peeled clementine oranges, and my father and I ride back to the valley.

BMI is taking the aversive concept to dangerous extremes, "spanking" the clients for transgressions, in Noah's case when he scratches other clients. In other instances, they exile him to the concrete, shadeless backyard, where temperatures reach 120 degrees, and refuse him water. There is a capriciousness to their cruelty. According to their internal protocols, Noah could be "spanked"—the marks look more like beatings—ten times in any five-minute period. He is being beaten fifteen times a day. Another client's mother tells my parents that her son was beaten, according to BMI's own records, 177 times in one day. If my father had brought Noah to a physician, the doctor would have had to report Noah to the police as a potentially battered child. My father, always concerned about his own health, and my mother, always concerned about Noah's health, now realize they have to get Noah out of BMI at precisely the time when they feel they are no longer physically up to the task of caring for him.

Autistic parents, I have noticed, do not like to consider the future. As they degenerate into their own infirmities, who is there to ensure the well-being of their perpetually disabled offspring? And what about after they're gone? So many autistic parents, when they meet me and listen to my concerns about Noah, seem grateful to see a sibling taking an interest in his autistic brother. For while they never urge it upon their normal children, if they have normal children, they secretly wish for a son or daughter who will care for the autistic sibling left behind. I rarely confess to them my own doubt at whether I will ever be the kind of advocate my parents are. I have my own children, my own family. How can Noah ever preoccupy me as do my daughters? I don't tell my own parents this, but I know it: once you are gone, your autistic boy? He will be less loved. For a brother does not love as a mother or father.

84.

My father has a burning sensation in his throat and shortness of breath when he walks, so he goes to his doctor, who suggests a stress test. After failing the stress test, an angiogram is ordered, and he is found to have complete blockage in his right coronary artery. His own father died in his early fifties, and he is now just that age. His cardiologist prescribes medication, a change in his diet, and a rigorous exercise routine. My father does not need any encouragement to fall into hypochondriacal introspection. He is prone to steady, hand-wringing self-examination, reviewing and reliving his mistakes and errors, or the mistakes and errors of those around him—my mother, me, my brother. We do not learn anything from our pasts, he is sure, but still, he ruminates, dwells, deconstructs, and reconstructs. It is a mental exercise as much as anything else, the past as a kind of rosary, slipped through the frontal lobe, scenes passing as if on a string.

I see this change in him, and I understand viscerally, for the first time, that he is going to die. Not today or tomorrow, as he seems convinced, but eventually, sooner than I would like. He suddenly seems so frail, slight, with his spindly upper arms, weedy legs—a tiny man, even in my adolescent eyes. Already I am becoming aware of how unlikely a success story he has been, earning a living as a writer in diverse mediums. He has been an exemplary provider for our family, yet now, there are times, as I watch him stir his low-fat soup in a pot, his glasses fogging up, when he seems to lack the strength to leave the house.

For the first time in my life, I am considering becoming a writer, wondering at that alchemy that transforms words into books or movies or, even more amazingly, money. It is a tribute to my lack of imagination that I want to become a writer, but it is also a tribute to my father becoming—how? when? what?—a role model for me. Yet he has always been stern with my writing, criticizing my poor grammar, my lazy lexicon, my imprecise diction. Almost everything I show him, he dissects, using an expression that he would use throughout my adult life when he was criticizing my work: "Baby sentence." He taps the page. "Baby sentence." Tap. "Baby sentence." He may be frail, but he is still ruthless with me. And in his newfound ailment—he is so hysterical that he will actually hold his hand over his chest during arguments with me or my mother—he becomes more self-centered, less generous. He doesn't have time to worry about his son's work. He no longer even worries about his own. He is sure he will soon be dead.

Now, just as he imagined he was breaking free of Noah, the price of that freedom is manifest in tiger-stripe bruises on Noah's buttocks and back. Yet my father now sees it as a stark bargain: his own survival versus Noah's. Take Noah back home and risk dying; leave him at BMI and who knows? Perhaps Noah will die. "I don't know what to do other than to sacrifice him on the altar of my condition," he writes in his journal.

85.

My mother is terrified, driven to a kind of panic about the abuse. What mother wouldn't be? The "spankings" are, of course, illegal. But what can she do? She talks incessantly about it, the steady, self-absorbed aloud fretting of a worried mother, outraged by the predicament. Complain too vociferously to the administrative director, and then face the prospect of withdrawing Noah immediately from the residence. And then what? Noah is actually regressing at BMI. Urinating on the floor, scratching, lashing out. Whatever they are doing, my mother points out, it isn't working.

My father drives out to the valley to collect Noah on weekends. When he is back home, my mother cooks his favorite meals, the *gyoza* he likes, the *onigiri* rice balls, Japanese comfort food. He is surly, grudging, seemingly aware that some injustice is unfolding. Why is he there? he would surely ask if he had words. He regards me with disdain. The lucky brother, the fortunate one, who stays home with mommy and daddy.

The administrative director has promised to use a squirt bottle instead of spanks, but then, as my mother is changing Noah, she notices a series of bruises down his spine. Why?

"We have to hold him down to administer the aversive."

"The water squirt?"

"Yes."

He is being abused. We know it. Yet my father dutifully drives Noah back to the hot, forlorn little house in the valley, to the staff that is not so much cruel as overworked. "I feel like Fagan returning Noah there," he laments. At times, there is just one caregiver for seven clients. There is no instruction in that little house, forget teaching. What they are all doing there is surviving, by any means necessary. The administrative director is adamant that such aversives are central to their program; they are, of course, dogmatic behaviorists, true believers in operant conditioning. In theory, the aversive is supposed to be phased out after the client's behavior has normalized. In reality, that is rarely, if ever, accomplished. BMI is committed to a program bent on breaking the kids spiritually through aversives. The more my parents stress that they don't want Noah hit, the more the administrative drector asserts that BMI can't implement its program—and treat Noah—if my parents don't go along with their methods. She hints darkly that perhaps they need to withdraw Noah, a prospect that panics my father—who will put his hand over his heart even as he hears this—and worries my mother. They threaten to expel him. "We can't take him back," my father believes, "we can't leave him there."

What am I to make of this knowledge that my brother is being systematically abused? That his life has gone in an undeniably dark and cruel direction? I distance myself further from Noah. I am unable to offer justifications or equivocations. Instead, I shirk from the obvious: Noah is being hurt—a little or a lot every day. And I learn to avert my attention from this reality.

86.

It is an early lesson in survival, in how easy it can be to carry on despite the hardship inflicted upon my brother. While I sleep late, eat a big breakfast, grab the sports page, Noah is suffering. While I smoke marijuana with my friends, or fail to dispatch my incessant algebra homework, Noah is being slapped around. While I struggle to come to terms with my nascent sexual needs, Noah is already—so young!—into his bad years. For how, really, does it get any better from here? It doesn't, and I already know it. My ability to turn away from what is happening suggests to me how I would act in the face of any number of great injustices. If they were to come for my neighbor, I would not speak up. They came for Noah, and what did I do? Nothing. Because this is what I discovered: it doesn't matter if you speak up; it doesn't matter at all. They will come anyway. Noah was taken quickly, over my objections, and was already being stripped of the little humanity he had. Of course, to those who didn't know him, he never seemed human. But he was as capable of feeling happy or sad, of experiencing pleasure or pain, as any of us. And therefore, wasn't he worth a moral stand? But I never made one.

I learn, still a boy myself, that you do sometimes turn away from the obvious suffering taking place right beside you. I never talk about it with friends; it vanishes from my consciousness when I am not at home. In the documentary *Without Apology* about Letchworth Village, the home for the mentally handicapped in New York, the parents of Alan Hamovitch implausibly insist, despite the horrifying images—the men rolling around in their own feces or tied down in filthy beds—that were then emerging that they didn't know how bad it was. BMI is no Letchworth Village, but we know, my parents and I, we know.

My parents want to remove him but believe that in their fragile health they cannot survive for long with Noah at home. My father is fifty-three, my mother is fifty. Both are worn down from years of sleeplessness and worry. And I, of course, in my teenage surliness, my stoned, conscientiousnessless-objector status to virtually everything to do with my family, only fatigue them more. I hate them. As a teenage boy must. And part of the reason, I believe, is for what they have done to Noah. And for what they have done to silence my better self.

87.

"I love Noah," my father writes. "But not the way Foumi does. Because I am a man. Because of my heart condition. I can be Abraham only too ready to self-servingly sacrifice my Isaac. Not only can I survive without Noah, but not having Noah around may be necessary for my survival."

Noah, for better or worse, held us together. When there are just the three of us, we spin off into our own spheres. My mother begins working on the novellas that will eventually win her fame in Japan, work that, not surprisingly, is about Noah. She seems to have washed her hands of me, her terrible disappointment of a son; she considers me a druggie, a cultureless wastrel whose interests are incomprehensible to her.

My father dreams of getting back to work on a novel. He supports our family through strange writing projects that never get produced: a script about a man who walks across America, another about a man who builds a Viking ship to sail back to his native Norway, another about the female owner of a football team. These projects are all brought to him by producers, and he takes them on grudgingly, at the same time complaining incessantly about how much money I am spending. He plainly dislikes this work, admits he is not good at it, and as he sits in his bedroom riding his Exercycle and watching basketball games, he can't help but wonder not at how he got here but at how to get out. He says there are only two reasons to write for Hollywood: to earn money and to get into position to direct a film. Neither, he believes, is sufficient to propel a real writer. So he listlessly sketches in the dialogue to made-for-TV pictures that go nowhere.

He is a few years past his greatest successes and finding it harder and harder to "be a fify-three-year-old promising writer." I don't know it then, but he is already in the midst of a long, commercial decline. He will never again have publishers and producers vying for his services. So the pressure he is feeling, about money, about better writing never written, is real, and it comes just as his first grave health warning appears.

I find both my parents exceedingly odd. They always seemed curiosities, with their bohemian values, their indifference to fashion and style. They are embarrassing, my mother in her Japaneseness, my father in his Jewishness, both of them in their strange combination of artsy-fartsyness and conservatism. My mother wants me home at eleven; she wants me to do well in my studies, to care about my classes, yet she also wonders why I care so much about my appearance, about peer group approval. I am a lousy athlete. I don't have any noteworthy attributes or skills. I am lacking, in other words, in any ability that might give me a measure of self-confidence. I am a failure academically, a disappointment athletically, and a misfit socially. And now that I have put away my toy soldiers and model ships and all the military models that took up so much of my time, I am left with two major talents: smoking dope and taking drugs.

88.

There were kids, friends of mine, who could smoke marijuana and walk into a trigonometry test and ace it. I, unfortunately, was never one of those. I was addled by bong hits, my thoughts muddled so that the computations, the sliding up and down along numerical scales, the measuring of angles, the estimations and recalculations, all of that became like a complicated story in which the main characters were constantly changing names and identities. I couldn't follow any of it. I took to reading paperbacks that I would hold beneath my desk in my lap during trigonometry class. I wished that I had one class I could look forward to, one teacher who inspired me or excited me. Years later, when I would meet other adults who had gone to Palisades High School, professionals in their fields—attorneys, executives, bankers, good students all of them—they would remember high school as being equally frustrating, even those who had taken advantage of the resources the school had to offer. In truth, the knowledge pool had been shallow. They had gone off to higher education ill prepared compared to their peers from good schools.

We had all been unlucky. The public schools were still reeling from Proposition 13 and the teachers' salaries were then near their historical lowest—it was often remarked that at Palisades High School, the student parking lot had better automobiles than the teachers'. In the one subject at which I excelled, history, Palisades High School had institutionally lost interest. I had a physical education teacher instructing me in American history in tenth grade; he knew nothing. All my investigations into the practice, theory, and history of war had left me with a remarkably comprehensive timeline of European events from Rome until the present. I could go for hours talking geopolitics with anyone who would listen, but in Pacific Palisades in the early 1980s, there was no one who wanted to listen. I stopped going to my history class, instead hanging out with a few other stoners at a friend's house who lived near the school and whose mom worked days and was never home.

Explaining Noah to everyone I meet is the worst combination of embarrassing, difficult, and boring. In some ways, it was easier when Noah was on TV or in the magazines or newspapers. Then I didn't have to talk that much about him because my classmates and peers already knew. But as I get older, I have to explain my family situation to friends, even to girls. It's not a pleasant or happy topic, doesn't really make sense, and can only put me in a bad light, I feel. Who, at fifteen, wants to be touched by tragedy? We all want to be golden children, blessed, strong, cool. There is nothing cool about being associated with autism, especially back then, before the celebrity endorsements and the NASCAR races sponsored by Autism Speaks. My brother is a freak, and I know it. Look at him, when he comes home for the weekends, all beaten up, bruised, angry, spitting at me. He is, plainly, some kind of monster. And I am related to him. I share his blood.

89.

We know that he has to come home, that he can't stay where he is. My parents urge the administrative director at BMI to have the staff refrain from using any aversive more severe than a water squirt, and for a few days a wobbly truce holds. My mother, always health conscious, also insists that they forgo using candy and sweets as rewards. She worries about his health and for several years has believed that a healthy diet can alleviate or prevent almost any ailment. She has frequently introduced various vitamins—ginkgo biloba, B_{12}—believing they might stimulate brain development, and wants BMI to take a similar nutritional approach to feeding Noah and not turn food into a reward for good behavior.

BMI finally sends a registered letter saying they will terminate Noah's placement in thirty days if they are not allowed to use their "treatment procedures." "In other words," my father writes, "the beat-up Noah procedures which according to law they aren't allowed to use anyway." My parents want to buy time, to come up with some other solution. They make the rounds, visiting the same shabby institutions they already know too well. The Noah question, of course, never really went away. But it has returned now and has forced our family to consider how long we can live with Noah.

BMI sends a letter with the following conditions: They can apply to Noah as many aversives as they wish, including putting him in restraints. They can feed Noah as much junk food as they wish. We cannot visit Noah at all during the next three months. During the following three months we can visit once a month—but at their discretion. Home visits will be solely at their discretion as well.

The conditions are, of course, unacceptable. And for the first time my parents worry that Noah might actually die if they leave him there. Certainly, withholding food as an aversive has made Noah gaunt and dangerously skinny—the beginning of a life of worry about Noah's fluctuating weight. My father, fortunately, feels that he is returning to health—his intensive cardio rehab program at the hospital, his new diet, his hours on the Exercycle have restored in him some small confidence. But even if his heart were failing him, I conclude, he can never let go of Noah. It goes against all logical thinking, but he still imagines that some day he will reach out to Noah, or that Noah will reach out to him. As a father, he can't help but wonder at the son he can never, really, know. If Noah stays at BMI, my parents realize, he will lose the few gains so hard fought for over the years. He is losing his toilet training. He no longer uses utensils to eat, so hungry is he from being denied food as part of BMI's "institutional procedures." He grabs the food and shoves it in his mouth, like the starving boy he is.

My father, in fleeting moments, envisions leaving Noah where he is. It is a fantasy of his, if he could let go, if he could forget about his son, then, he believes, he could get on with his own life. He could write novels and plays, rather than television movies. He would not be tied down to this family, this quotidian trap. From a distance, I can see his calculations and resignations for what they are, just a starker version of the dilemma every father confronts once a marriage has settled into its most familiar topography; what in its darker moments can seem a vast plain of disappointment when we don't become what we wanted to be when we were twenty. It is hard to separate those parts of a family's trials that are due to autism from those that are due to just being a family. I can only begin to parse the distinction now. Father as I am to children who are healthy, I dream of freedom as longingly as my father did then. He imagined Noah as his jailer, but he was wrong. It is the family that traps us, healthy or ailing, happy or maudlin, for better and for worse.

Where does Noah end and normal begin? That is a question none of us can ever begin to answer. Perhaps Noah ends when you decide he does. When you say, Enough. Noah's path is his own, charted by whatever environmental or genetic catalysts, and eventually he has to live out his own destiny, as unfair as that is. I'm not justifying the actions of families like mine, I'm just observing that Noah is not entitled to better treatment than the rest of us—a habitual drug user, a criminal, any of the many unfortunates who can't seem to help themselves. Noah will simply have to settle for some version of the life that is the lot of those who don't fit in anywhere. We will do what we can. And that will plainly not be enough. Every decision about Noah becomes this bad-versus-worse calculation. How much can my parents take? How much is Noah suffering? Where is the equilibrium point? It is the steady B story to my life. Noah is doing a little better or a little worse. Should we move him? Is he being mistreated? The answers are always awful, and I begin to learn, as a teenager, how to compartmentalize what is happening to Noah. I try not to let it get to me.

My mother is unable to equivocate. She is a moral absolutist, and insists that as long as Noah is at BMI, we have to consider him as we would a Holocaust victim. We can't knowingly turn our backs on him. He is not an abstraction, an image flickering into our living room on the evening news. We have to do what we can to save him. Her simple argument carries the day, and soon, we are preparing for Noah's return. We cannot, as a family of good moral conscience, abide by BMI's guidelines, and so we will not capitulate. We will not surrender. Not yet.

90.

So he comes home, my father driving out to pick him up for the last time. Noah is brought out and handed over as if this were a prisoner exchange, his suitcase full of raggedy clothes already packed and waiting next to the front door. The administrative director stays in her office, not bothering to say good-bye to Noah, whom she claimed to care about deeply in so many earlier discussions about his treatment. My father neglects to check to make sure all his possessions have been returned, though he does collect the rice cooker. When my mother unpacks, she finds that several pairs of Noah's pants, elastic-waist corduroys that she has to sew for him herself since he can't use a belt or buttons, are missing. They have been replaced by shoddy, donated pants, other kids' trash.

91.

I didn't become a grown-up without a fight. Every stage of my development was more a reluctant surrendering of childish things—toy soldiers, model railroads, baseball cards, video games, skateboards, drugs—than it was excitement about a new phase of life. So many of my peers seemed to find maturing to be a natural process; they couldn't wait for childhood to end so they could drive cars, drink beer, and chase girls. While all that sounded like a great deal of fun, I already knew that there was a catch.

I can still remember when, sometime near the end of eighth grade, when I was thirteen, and we were all just this huge cohort of kids going to school together, playing soccer, skateboarding, and then—it seemed like it happened over the course of a few weeks—suddenly there were cool kids and everyone else. I had been friends with plenty of these cool kids, been a pal to a few of the girls, even. Now, these Barbaras and Rommys and Brits held me in obvious contempt. What happened? I would have asked, if they hadn't so suddenly intimidated me. It was as if a few of the kids realized they could be cruel, and so they were. You take what advantage you can. At thirteen, your tribe's dominant male and female are manifest with such clarity that you don't even wonder at their status. And during those years, the tribe will unerringly throw up these figures with such precision that there is never a doubt as to their legitimacy. Very rarely, in adulthood, is there such an efficient selection of leaders.

I know that this mystical process will never anoint me. My teen years have not been distinguished. I have become farsighted and need to wear glasses. And now that this very rapid winnowing of the socially successful from the less desirable has occurred, I am aware that I am cut off from the main current of my little town. Why, then, am I expected to give up my toys? My Panzer Mark IV tanks and Akagi aircraft carrier and Kawashini flying boats? I haven't gained anything in return. I want to hold on to my toys for as long as I can. Never give up childish things. Never surrender.

But I have to. Even though I realize that I am that most disappointing of all teenagers: the nerd who is also an academic bust. It is an astonishing scope of failure, in and out of the classroom, on the field, with the opposite sex. I don't know how much of this my parents can actually see, and perhaps they let me continue my childish play as long as I do because they understand that I need *something*, anything.

I then make a conscious decision to grow up. I will try to socialize, to participate, however I can. I put away childish things, my tanks, my armies, my baseball cards. I am going to have to pretend to be more than a boy, though it is a charade, of course. And I spend the rest of my life thinking that once this is over, this whole pretending to be a grown-up, then I can start painting model tanks again and marching little armies of HO-scale soldiers across my desk.

I piece together a more appropriate persona. My long hair is shorn; I secure a contact lens prescription; I start wearing the Izod and Polo shirts that seem to be popular. It's calculated, and even while I find myself trying to blend in, I am disgusted by my own failure, not because I am a phony or inauthentic, but because I can tell I have just manufactured of myself a crappy version of the cool kids, a second-rater in every way, and it is easy for me to measure how far short I am falling.

Just once, I tell myself, just once I want to know what it feels like to be someone who can easily join. I want to slip in and out with the current of easygoing men and women and participate with the thoughtlessness of a pretty, dumb girl. How wonderful that must feel. To not have to try or study or observe but to just be and for that to be enough.

92.

Many parents of autistics rightly fear the onslaught of puberty for their more profoundly afflicted children. If adolescent boys are a handful when they are in the best of health, then an autistic boy who is already hormonally, immunologically, and neurologically haywire at the best of times can enter into a period of unsoothable turbulence. The boys don't understand the changes they are experiencing, can never grasp that adolescence is a process, that this awkwardness, this discomfort, layered on top of their preternatural discomfort, is a universal experience rather than some anomalous and unjust suffering. What is Noah to make of his first erection, his nascent sex drive, when he cannot understand the basics of human reproduction. He experiences the frustration of the raging adolescent without even the slight amelioration of understanding that he is yearning, longing. And what is better? If he knew the great carnal celebration that he is so likely to spend a life being denied, wouldn't that make his state of teen tumescence even more discomfiting and enraging? There is no playbook for this particular familial complication. Even today, the most popular medical textbook for autism, the 1,400-page *Handbook of Autism and Pervasive Developmental Disorders*, offers just four paragraphs dealing with sexuality, citing a few papers that helpfully point out that the most common sexual activity of the autistic is masturbation, and documents "parents' concerns" at the tendency of their severely autistic and mentally retarded offspring to masturbate in public. Many parents, apparently, would prefer to live with the rage of unsatisfied longing than put up with a chronic, public masturbator. Stark choices, certainly. In her book *Making Peace with Autism*, Susan Senator, to her credit, wrote that she and her husband told their autistic son Nat to masturbate in his room. Nat, who was middle-functioning and verbal, began to call whacking off "making privacy." Still, when Nat's younger brother Max came home with a friend and found Nat masturbating in his room, his mother had to stress to Nat the importance of closing the door.

I never saw Noah masturbate, and consider myself lucky for that. I understand from my father that Noah learned to masturbate by watching a roommate at a group home. We are fortunate that Noah, for all his misbehavior, was never a public masturbator.

The issue is related to one that has inspired some contention in the autism community, where desperate parents sometimes seek a diagnosis of precocious puberty, in part because of a belief that elevated levels of testosterone increase mercury toxicity, itself the subject of endless and passionate debate as being a possible catalyzing agent for autism. The treatment for decreasing testosterone levels is the hormone Lupron, which is used most frequently as a treatment for early puberty. Lupron therapy, ostensibly to remove mercury but with the additional effect of delaying puberty, is becoming a faddish alternative treatment among autistic parents. Proponents of the therapy insist that precocious puberty is a common symptom of autism, explaining that any early sexual changes before age eleven—meaning masturbation; aggressive behaviors; hair on the legs, upper lip, or armpit; growth spurts—are all, according to controversial autism specialist David Geier, "not normal" and could be treated by Lupron, usually administered as a slow-release implant or a monthly subcutaneous injection, which could presumably keep your autistic boy a boy forever. It's a fascinating notion, that of intentionally delaying your autistic son's puberty so that the harder issues of his public masturbation may also be postponed, pushed off into the indefinite future, all in the name of fighting that dread bogey metal of autism, mercury. By now, the prescribing of Lupron has become more common among autistics. One parent I know who brought her autistic daughter to a pediatrician when she was ten was told, based on an X-ray of the growth plate in her hand, that she should be taking Lupron, "So she wouldn't face the social stigma."

There is no easy answer here, and there never will be. But in all my visits to autism conferences and behaviorism conventions, I have never heard the issue discussed or seen a paper on the subject. There is no scientific research or long-term studies to justify this protocol.

Most of the boys who are granted puberty eventually do discover masturbation in the traditional manner: repeating a movement that feels good. Others have to be taught or learn by observing. Noah, at this point, is still perplexed as to why his penis periodically hardens, and he is driven to fits of anger during these erections, turning over chairs and our living room coffee table, which is a favorite object of upending. In my life with Noah, I don't recall our family ever leaving anything more valuable than a magazine on any flat surface in the house.

We do not expect that Noah is ever going to be in love or will ever be in a consensual sexual relationship. Never being able to experience that thrilling combination of sex and love as the basis for companionship is one of the great sadnesses of most of the severely developmentally disabled. Intimate love is the great mystery and source for so much of our daily lives, the surprise, the joy, the motivation, the pleasure, and yet it is a world that Noah does not understand. It is, I sometimes suspect, the reason he prefers men to women. There is some tension between Noah and females, the unresolved stress of wanting and not knowing what he wants. There is that instinctive desire, I am sure—women have told me that they have felt that emanating from Noah—but he is unable to put thoughts to it, to verbalize it, to contextualize it, and so is left with an angry longing that he can express only as a kind of anger.

93.

"With Noah around there's never any rest," my father writes. "We constantly have to be on his case. Making sure that he goes to the bathroom. Wiping him when he does. Checking to see that he has not put any foreign objects into his mouth. Yet somehow the house, our home, feels more like a house, feels more normal with Noah around. Perversities and infirmities. Infirmities and perversities. Walk around with a pebble in your shoe long enough and eventually it feels right."

Perversities: Noah is as prone to being a terror as ever before. And now that he is back it feels like he wants to have another go at me, that maybe, despite my height and reach, he can finally dispatch his big brother. He is jealous of me; he has to be. While he was suffering in that sweltering valley ranch house, here I was, back home, still with our parents. Or perhaps I am ascribing to him motives that are beyond him. (I never know if I am underestimating or overestimating his intelligence. Is he dumb as a fish? Today, I meet parents all the time who assure me there are intelligent men and women locked away, lurking inside their low-functioning autistic children. Really? I don't believe there are intelligent men and women locked away inside most of the normal people I meet.)

He comes at me, grabbing a handful of hair. I don't retaliate. I no longer take a shot at him to make him let go. I am Gandhian in my nonviolent response. I try to pry his fingers loose, which is always a Sisyphean act. As soon as one hand is wrenched off, he grabs on with the other. When he has both clamped on, I know I am in for a long, hard struggle. Sometimes, I can grab a handful of his hair, and we stand like that, heads pulled low by our mutual leverage, breathing heavily, like wrestlers before a takedown. Now, he pulls my head closer to his, trying to bang our heads together. I can't see his face, but I know its contorted rage, lips peeled back over gums, wide insane grin, like a jack-o'-lantern made flesh.

"I hate Noah," I tell my father when I have finally extricated myself. He tells me that it's normal.

But there's nothing normal about it. A brother who attacks me randomly, without warning, and against whom I feel it is unfair to retaliate? Noah is a bigger, angrier, surlier version of the boy he was. He has filled out in the chest, though his arms remain as bony as mine. He will never be a large man, that much is thankfully clear, but he already has a man's walk, a side-to-side shuffle that doesn't propel him with any great haste and is indicative, I believe, of his never really having anywhere he is in a great hurry to reach. He likes to plant himself in the backyard, rocking back and forth on a patch of grass in the afternoon sun, a twig or a leaf rolling between the fingers of both hands. Occasionally, he will leap to his feet and begin a gallop around the yard, an aimless peregrination that concludes, usually, with his retaking the original spot. There is the wicker basket swing hung from a carport beam that he likes to rock in, the gentle creaking motion calming him for a spell while my mother, wearing a straw sunhat, sunglasses, and an apron, works in her vegetable garden. Our cat, TG, slinks close and wiggles its haunches as he pretends to stalk my mother while she digs and trowels. Sometimes, he will sit at the edge of the lawn and observe Noah, his repetitive twiddling of a leaf, and despite the uneasy truce established between Noah and the feline, he sometimes will be so mesmerized by Noah's twitching and self-stimming that he will stalk and pounce, getting in a scratch or two on Noah before my brother gets up and gallops away, sometimes coming over and leaning his head against my mother, murmuring "Buh-buh-buh-buh-buh-buh-buh," as if trying to tell her the cat is a bad boy.

94.

The Palisades Day Care Center has been closed down. My mother continued it for a few months after Noah was placed in BMI until her last, best staffer quit. The parents of the remaining children weren't interested in maintaining the program, more concerned, as they were, with finding longer-term solutions.

We now begin that familiar trek from residence to special school to group home, looking yet again for a place for Noah. The options, of course, haven't improved. They never do. I babysit Noah for long afternoons as my parents drive out to the valley, up to Santa Barbara, down to San Diego, scouring southern California for a solution. My father flies to Georgia, to South Carolina, to Pennsylvania; my mother goes to Japan, inspecting various residential facilities. They sadly conclude that each of them is designed for higher-functioning autistics than Noah.

The best option, surprisingly, is a public school for the deaf called the Marlton School. Because it has been decades since the scourge of rubella caused epidemic-proportion deafness among the newborn, Marlton has expanded to include a program for other developmentally disabled and retarded children.

They like what they see and entertain the notion that perhaps Noah, who has shown no great ambition to speak, might be taught to communicate by signing. It is still their fondest wish, of course, to talk with Noah, by whatever means that might be, to "hear" their son's voice, whether audibly or visually. I don't tell my parents that I find this aspiration ridiculous. This is a boy, after all, who still can't tie his shoelaces. The school for the deaf is untainted, in my parents' view, by modish behaviorism; the staff is ample to teach the dozen special-education students a curriculum that is a modified version of what the nondevelopmentally disabled deaf children are learning. There have been stories, first circulated among parents and then written up in newspapers, of autistic children making breakthroughs in sign language, the neural circuitry involved being different than it is for verbal communication. My parents, amateur neurologists that they have been forced to become, find this novel approach exciting, and both enroll in sign language classes in the evening when Noah starts at Marlton.

They ask if I would like to learn American Sign Language (ASL) as well. I'm not interested. Not because I don't want to speak with Noah, but because I have seen enough of these false starts and doomed hopes. For my mother, it is a relief to be working at something, anything, rather than just abject surrender, hence her elaborate preparation of Noah's favorite meals, her careful consideration of his diet, her research into the appropriate vitamin dosages, and her meticulous creation of his American Sign Language flash cards. She likes projects, despite her protests to the contrary, and Noah is a lifetime's worth. Her industriousness is itself an affront to my laziness and makes our home a difficult one in which to while away hours watching television. And in these years, before her writing career had flowered to fill up her days, and when Noah is there to occupy her, she shows her love for her son by staying almost diabolically busy with sewing, cooking, gardening, cleaning, and compounding the difficulty of each of these acts by insisting on particular methods—clothes must be hung out on a line in the sun rather than machine dried, her garden is composted, the store-bought food should be organic. It makes for extra labor, chores my father and I are reluctant to perform. And Noah, of course, never has to lift a finger.

So she takes on sign language lessons as yet another duty, a mother's job like any other, and she is determined to complete this task with the same diligence with which she approaches any of her self-appointed, virtuous machinations. My father, on the other hand, commences this process of learning ASL already knowing he will not follow through. He has his worries about his heart condition, and then the diagnosis from a GI specialist that he has an ulcer, and he is lousy at learning languages anyway. The truth, I suspect, is that he is as skeptical as I am.

95.

But no matter the language, the school seems a good fit for Noah. He wakes up at about 6:15 A.M., an hour earlier than my usual alarm bell goes off, slides on his baggy corduroy trousers—my mother sewed him a few new pairs—a chewed-up T-shirt, and his vinyl windbreaker; my mother brushes his hair and teeth and gives Noah a peeled pear or apple (he has breakfast at school) and then stands with him by the palm tree in the strip of grass between the sidewalk and the street while they wait for the bus. He looks, for a moment, like any normal kid waiting for the bus, albeit with a telltale stylelessness that betrays the fact that he doesn't choose his own clothes.

Some mornings, when my parents are too tired, I make sure Noah is dressed. I don't worry so much about brushing his teeth or combing his hair and Noah notices the change in routine, but when I ask him if he cares, he doesn't respond. He can already make a few rudimentary signs, raising his fist to his mouth to indicate he wants a drink, putting bunched fingers to his lips to indicate he wants to eat. In the mornings, when I'm in charge, I don't bother with the snack, but I give him a glass of juice when he makes the sign for drink and then take him outside and we sit on the sloped lawn in the sun while we wait for the bus, Noah rocking back and forth and me reading the sports page. Sometimes he puts his head on my shoulder. Those are good moments.

96.

Noah is often up late crying. Or chirping away. He doesn't seem to need much sleep and he keeps my parents up, both of whom are apt to stay up late worrying and talking about Noah and me anyway. We are a handful, Noah for the obvious reasons and me with my pattern of dope smoking and academic failure. It is too easy for them to feel like failed parents. Both boys are disappointments in their respective fields: autism and adolescence. It's impossible for me to dismiss how deformed our family has become by Noah and our response to Noah. I hate our introverted conversations and concerns, our tight-wound, busy state of constantly computing an insoluble problem, our typical suspicions and angers—my parents at their worn-out marriage, my own predictable rebelliousness, Noah's hogging of all overt worry so that the rest of our issues are always battling for second place.

And the years of physical and emotional toil have been harder on my parents than on me. I'm vital, growing, my energy, despite my dopey catatonia, on the flow rather than ebb. But they are both over fifty, and they find the sleepless nights and endless tussle of Noah, and the attrition of fighting with me, to be cause for a dispirited appraisal of their lives. My mother keeps busy, keeps fighting. But my father, writing his television scripts, worrying about money as he sees the indefinite expense of Noah extending out forever into the future, seems to tire. He loses some of the verve that had driven his earlier successes, stops nurturing the connections with New York literati that had allowed him to maintain a career in letters as he built one in film and television. It is the disappointment of the films he gets made—*Oh, God! Book II*; *Lovey*—and those better projects that he doesn't. He is too aware that his successful books have both been day-to-day accounts of his life with Noah, not the great novels he admires. He is, as he repeats to me, a minor writer. And though he professes no great disappointment at this fate, my father finds each restart a little harder, even as the family needs the money more and more and Noah keeps him up at night with his angry howls or steady bleats. "I am falling apart," my father writes, "and poor Noah's fate is that he goes down with me whether it's his fault or not." Now that his ulcer has been diagnosed, he withdraws from taking care of Noah, leaving more of the daily ritual to my mother and me. Yet remarkably, even as he frets, he is making six figures a year from writing these films and teleplays that go nowhere. "Not bad," he says, "for a guy too old and too white and too short to play in the NBA."

97.

There is no solution out there in the world, in the dozens of institutions and group homes my parents investigate. Benhaven. Camarillo. Ojai. The pattern is that the good places don't want Noah, and my parents won't put Noah into the kind of places that will accept him.

The stopgap my parents devise is as prescient, in its way, as my mother's insisting that we recycle all our paper and glass years before there is a city program for such matters. (This is a woman who descends from a long line of too-early adapters. Her father, an entrepreneur in prewar Japan, was among the very first in his country to manufacture golf balls, years before Japan's golf boom. Of course, in between his importing of a peculiar machine to wind synthetic thread into hard-shell spheres and Japan's mid- to late-twentieth-century golf craze would be a world war. My mother still recalls cowering in her parents' house while a not-too-distant bombing raid devastated parts of Osaka and, all around her, golf balls bounced crazily atop the hard wood *genkan* and tatami mats.) Her idea is simple yet terribly expensive: we should find another house in the neighborhood for Noah to live in with a full-time caregiver. That way, Noah can continue to attend his school, Marlton, which so far has been a good fit. More important to my parents after Noah's last experience, if we are living nearby we can continue to monitor Noah without the physical stress and strain that is wearing down my parents. All that is required is a house and a person to live in it with Noah.

Instead of visiting various facilities for the developmentally disabled, they begin a more pleasant search, this one for a new house. Initially, the plan is to move Noah to this new residence while we will stay where we are. That evolves, after some consideration, into the rest of us moving while Noah stays put, the idea being that Noah will be more comfortable in this familiar home and that our neighbors are already accustomed to the autistic boy next door.

What they are proposing to do would become known, years later, as supported living, a version of which is now among the encouraged long-term solutions for adult autistics. In the early 1980s, when large, centralized facilities or group homes are the only two options, such a plan is radical and relatively untested. It was a desperate half measure, of course, a complication rather than a solution. I sometimes think to myself, Why are we contorting ourselves in this manner? Wouldn't it be easier to put Noah away? My life, which should be more encompassing, is instead diminishing to just this family, and in our surly comradeship I find myself hating my parents and Noah for the ridiculous measures undertaken.

Now there is this, the purchase of an additional house for my brother. While I have to lobby my parents for a skateboard or a stereo, an entire home, albeit heavily mortgaged, is purchased for Noah. We are fortunate, of course, because of my father's begrudging gift for writing screenplays and teleplays. And the beneficiary of that good fortune? Noah, of course. He always gets the first cut.

But when I walk over to the new house, still unfurnished, and sit for a while in the dining room as the sky turns dark and the neighborhood lights flicker on, the reflections glowing in the shimmering pool, I am excited at the prospect of moving. Fine, Noah can have the old house. We can leave him behind. And we can come and live here. Perhaps this is just what we need, a new beginning. The old house, as beautifully situated as it is near a bluff overlooking the Pacific, is too freighted with memories. And in my family, I have accepted, the memories are always of Noah, of the various phases of Noah, of his moods, his violence, his anger, and, fleetingly, his joy. But as long as we were there, in that house, it would always be Noah's house.

Now, in this silent new house, smelling of fresh paint, the screen door still shiny, I dare to picture a life without Noah. My life, I convince myself, can change. I am studying for my driver's license and getting my contact lenses. I am taller, leaner, and, for the first time, comfortable and occasionally adept at talking to girls. I don't feel, in other words, like a runty embarrassment. This hasn't anything to do with Noah, I know, but is instead a kind of emerging from the entanglement of Noah, from the autism-centered morass that is my family. Why, if I lived here, I could even have friends come over.

98.

It takes us six months to buy furniture, to move, to provision both houses and, most difficult of all, to find a caregiver to live with Noah. A classified advertisement is placed in the *Los Angeles Times*, seeking a full-time, residential caregiver for a developmentally disabled child. A parade of the maladjusted responds, the careerless, the aimless, those who see the possibility of three squares and a roof over their head, along with a little dosh, to be a fair trade for having to look after a retard. As I consider these applicants, who arrive in their variously beat-up automobiles—in Los Angeles, it is always too easy to judge the economic condition of those who park in your sight—I go from wondering at who would want a job like this to realizing with a start that what I've been doing for my whole life—living with Noah—is something that people expect to be paid to do.

My mother is a keen judge of character, quick to dismiss anyone who treats her condescendingly because she is Japanese and speaks halting English. She believes there is a correlation between intelligence and good character—I will never be convinced of this—and so is disappointed at who turns up. But this is not, of course, the type of position one seeks on the back of a sterling résumé. It is a low-achiever position, involving as it does some cleaning, some rudimentary cooking, and some ass wiping.

My father, trying to be pragmatic, reminds her that she mustn't expect A students. We must settle for reliable, trustworthy, and every candidate is a compromise. Finally, my mother settles on an energetic and cheerful Tunisian fellow newly arrived in the United States, convinced, as so many are initially, that he will be able to reach Noah. My mother likes that he is a foreigner, unsteeped in what she views as lazy American ways. He will, she hopes, have a little of what she presumes is his old country's work ethic, though my father warns her that Tunisians are no more renowned than Americans for their diligence.

Still, Shedley seems to get along with Noah, and so our experiment gets under way. Shedley will live with Noah for five nights a week, and then Noah will come stay with us in the new house for the weekend. (We quickly amend this so that either my mother or I will instead stay at Noah's house, our old house. My father, who is just emerging from the worst of his health crisis—his diaries for this period are steady assurances that he is near death, "I'm just trying to make some money for my family before I die," "I feel my death is imminent"—will soon join the rotation.) During the day Noah continues at Marlton, where he is receiving passing marks in his two classes, autistic core and physical education. Better grades than I am getting.

So we are moving away from Noah instead of Noah moving away from us. We can see him daily, visit him, but we will have our distance. I spend a great deal of time riding my bicycle back and forth between the old house and the new house, we divide our meals between them, even spending one night here and one there, with Shedley staying in whichever house we aren't. He is short and stocky with a rectangular head and wiggle of brown hair that is neatly combed and pomaded. He belts out his curious English in a deep baritone, expressions like "good grief" and "oh brother" that he gleaned from the Charlie Brown books he read to learn English.

99.

I don't move my bedroom furniture. Instead, my parents agree to buy me wonderful new belongings, a new king-size bed with a built-in bookcase/headboard and tracked lighting system, a new desk, chairs, a fancy stereo—Yamaha amplifier, Technics turntable, Sony cassette player and JBL speakers. We buy new sofas, Asian rugs, televisions, and a new Volvo. I don't know why we suddenly feel prosperous, but perhaps it is the general mood of being unfettered and free. One burden—Noah—is lighter, so the rest of our worries suddenly seem trivial. My parents open the financial spigots, and for the first time I begin to suspect we are rich, not wealthy, I know, but certainly not poor, never struggling. It is a dangerous notion for a lazy son like me to entertain. I don't need any more disinclination toward hard work.

One weekend night, the older brother of a friend of mine picks us up in his Honda Accord to go to a concert. The Canadian power-rock trio Triumph is playing at the Santa Monica Civic Auditorium. We buy a few sixers of Moosehead at a friendly liquor store and smoke a joint while parked at the top of one of those innumerable canyon roads—Kenter, Mandeville, Amalfi, Capri, Chataqqua. Brett's older brother is only humoring us in taking us to the Triumph concert; he actually hates Triumph, he explains to me, or, really, doesn't care about them enough to hate them. While we are sitting in the car, windows rolled down, passing the dope around, we listen to a song Brett likes called "I'm So Bored with the USA." I've heard of the Clash but never listened to them. I have spent my teen years listening to arena rock, the distant, virtuosic music played by official rock stars, songs about Mordor and the Temples of Syrinx and By-Tor and the Snow Dog.

I am a little drunk and stoned, but the guitar rock on Brett's stereo is completely different. It describes an idea I have actually had and, through a combination of words and music, explains and embodies that idea. I can't make out the lyrics, save snatches, *"Yankee detectives / Are always on the TV . . ." "Yankee soldier / He wanna shoot some skag . . ."* and, of course, *"I'm so bored with the U . . . S . . . A . . . / But what can I do?"* What a revelation! Triumph sings songs about being in love and how "there's a hole in the sky that leads nowhere" and "the magic power of the music." Frankly, besides a vague idea about the virtues of rock and roll, I don't know what Triumph sings about. But this band, the Clash, is singing about a familiar feeling that I really have. I'm bored. We're all fucking bored with the U.S.A. Brett's older brother plays that song over and over again on his cassette player, and after a while we're drunk and we're singing along. When we finally do make it to the Triumph concert, we're not interested in the band anymore, but we already have tickets so we park and dutifully join the crowds of stoners making their way into the Santa Monica Civic Auditorium. But while we're shuffling toward the venue, I keep thinking about the Clash and how much I wish we were going to see the Clash instead of Triumph, who suddenly seem irrelevant. My friend Brett, who is drunker than me, apparently feels the same way and climbs atop a parking stanchion and shouts out, "If you're from the valley and you hate the Clash, you suck." His older brother pulls him down, but Brett climbs onto the hood of a car and shouts it again. The denim-clad, long-haired rockers heading into their pop-progressive rock show don't want to hear some skate rat mouthing off about the Clash, and they start to boo. Finally, Brett's brother grabs him and tells him to fucking maintain. Brett falls asleep during the concert. I watch it from a seat near the back, finding the long guitar solos to be ridiculous.

I leave my old posters behind at the old house, no more Zeppelin or Rush. I buy new ones, the Clash and the Jam. There is a kid up the street, Mike, who tells me about other bands, the Sex Pistols, of course, but also local bands, the Circle Jerks, Catholic Discipline, the Germs. He gives me a cassette of the Germs ("Forming," "Fuck You," "Germicide") and I dislike it. I prefer the UK bands, the Clash, Killing Joke, Siouxsie and the Banshees, for one thing, they have much better-sounding albums. The local acts don't sound professionally recorded, and the lousy quality is jarring to me after years of listening to impeccably mixed and produced studio rock. But the idea of a band saying, "We don't care what you say, fuck you," is so bracing that it is impossible to totally reject it. We have been told, by countless rock magazines like *Cream* and *Circus*, that what matters is great guitar playing, fast guitar playing. Hendrix. Jimmy Page. Eddie Van Halen. They are the greatest rock stars because they are the best guitar players. These new bands don't even have guitar solos; they barely seem to be bands at all. But their thesis—"they call us stupid, they call us lazy"—is so much more interesting.

I wish I could call all this an awakening. But it is more a segue into a more profoundly indifferent adolescence. I leave behind the topography of the old house. The imaginary, ongoing war between pretend empires stays there. I don't want to daydream imaginary wars all day, or play with pretend football leagues. I take the bus into Santa Monica to attend driving school and eventually pass my exam and am given my dad's old car. The Mazda station wagon, an RX-3 with a rotary engine, is surprisingly fast, with a tendency to fishtail around curves. I load an expensive stereo into it with four speakers. I drive myself and Mike, from up the street, to school. He plays me his Dead Kennedys cassettes and I play him U2's *Boy*, which he says totally sucks.

100.

And Noah, for the first time, begins to recede from my life. When I have to sleep at the old house to care for him, I usually make sure to bring a joint, which I smoke on the back porch, beneath the eucalyptus, biding time until he goes to bed. But now, I am understanding that Noah does not define me or my life. He has his life, here, and it is fine. He's not being beaten; he's not suffering as he was at BMI.

This is a strange kind of bliss. No one in my family feels a great deal of guilt. Nor are we as ruthlessly taxed by Noah's demands as we were. My parents feel they are doing what they can. I don't feel any shame that my life is so much better than Noah's. And Noah is learning a handful of signs at Marlton—he can rub his stomach if he is hungry, indicate drink or eat—and we hear from his teacher Mark that, after a difficult start, he seems to have settled into his routine at school and to enjoy it. Still, Noah struggles with sign language because of his inadequate finger coordination; he doesn't move his fingers well, or doesn't seem to want to. (Though I've seen him do rather complex movements when he is stimming with a rubber band or string.)

101.

During a visit to Noah's school, yet another new teacher—how many new teachers have my parents and Noah had to break in?—proposes that Noah start to use a communications board, a kind of augmented communication system whereby he can point to a picture of what he wants to say. The advantage of this system, assuming that he ever masters a large enough visual vocabulary, is that he would be able to communicate with anyone as long as he had his picture board; with sign language one is limited to those who can understand ASL. The disadvantage, of course, is that if he is without the board, he can't communicate. Certainly, the system provides for easy reinforcement of itself; Noah points to cookie, Noah gets cookie. From a behaviorist standpoint, it is easier to teach than sign language. Also, for a child who is not socially engaged, the picture board system, my parents are told, is a great means to integrate Noah into a social milieu. Still, it is not really a language.

This period, the late 1970s and early '80s, marks the first flowering of these so-called augmented communication systems as a vehicle for teaching language to the autistic. "There is significant evidence," writes Chris Kiernan in 1983 in the *Journal of Child Psychology*, "suggesting that both signing and symbol use provide a means of communication and language development for autistic individuals." Those children who are nonverbal, like Noah, become the participants in benevolent experiments using different communications systems. The sign language that he was vaguely learning was inspired by Margaret Creedon, of the David School in Chicago, who began teaching autistic children American Sign Language as early as 1969. There, an immersive approach was taken as teachers used signs and words simultaneously, not only when instructing students but also when communicating with each other. Creedon, according to her own published work and glowing newspaper accounts, was able to teach sign language to twenty-one autistic and severely retarded children: "Sentence forms included adapted information, questions, answers, emotionally toned remarks and social phrases." According to a 1976 paper, by the end of the project, two-thirds of the students had gone on to develop speech, and eight children developed what she termed "fluent speech." The success of the David School had made sign language and other augmented communication approaches fashionable, just as the difficulties of the Lovaas-led behaviorism approach were becoming more widely understood, at least among some parents. While Lovaas's methods were still dominant in the field, parents whose children were struggling with a pure Discrete Trial approach now had another, innovative option.

The early 1980s, however, was the era when Lovaas was considered the best therapist for a young autistic. He had already begun the programs that he would famously write about in his 1987 paper "Behavioral Treatment and Normal Educational and Intellectual Functioning in Young Autistic Children," introducing the idea of "recovery" for autistics. In that study of early-into-treatment young autistics, about three years old at the start, he concluded that in his Discrete Trial treatment program 90 percent of those who received intensive, early intervention would show "substantial positive improvement." (The methodology of Lovaas's study was later widely called into question, especially the notion he and his staff had been cherry-picking higher-functioning, younger autistics into the intensive intervention study groups.) Still, among parents of the slightly older autistic, there was a growing community of those whose children had "flunked" Lovaas, or simply been nudged out when they grew too old, as Lovaas was determining each year that ever younger autistic children were too old.

For the Noahs of the world, the possibility of another approach, still with a behaviorist core, but one that might skip over some of the cognitive issues that had held them back from developing speech, seemed like a harmless alternative. Throughout the 1970s, papers had been sporadically published, emphasizing that, through augmented speech programs, small groups of autistics were developing the correct use of pronouns, complete sentences, emotion, and context in language, that the nonverbal were beginning to talk, the already verbal were conversing. The *Journal of Autism and Developmental Disorders* and the *Journal of Child Psychology and Psychiatry* regularly published papers extolling speech- and communication-development breakthroughs: three in six autistics producing words, four out of four children showing "improved vocalization," according to the *Journal of Autism and Childhood Schizophrenia*. These studies indicate that "speech can readily develop in the context of a signing program," wrote Chris Kiernan. The hopes, of course, are that though verbal communication has proven a frustrating challenge for too many autistics, perhaps another mode, that doesn't use the same parts of the brain, will be more effective. The language cortex is situated on the left side for 95 percent of people, but other parts of the brain are also involved, Wernicke's and Broca's areas, as well as a fissure that divides the temporal and frontal lobes. In autistics, according to some theories, any or all of these areas may be afflicted. Making sense of spoken language is a complicated and multifaceted process: voices must be distinguished from other sounds, then those voices must be broken down into words, and then those words must be understood and then put back together into sentences. For those of us who have that ability, or learned it, it is natural. But for a Noah, who had never picked up the knack, it seemed that, somewhere in that process, the transfer of synaptic impulses from auditory cortex to thalamus to language cortex is not happening. Normal people who experience damage to certain areas of the brain lose their speech, or aspects of language. People with damage to Broca's area, for example, can understand what is said to them, even know what they want to say, yet be unable to say it. Additionally, another symptom of autism, echolalia, the constant repetition of what is said to someone, may be due to hypertrophied connections between Wernicke's and Broca's areas. Noah's communication problems are so profound that we have virtually given up trying to teach him to talk. So perhaps if communication could be rerouted, as it appears to be in deaf people, who use different areas of the brain to process language, then Noah could use language.

Language may be the defining human characteristic. Self-consciousness, according to child psychologists, starts to emerge in children when language does. So where does that leave Noah? He does seem to lack a certain self-consciousness, an awareness or concern about his appearance, of how his behavior is being perceived. Does he even lack consciousness? The latter is a more troubling idea, and one that, for the first time, when I am spending weekend nights taking care of Noah, I start to wonder about. It is very hard for me to separate the idea of consciousness from self-consciousness: if I didn't have to interact in the world, I would certainly be conscious in a very different way than I am. Who is Noah if he is without language?

It is an ancient question, of course: what came first, language or consciousness, words or thought? Even Aristotle, as he hierarchically divided human from animal, placing humans on a higher plane because of their faculties of intelligence and understanding, of judgment, admitted that it was language that allowed us to exert the will, that gave us the tools to make judgment, that it was language, in a sense, that elevated us. Percy Bysshe Shelley wrote in *Prometheus Unbound* that God "gave man speech and speech created thought." It is the recurrent theme in romantic literature, that language precipitates consciousness, that words make thoughts. Years later, when I would ask my daughters, "What are thoughts?" Esmee, at eight, would answer, "My voice talking to myself." That notion, of the voice inside the mind, of words somehow providing both the foundation and organizing principle of thinking itself, is constant throughout much of developmental psychiatry. "The internal aspect of the thought . . . for the child consists essentially in the articulation of words," wrote Jean Piaget in *The Child's Conception of the World*. "To think is to speak."

The evolution of consciousness itself is now supposed, by some, to have been a result of language, of man essentially talking to himself, and building up the neural networks that allow for the give and take of thought. Cognitive scientist Daniel C. Dennett postulates that early thought actually was spoken aloud—a hunter-gatherer, using the same sounds that he used to communicate with his tribe, warned himself upon seeing a predator, or informed himself when he was near a food source—and that over time the sotto voce version of this feedback loop would become preferable. "The silent process would maintain the loop of self-stimulation, but jettison the peripheral vocalization and audition portions of the process, which weren't contributing much," Dennett speculated in *Consciousness Explained*. Gradually, over the incomprehensible stretches of time that such things require to unfold, the hunter-gatherer brain, like an animal brain—basically a reaction machine, devoid of much more than sophisticated sense memory—becomes rewired to handle this internal discussion.

Neuroscience in the late twentieth century would go even further, exploring how the wiring of the brain itself is transformed by language. Animals do not have similar left hemisphere bulges in their brains (save for a few primates who have little buddings in these areas), the areas we know to be our language areas. This area possesses deep connections with a wide array of brain structures, those that process sensory stimuli, that store sound and sensation. If our ancestors were somehow similar to today's primates, then language developed in a kind of synaptic vortex where important functions all converged. Once language took hold, however it did so, it quickly colonized the human mind, expanding to take over much of the left hemisphere, either as beneficiary to or cause of the massive brain growth that humans experience and one of the reasons the human brain is asymmetric in function.

It is possible that a similar process must happen in the individual for there to be thought. "Before my teacher came to me," wrote Helen Keller, "I did not know that I am. I lived in a world that was no-world. I cannot hope to describe adequately that unconscious, yet conscious time of nothingness . . . Since I had not power of thought, I did not compare one mental state to another." If the child does not develop language, then how does the brain develop? How does he think? And years of such neglect of the brain could only result in a stunted mind. I found myself despairing of whether Noah could even have thoughts, ideas that I would recognize as human.

Does Noah think? Does he dream? He knows me. He remembers people. He is capable of love and of being loved. But to communicate would be to become a person and take his rightful place. As it is now, he has become like a force, murky, complicated, extending beyond his own physical vessel to every single area of our life and consciousness. Our family's El Dorado was the idea of Noah developing functioning language. We already doubted such a place existed, but still, give us a map and we cannot help but start charting an expedition. Noah talking is the most common, recurring dream of my father.

I often have that same dream.

And so, I'm sure, does every sibling of a nonverbal autistic.

102.

The tasks of keeping both houses running, keeping Noah and his caregiver fully fed and provisioned, and arranging for the gardeners and cleaning staff are taken on by my mother. My father spends some of each day driving between our two houses, which are just a mile apart in Pacific Palisades, shuttling bedding, food, small bits and pieces of furniture back and forth.

And while my father labors away on his scripts—a movie about a man who gets a heart transplant and falls in love with the donor's wife, a drama set in a medical school—there is a genuine artistic flowering within our home. My mother, the former painter, for the past several years has been writing when she finds snatches of time, and now she throws herself into writing fiction in earnest. She has translated *A Child Called Noah* into Japanese and soon embarks on her own career in Japanese letters, working on the fiction and nonfiction that will eventually win her fame in her native land. She works in the sunny room in the new house that had originally been meant for Noah. (We still called it Noah's room, even though Noah had never spent a night there.) She curls up beneath a *kotatsu*—a table with a built-in warmer—a pair of black-frame reading glasses balanced on her nose, and handwrites her kanji onto a lined pad. She has always been studious and diligent, and now she applies those energies to writing fictional accounts of a Japanese woman, married to a Jewish man, who is raising an autistic son in the United States. She reads these stories aloud to my father and me, translating them in her halting English as she goes—"and then, whileawhile after, she comes back but she comes sick so she is benting her body, very discomfort. She thinks that's a stomach. That's her observation." My father and I interrupt her frequently, asking her to explain what she means, who is saying what, who is talking? I grow frustrated and lose interest, but my father, hands behind his head as he lies in bed, listens to her narratives and tries to help her plot her stories. I have to admit I don't take her career seriously. I underestimate her. Many people have.

She takes advantage of her respite from Noah to write her first novel, *Tumbleweed*, loosely based on my grandmother's coming to America to stay with our family. Since my grandmother never spoke any English, she could converse with only my mother during her visits. My mother uses those conversations as the basis for her novel. She submits the novel to numerous Japanese publishers, scarcely receiving even a rejection from any of them. When a Japanese magazine sends an editor to the United States to interview my father, she gives him a copy of her story, asking them to publish it. They never reply. Undaunted, she enters literary contests for new writers, a traditional means of breaking into the publishing industry in Japan, and loses all of them. Her problem is, she suspects, a basic problem with her language. She has been living in the United States and speaking English for so long that she now wonders if her written Japanese is somehow amateurish or, more likely, anachronistic. To catch up, she reads a huge number of contemporary books in Japanese, kneeling at her low table, squinting through her glasses. It is a monastic, autodidactic mission, and she sets for herself a clearly defined goal. She will write two new novellas, using her freshly rebooted Japanese, and if she can't get them published, then she will give up writing and return to painting.

She has her new routine, retreating with a cup of tea into "Noah's room" and writing after breakfast. My father has his office in town, above a bank. And I have my new room, and sometimes I sit down at an old Royal typewriter set up there on a wheeled typing table and begin to tentatively tap out little sketches, parts of stories. I tell myself I won't write about Noah.

103.

We are able to maintain the fiction of our peaceful little writing colony only as long as Noah is well. Even if he is out of our sight, if he is hurting, then we all hurt. If he is content, healthy, then we can guiltlessly ignore him. Therefore, recruiting caregivers for Noah becomes a constant need. They are a procession of similarly unsteady performers, Shedley giving way to a Canadian named Ben, who from the start seems a lost man-child. Slow-speaking, stuttering, tall, and well built, he wears thick-frame glasses and dips his head a little when he enters a room. It should be a warning sign, I guess, when his parents come to visit my father after he is hired and thank him for taking on their son. He has, they tell him, not gotten many good breaks. Still, his references check out. He worked at a retirement home in Washington, a hospital here in southern California. A good worker, quiet, punctual.

Ben is not clever. He struggles to operate the washing machine, for example, and instead of asking my mother or father how to operate it, he decides it is broken and takes it apart to diagnose the problem. One afternoon while Noah is still at school, I arrive at our old house to bring some clean clothes for Noah and find Ben sitting on the linoleum floor of the little mud room, the oily gears, belts, and flywheels of the General Electric spread out on newspapers. Ben complains that the problem is a missing part.

"Maybe you lost it," I tell him.

He purses his lips, his stubbled cheeks tensing up. I can see he is frustrated. "It's not here. IT WASN'T HERE WHEN I TOOK IT APART."

I've never seen anyone take apart a washing machine, and I can't imagine how he will put it back together. When he stands up, however, I am again immediately aware of how large he is. He walks over to the sink and stands with his hands at the front of the basin, leaning forward and tilting his head downward. He doesn't like to be challenged, I can see, and for a moment I wonder how he can put up with Noah.

I leave the clothes on a dining room chair and drive home. My father calls a repairman who comes over, presumably with the missing part, and fixes the washing machine.

Still, my family so wants Ben to work out, for one of Noah's companions to turn out to be the kind soul who will see through the increasingly irascible and difficult man-child and find the brother and son who we believe is there. And Ben, though there is that menacing silence, also seems to like being around Noah, to be so important in someone's life. He is kind and usually soft-spoken. I end up watching the World Series with him, and we share Thanksgiving at Noah's house, my parents bringing over a turkey while Ben prepares an oyster stuffing of which he is proud. Still, it is a relief when we can leave, can return to our new house.

Noah doesn't seem happy with Ben. But neither did he seem happy with us. He is agitated, my mother notices, more agitated than he was when Shedley was around. Even at school, the progress that he had begun to make toward augmented communication, the pointing at shapes and pictures of food when he hears the correlating word, has slowed down. Ben tells my parents that he is fine, that he and Noah get along. But it is odd that Ben doesn't seem to have any friends, no one he is in a hurry to visit on his free weekend nights. His only extra-curricular activity, that we know about, is a weekly basketball game. He's a loner, my father observes; perhaps it takes a strange person to relate to Noah.

I don't like him. He seems to see me as some kind of rich kid, a boy who has been given every easy opportunity. It's not true, not by my reckoning, but I'm not interested enough in Ben's opinion to bother to engage him. I don't mind relieving him on Friday night, sleeping in the den, and watching Noah for an evening. But Ben is not an easy person to be around. His long silences and halting conversation make me uncomfortable, and I don't know why I feel this, but I believe he is judging me.

104.

One evening while my mother is bathing Noah she notices what appear to be bite marks on Noah's shoulder. Perhaps a boy in Noah's class has bitten him, she thinks, and looks through the kitchen for the notebook that accompanies Noah back and forth from school, where his daily activities are noted. When Ben returns from his game, she asks him if he has seen the notebook.

"I misplaced it," he tells her. He is wearing gray sweatpants, a long-sleeved shirt, a pair of high-top canvas sneakers. His glasses have an elastic band on them to keep them from falling off while he plays.

My mother says she will call Maggie, Noah's teacher, to ask if she knows anything about these marks.

Ben then admits that he bit Noah. "I was frustrated."

"Because of Noah's behavior?" my mother asks.

"No," Ben says, "my own frustration."

My mother doesn't respond, hurriedly gathering her purse and car keys and driving back home. She recalls that while she had been undressing Noah and putting him in the bath, he kept reaching for and touching his anus, a telltale sign, they have been told by other parents, of a child who has been raped.

"The irony of it," my father writes, "we take Noah out of BMI, we try to keep him out of Camarillo, because we are afraid of such abuses. And they happen in our own home."

The next morning, Noah's school nurse, who had also noticed the marks, calls and says she is reporting the incident to the police. My father tells her to wait until he can get Ben out of the house. Ben's quiet anger is suddenly menacing. He's a large man and in a rage, who knows what he can do? We don't want a fight; we just want to be rid of him. We can't prove what we suspect happened to Noah, much less press charges against Ben.

"I want him out of the house with no problems," my father says.

We can't trust him. Noah can't trust him. When Noah goes to school the next morning, we drive over to the old house and gather in the kitchen. Ben comes in. My father tells Ben that Noah's school nurse has called and she will be reporting the incident to the police.

"You're going to have to leave."

Ben looks down at the floor. "That's what I get for being honest."

Then he goes into the master bedroom and locks the door.

"What are you doing?" my father shouts through the door.

"Packing."

He finally emerges, a leather shoulder bag over his arm, his clothes shoved into two cardboard cartons. It is alarming to my father that he seems to know how to leave quickly, as if he's been run out of workplaces and living spaces before, as if he expected to be found out and sent packing.

When he is gone, my father sifts through the trash he left behind—hundreds of business cards, some real, others suspicious. Cards from homosexual prostitutes, and many cards with the same name with several different, apparently fictitious, law enforcement affiliations: the FBI, the LAPD, the Treasury Service. "A strange assortment," my father would write that day, "I don't know what they mean. We certainly housed a looney."

What did happen to Noah? We don't know, and I don't really want to know. My parents always stress to me that it is possible Noah was raped; they are careful not to state it in the definitive. But it is hard for me really to posit that crime, that kind of hurt. How has Noah, my brother, in the next room from me for all those years, how has he fallen to this level of suffering?

First, who is to blame? Ben, obviously. But my parents, who hired Ben, who let him near Noah and who now aren't sure how to proceed. Noah can't testify. I think that we should somehow punish Ben; he should be tried, jailed. Who would violate a brain-damaged child? But we still don't know what really happened. My parents don't have the stomach for a police investigation. What will Noah gain by this? How will his life be improved?

This is a turning point for me. I am seventeen and almost out of the house, the tortuous process of college applications finally completed—my father goading me to write my essays and then finally writing them for me himself. One way or another, I will be leaving, no matter what lowly college deigns to accept me. (My father eventually pulls some strings, and through a connection of his I am admitted to Sarah

Lawrence College outside New York City.) I have to get out of here. I don't want to face the reality of Noah, of what is happening to him, of the abuses he is suffering, the tragedy of his life. What can I do about it? I'm only a kid, just a year older than he is, how am I going to change his circumstances? I've never written or talked about that rape, his first rape, until now. I've barely admitted its occurrence to myself. But what else can I do at that age but say, fuck it, I'm going on and getting out of here, I'm not going to let Noah and his miserable fucking life slow me down for a moment. He's a wreck, and it will be wreckage from here on, I am pretty sure.

It's not that I tremble with sensitivity. I want to live without feeling guilty every moment because of the suffering of Noah. Anyway, how can my concern make a difference? I've done what I can, seventeen years' worth. Now, with my new music and my new friends, with the cocaine and amphetamines that are now a part of my life, the Valium and Darvocet, the quaaludes and Mandrax we can occasionally score, I have wonderful chemical solutions to my Noah anxiety.

My brother was raped? I barely pause to consider what that means. All I have to do is kill a few months and then I will be gone, to college, away from Noah, and good fucking riddance. I can't wait.

105.

Exasperated by the cycle of classified advertisements, the disappointing candidates turning up, the Jehovah's Witnesses, the manically depressed, the swingers, all of whom are interested more in the free room and board than any affinity for the developmentally disabled, my mother now explores a new option: hiring students from Japan who are seeking degrees in special education. My mother, after years of living in America, is more certain than ever that a Japanese will work harder than his American counterpart, will be more reliable, dependable, trustworthy. She is disappointed by years of dealing with American bureaucrats—those counselors and case managers who have been passing Noah's files along to one another for a decade—and now by this run of disappointing caregivers. Another fellow had followed Ben, this one with a riverboat gambler name and a blond helmet of hair like one of the guys in Abba. He smoked dope and did blow on weekends, we knew that, we just hoped he wasn't loaded when he was taking care of Noah. He lasts about six months.

Americans are lazy, my mother has concluded. She will now trust her countrymen. And on visits to Japan, she has made some connections in the special-education community there. She asks an administrator in the appropriate department of the Japanese Ministry of Education if he can find any students of special education who would be interested in working with Noah. It is a great opportunity for a Japanese person to see America, to learn English, and, if the person were inclined to pursue a career in teaching the developmentally disabled, he would have a year of good experience under his belt. The salary isn't great, but the hours are not terrible. Noah is at school from eight until three thirty. He goes to bed around nine. And weekends are free.

A professor in Tsukuba, in northern Japan, has a candidate from Hokkaido, a skinny-faced, wiry man with a thick, straight hair that extends from his head like bristles from a brush. He takes a train to Tokyo, where he meets my grandmother and my aunt, and they both say he will be fine. He seems earnest, hardworking, and so he is hired, given air fare, and flown to Los Angeles to live for a year with Noah in my family's old house.

This arrangement, logistically unlikely, expensive, requiring complicated negotiations over two countries and different languages, ends up the most satisfactory yet. These Japanese fellows are hardworking, and in their isolation—they don't speak English—they have very little to focus on outside of Noah. They make Noah their project, and actually begin to learn their rudimentary English while working with him on his various augmented communication programs, his ASL and flip card pictures. Our family fortune dwindles into Noah's treatment, yet just now, somehow, with this intensive one-on-one therapy provided by these tough, little Japanese helpers—Taketoshi follows Shinji a year later—Noah is improving. His teachers at Marlton are happy with his progress, though there is another clock ticking there, as Noah will soon age out of that school and we will have to seek another placement. And Noah is happy; that is what is striking. He participates in the Special Olympics, earning a modest participation plaque in the Frisbee throw. He likes his teachers, and he is listening, forming words beyond single syllables: "muh-muh-muh," becoming "my-my-my," becoming "my name, my name, my name," becoming "my name is Noah."

Shinji has Noah running around the track at my high school, has Noah doing sit-ups, has Noah physically fit. Taketoshi, when he comes, will actually teach Noah to swim in a messy dog paddle, but still, Noah can't be left in the pool without a life preserver. It is a remarkable achievement, and my mother can feel, for the first time, Noah coming back to her a little. He is forming small words, making little sentences, first in conjunction with his signs, but then without the signs. He can say, "I want juice" or "I wanna eat" or "I wanna go." He says "Momma," "Josh," " "cat," "Taketosh," "car." He has words, and he is beginning to put them together. "No," he will say when I ask if he wants to come inside.

"G'bye," he will wave when he wants me to leave him alone.

Of course, it is rudimentary, less language and a smaller vocabulary than chimps have learned, but compared to what we had, it is something, a crack in the silence.

2002

106.

That Noah is taking an airplane is remarkable; we didn't dare take him on a flight after he hit puberty. And now he is jetting around the planet. Even more surprising: he tells me on the phone before his flight that he is not nervous.

Noah speaks.

"Karl," he says, "Karl. You're coming." He has trouble with his pronouns, frequently mixing up "you" and "I."

"*I'm* here," I say. "*I'll* meet you."

I am living in Hong Kong with my wife and two daughters. Noah's visit, carefully planned, the itinerary mulled, the entire trip seeming a preposterous fantasy until the day arrives and my father drives him to the airport. My mother, not surprisingly, was against it, warning that in the event of a tantrum in these post-9/11 times, who knows how a federal marshal on the flight might react. Noah could be tasered, or worse. But Noah wants to come, has been repeating his request—he tends to remain fixated on single ideas, and when the concept of his visiting us in Hong Kong was broached, it took sturdy root in his mind as a fixed objective. His first Asian voyage. He had flown on planes before, coming along with my parents to visit me when I lived in New York. But this journey, thirteen hours in a plane, is on a different scale.

"You're coming," Noah said to me on the phone. "Hong Kong. Karl, you're coming."

At first I had dismissed this as literally one of Noah's occasional flights of fancy. For a time, he was obsessed by bus travel and planned a route across the United States, one that my father, upon inspecting it when he saw Noah's flat map of the country, realized was not grounded in any real bus routes or schedules but was Noah's idea of a bus ride, projected onto a map—a squiggly line making its way across the United States to New York. He took the plane with my parents instead, my parents securing him an aisle seat, my mother preparing for him a bento box with *onigiri* and California rolls. He was reluctant to use the bathroom, and finally would do so only as my father stood outside, waiting for him. Noah exited with his pants around his ankles, prompting my father to bend over and pull up his trousers. The flight attendants working the rear galley barely seemed to notice, so busy were they with their sliding in and out the various serving wagons and trays. They had surely seen this before.

But this trip would be different. Noah's most ambitious and risky yet, hours on an airplane. Solo. My father and I had agreed to share the cost of a business class ticket. We would spare Noah the discomforts of flying that great a distance in the back of the plane. And the video monitor might provide for him some diversion; he loved movies. He could also divert himself for long periods of time working on word searches and crossword puzzles. In preparation, my father ordered six volumes of word searches from Amazon. The calculation was that as long as Noah took his meds—his Ativan, his Haldol—pulled up his pants upon exiting the toilet, and had enough rice balls and sushi to last the whole flight, he might make it the whole way without a major mishap. At any rate, my father argued, we had to treat Noah like an adult, even if he was still more childlike. This was Noah's decision, and he claimed to fully understand the risks.

My wife, much less risk averse than my mother, so much so that they almost seemed like two different species, was in favor of the idea of Noah's flying by himself. Though what we would actually do with Noah once he arrived was a source of some mystery to me. He had never really shown much interest in my daughters, barely acknowledging them when they were babies and struggling to interact as they grew into walking, speaking creatures. I suspected that he sensed in them some competition, as if he was supposed to be the child and the girls were usurping his role.

My parents were sensitive to this, always buying Noah a present when they purchased one for Esmee or Lola. Esmee and Lola, for their part, saw Noah as just another adult, and they had already noticed in their interactions with grown-ups that they would either be the center of attention or largely ignored. Noah ignored them, though I could detect in him a certain annoyance at their skittering movements and steady progress. They were growing effortlessly up, mastering walking, talking, eating with utensils, toilet training, all areas where Noah had struggled.

107.

He wasn't prone to reflection. It never occurred to him to ask after our childhood, about who exactly he had been. He didn't even understand that my father's books were about him, about our family, when I suggested that he might try to read them. Perhaps that had been a bit ambitious. Noah could read words; he had trouble following a written plot or narrative.

Still, this was our family's greatest triumph, Noah's talking, and we took pains to remind ourselves, when life's hardships would again intervene, that we should be grateful for what had happened, for this surprise. We weren't the types to use expressions like *miracle* or *gift*, and it certainly had never seemed like a miracle, won as it was in piecemeal advances, slow accretions, minute gains. From signs and pictures to words to understanding our words, to, finally, sentences. It hadn't been a miracle; ask my mother, who had spent years, along with her imported Japanese graduate students, patiently teaching Noah, the signs, the pictures, "My name is . . . Noah." That halting series of grunts, as signal as the trickle of water on Helen Keller's hand, that was the dawning of speech. And Noah's dawning, slow but unmistakable, to the mechanism of language, to the labeling of things, to the compounding of those labels into words—it had been the surprise that we had been waiting for our whole lives.

My father's pessimism had been unfounded, my willed indifference unhelpful, my mother's unbending effort ultimately rewarded, as she never ceased to remind us. At first, when I heard these reports, busy as I was with college and my junior year abroad in Paris, I always waited for the inevitable regression. Noah had made progress, I admitted, I saw, I felt, but still I waited to be told that he had slipped back again. His latest teacher had returned to Japan, his work-support partner had found a new job, and so Noah retreated into a sulk. And while there were setbacks, none were so severe as to wipe out the gains, and the gains were reinforced, widened, so that what emerged after a while was my brother.

I was preoccupied, of course, with my life, with my own aspirations, goals, wants. Noah was absorbing a disproportional amount of our family's resources, I believed, with his own home, his own live-in help, and I still resented it when my father complained to me about how much I was spending. I was fortunate enough, for example, to spend a year and a half of my college career living in Paris, yet my allowance, including my rent, was $500 a month, while Noah, I assumed, was going through thousands. I kept such complaints to myself, and soon, by the time I finished at Sarah Lawrence and returned home to visit my parents, I had to admit that what was happening with Noah was the great surprise of my lifetime. It was the summer after my senior year, and my father had just picked me up at the airport.

"My . . . name . . . is . . . Noah," he said, his head bobbing back and forth, still thumping his own chest with his open palm as he spoke. "My . . . name . . . is . . . K-k-k-karl," he then said to me.

My blood jumped.

"My . . . name . . . is . . . Foumi," he said to my mother, who was standing by us.

"I wanna . . . eat," he continued, making the fingers-to-mouth sign for eating.

I looked at my mother, who was half smiling, half crying. My father was standing behind me, wearing one of his captain's hats. I turned around, and he shrugged, smiling.

"What did I tell you?" he said.

We were standing in the entranceway to our old house, the one I had lived in through my childhood and into my adolescence, the house we had moved away from and left to Noah. I was bewildered.

"Good, Noah," I said, hugging him. "Good boy."

He leaned into me, returning the hug his way. "G-g-good boy."

He had a hundred words, maybe more. Nouns were flooding in, a dozen or more a day. Pronouns were a struggle—you, me, I, him, her—he never really got the hang of them. Verbs might never be correctly conjugated, but that seemed a ridiculous luxury compared to where we had come from.

My father's journals from these years become more sporadic, irregular, as if now that he can talk to Noah he no longer needs to make this steady conversation with himself. When he does write, the refrain is constant, the usual worries about stature and money, as in this entry where he discovers that the actor Jon Voight is employing a different writer for a project. "In the trades this morning I read that Voight and Schaffel [his producing partner] are making a movie about Wallenberg. And they have already chosen their script writer. I am slightly hurt. I had thought they might come to me. But at least I did get a good ride out of *A Change of Heart*. Financially, I mean. I only wish I could give something any work today. But I am really tongue tied. But the money worries and the indignities of being a minor writer I'll take for the longshot we've brought in with Noah. I feel like I should become a degenerate lottery player or handicapper, so hot must be my hand now." He is not used to the persona of winner, yet that is what he now admits he has become, late in life: if his success as a writer hasn't amounted to quite what he had once hoped, even better, he has found his son.

Or, I should write, found a way to his son.

108.

Noah, at first, would speak only to Taketoshi, his Japanese caregiver, and my mother. Then, my father. At first, he was reluctant to speak to me, or even to acknowledge me. He resented being separated from the family, and seemed always to forget that instead of living with my parents at their new house, I was actually living in another city, in another part of the world. He did have a memory of our youth, our adolescence, I realized. Enough to harbor resentment. So that meant there was more, that during those years before language, when I speculated that he possessed only an animal brain, one that processed sequentially and associated sensory data with food, pain, warm, cold, there had also been a prelinguisitic emotional consciousness; that meant there were memories, of people, of events, and we could gradually pull those out, even talk about them.

But I was getting ahead of myself. Noah was barely verbal, and the vast majority of his language was still echolalic repetition, and when he was tired and you wanted to speak with him, he would give a peremptory nod and say, "My . . . name . . is . . . Noah," his way of saying leave me alone.

And he was still subject to tantrums, to explosive outbursts, during which this gift of protean language paled against the reality of a grown man, sprawled on the neighbor's lawn, pulling down his pants. But the frequency, I pointed out to my parents, was decreasing. It was hard for them to gauge, mired as they were in the day-to-day of Noah, but even Taketoshi agreed: Noah was becoming easier to handle.

It was obvious why his behavior was improving: he was less frustrated. When he had a headache, was hungry, was too hot, he now had the words to express himself. It was nothing less than miraculous, while I was staying over at his house on a Friday night, giving his caregiver an evening off, to have Noah come toward me, stand awkwardly, bobbing back and forth, twiddling a rubber band in his hand, and, instead of spitting at me or slapping his own head, he would say, "I want water."

"You know where the water is," I said.

He shook his head. He wanted help. He had just learned to push down the button on the water dispenser and was not confident he could do it himself. When I went into the kitchen to check, I saw spilled water all over the floor. He had tried to drink from the little plastic tap without a cup.

"Here." I held an orange plastic cup beneath the tap. "You push it."

Noah shook his head. "Push it," he repeated, watching.

I did and filled the cup.

He drank. "More."

I shook my head. "You do it."

"Push it," he said.

"You push it," I told him.

"You push it," he said. And he did it himself.

There were moments like this every hour, and even though we were not a family given to hugging, I must have embraced Noah a dozen times a day.

109.

Intelligence is language, thought is language, everything is language, I concluded, watching Noah's emergence. With words he could process, establish fixed points in his mind's eye, recall similarities, differences, novelties. I have read the analogy that the human brain is hardware and language is the software, that language is loaded and then the brain becomes what we know as a mind. That is an oversimplification, of course, but there is some useful truth to the process of language entering the brain. The brain itself starts to rewire; I could almost see it in Noah as he became more confident with grammar and patterns of speech, as he comprehended the framework of language and how to put new words into that framework. The system had been down for so long that there was naturally a great deal of possibly permanent damage, but the brain is also a surprisingly resilient organ, and, as we saw, self-reinforcing. The hardest work of getting Noah to this point had been done by my mother, by Noah's teachers, by his caregivers, involving the hours spent every afternoon with signs, pictures, words, and always, the threat that Noah would regress the moment he walked away from the table. That had been Noah's pattern: one step forward, one step back. While it had never been entirely broken, the sign language had been a crucial bridge of retention. Noah held on to the signs he learned, equated them with sound, and actually began making the transition to speaking the sound and understanding the sound. The process was reinforced, at Marlton School, back home again with Taketoshi, and then again with my mother, even as my father and I had already been worn down by Noah's previous intransigence. We were skeptical; my mother had remained undaunted.

What was now possible? I wondered, that first summer of Noah's new life.

He still wouldn't speak on the phone, found television incomprehensible, and had a wide range of behavioral problems. But there was now possibility where before there was a desiccation of hope. As I thought of all that I wanted to ask him, talk to him about, I stopped myself and realized something: I had a brother. Those fantasies of my childhood came flooding back: What if Noah were normal? Well, he wasn't normal, but he was coming back to us. What would we do? What would Noah actually be like?

My parents and I enjoyed conjecturing in these directions, extrapolating, from small behavioral tics Noah was displaying, possible larger, grander characteristics—from a gesture we were conjuring personalities. He had always been more fond of men than of women, and now that he was beginning to speak, the only female he would address was my mother. Perhaps he was homosexual? my mother wondered. He had lately begun to show a preference for certain shirts and pants, and he refused to wear his old canvas sneakers. Superficial? We wiled away evenings with such speculation.

Oh, what might he achieve? Perhaps he would be able to live on his own. Cook for himself, wash his own clothes. This was the first year of his life in which he learned to clean his own rectum after a bowel movement. Just that achievement, for the immediate family, feels like a blessing. Add to that shoelace tying, belt buckling, tooth brushing, hair combing. Noah was already functioning like a six-year-old, and you could now treat him as you would a child, which was a huge stride.

110.

I took him to a hamburger joint in Pacific Palisades, where I sat down opposite him and asked him what he wanted to eat.

"Rice," he said. "W-w-w-wanna eat rice."

I shook my head. "No rice. How about hamburger?"

He rocked back and forth, shaking his head. He never really liked hamburgers.

"Hot dog?" I asked him.

He nodded, still rocking.

"Sit still," I told him. "Sit. Sit."

He slowed down, but still seemed to expend the same level of energy in his diminished movement, so the effect was as if he were vibrating.

I ordered a hamburger for myself and a hot dog for Noah, a couple of juices, some French fries. Noah never really liked fast food, and when the hot dog came he regarded it with a scowl, stripping off the bun and eating that as he continued rocking.

He still tended to attack his food, a vestige of his stay in the BMI, when food was given to him as a reward for good behavior and withheld when he was bad. He gobbled up his bread and his hot dog and stuffed French fries in his mouth, guzzling orange juice to wash it all down. He finished his meal in about twenty seconds.

"More, more," he demanded.

"Dessert?" I asked.

I knew that ice cream always posed a problem for Noah. He ate so quickly he would get an ice-cream headache, and never comprehended the cause. I ordered him a scoop of vanilla with chocolate sauce.

He spooned the whole mess into his mouth just a few moments after the waitress dropped it off, and then let out an angry, lamenting moan about his head.

"Noah," I told him, "your head, it hurts?"

"Yes," he said.

"Don't eat ice cream fast," I said. "Eat ice cream fast and your head hurts."

He didn't seem to be listening to me, busy as he was with pulling apart a napkin and playing with the twisted-up bits of paper.

But he ate ice cream slowly after that.

111.

For me, following that first summer of his great breakthrough, with each return visit I would see more and more of Noah's emergence. In the evenings, I would take walks with him. He still trailed behind me, frightened of dogs, eager to collect string and rubber bands, and compulsive about gathering trash and litter and properly disposing of it. But while I waited for Noah to catch up—he still walked in that same pigeon-toed gait—I could ask him:

"Wanna go home?"

"More walking," he would say, shaking his head. "More walking. To Gelson."

He always wanted to go to the supermarket, where he knew he could buy a doughnut or bag of chips. Where trips to the supermarket used to be cause for alarm, now Noah passed through the electric doors and marched down the aisles with a newly acquired, cool eagerness. Money was still a little bit of an abstraction for Noah. He knew how to pay but would often refuse to take his change or would leave it on the counter, indifferent to it now that he had the item that he desired. Our project was to familiarize Noah with currency, but that was proving difficult because of his leaky understanding of counting, adding, and subtracting. He still had trouble working with numbers larger than ten. And subtraction, unless he was working with counters like marbles or beads, was conceptually foreign to him. But he understood, very quickly, that money could buy you what you wanted, and that with money he could purchase, for example, peanuts or doughnuts or fruit juice. Every walk, therefore, turned quickly into Noah lobbying for a trip to the supermarket. He already knew the way himself, and would sometimes run ahead of me to direct us toward his desired destination.

The rushing in of knowledge, of understanding, of skill, was uneven and surprising. If in early childhood, as I have observed, there is a steady current of learning, a compiling that seems as natural a force as gravity, then Noah was going through a kind of much delayed early childhood himself, only one in which lazy and awkward behaviors, acquired through decades of poor neural wiring, had to be undone before newer, more appropriate behaviors could commence. He was still spitting at people, eating with his fingers, chewing on the front of his shirts, even as he was becoming *domesticated* in so many other areas.

Time was a source of endless confusion for Noah. If I told him that tomorrow I was going to pick him up to take him to his new favorite restaurant, Jack in the Box, he was likely to go immediately to the entrance, put on his shoes in expectation of his outing. He could not grasp the concept of time, or what it is that we are measuring when we talk about hours, minutes, seconds. He certainly couldn't tell time, and despite Taketoshi's efforts to explain it to him, Noah did not understand what the clock face or digital readout were supposed to represent. Tomorrow, today, yesterday, these were easier for Noah to understand, though he frequently confused tomorrow and today, and if I told him we were doing something tomorrow, he would likely come bother me a few minutes later asking if it was tomorrow.

Among the most remarkable transformations was the subtle change in Noah's appearance. He had always been sharp-featured, a handsome kid, though with his bobbing and rocking back and forth, the squinting of his brow, the occasional anguished contortions, the scratching, the teeth grinding, he had begun to look a bit grotesque, as if his insanity were altering his appearance from the inside. But now that he could communicate, the despairing, angry look that had been his predominant expression was infrequent, replaced by an expression appropriate to his mood: inquiry, curiosity, listening. We don't realize how much of our appearance is predicated by how we manipulate our facial muscles. Noah had kept his face in a state of extreme tension. Now, there were moments of repose, quiescences during which he beamed the tranquil curiosity of a boy. Those instances, as much as the speech, the understanding, the emerging mind, were a delight to observe.

112.

It is a cliché to describe it this way, but his horizon expanded, his consciousness like an ever-widening pool of light, creeping brightness over the whole of human endeavor. Imagine being a baby at age twenty, with the mind of a three-year-old, and then starting the long stumble toward the world. Noah accelerated, and I would be startled. He was drawing representational images. He was watching television, speaking on the telephone, reading.

My own accomplishments as I struggled to make myself into a writer were paltry. Even in college, I remained a lousy student, prone still to oversleeping and smoking too much marijuana. Though I had decided that I should be a writer, I was still not inclined to actually write. And what could I do, anyway, to take the fraternal spotlight from my brother? His every modest achievement was celebrated with infusions of his favorite foods, joyous clapping, hurrahs. I mean, my parents would sometimes just stop and gaze in admiration at Noah as he watched *Wheel of Fortune*, his favorite show. After I began to take for granted the wonder of Noah's quotidian progress, I considered for a moment his life and circumstances. He had a pretty good deal. His own house, basically, in Pacific Palisades, and because he would soon be completing his program at the deaf school, graduating as it were, he would be unemployed and living off the fat of the land. My parents were scurrying to find programs for adult autistics, and there were painfully few, though now that Noah was verbal and toilet trained, he was eligible for various supported employment situations, where he could, as the counselors said, "transition into the mainstream workplace." Until then, he could lounge around the house, watching Pat Sajak and Vanna White, eating his beer nuts, and drinking guava juice. I was a little resentful, as my parents railed at me for flunking a creative writing class and generally overspending. How much was putting up Noah in his bachelor pad costing? It was Noah, it turned out, who was living this life of a man-child frat boy, shacked up in his own place, with his parents applauding the fact that he could watch television.

Even more perplexing, my family had never been one to put great stock in ceremony, yet when Noah graduated from Marlton, receiving an embossed certification of completion, not only did they attend, they hired a photographer to shoot him in blue gown and cap with yellow tassel, as he walked across the stage in his toes-in gait, bobbing back and forth, neglecting to shake hands with the Asian woman who was the principal. There was, of course, another woman doing sign language captions of the whole event, and later, there would be a graduation dance for the deaf. But first, back home, my parents wanted to have a little party for Noah. My mother prepared plates of *gyoza*, *onigiri* rice balls, and teriyaki chicken to go along with pitchers of his favorite fruit juice. He stuffed himself happily, and it was a few minutes into the meal before I realized that he had stopped spitting while he ate. He was sitting there, eating, smiling.

"Congratulations, Noah," I said for the twentieth time.

"Congratulations to me," he said, using the correction pronoun, grinning.

"No more school," I said.

At this he stopped chewing, looking over at me. "No more school?"

I nodded.

"For Noah?" he asked.

He had been told, repeatedly, that he had completed Marlton, yet each time we reminded him of this, he was surprised anew. Routines were terribly important for Noah, and I knew that until he actually did not go to school, he would still, on a deep level, believe he would be attending Marlton. Not going would be the proof that he was not going. He was still struggling, at times, to intellectualize.

After our little celebration, it fell upon me to drive Noah to his graduation dance. I was surprised that Noah had wanted to attend, and I had to be coerced by my parents to agree to go with Noah. They finally agreed to pay me if I took him.

I don't know why, but I had imagined a dance for the deaf would be dissimilar to other high school or college dances. I assumed there would be no music. Why bother? I thought.

In reality, there was the usual noisy dance music, though with far less attention paid to the selection of tunes than there might be at, say, my own liberal arts college. Shannon's "Let the Music Play" was blaring when we entered, the bass turned up so that the hearing impaired could feel the rhythm through the gymnasium floor. And just as in my own high school, it was the African American students who were less inhibited on the dance floor, though I have to say I was surprised at the general happy mingling that was going on. The deaf were able to talk over the music much more easily than the rest of us, their hands, in their intricate, flashing, scissoring motions, doing a dance of their own. I had never seen Noah among his peers—and at Marlton he had been not in the mainstream of the school but in a program designed especially for the developmentally disabled—and few of his colleagues would be here this evening.

Noah had never danced, nor did he really understand what a school dance was: a pickup scene with frenetic movement. He was socially way out of his depth here. For one thing, I realized that to the "normal" deaf kids, Noah was still a retard, and therefore either embarrassing or at best invisible. The last thing the deaf needed was to be identified with the autistic. They would never notice Noah's great achievement, his breakthroughs. Who would? Unless you were watching closely. Unless you cared. So these deaf kids, dancing and signing to one another, didn't ignore Noah so much as just not notice him. And that's when I realized that Noah, by learning to speak, by becoming conscious in a familiar way, had taken a huge step into far more socially challenging terrain. I don't know if he was aware of how he was regarded by his schoolmates, but he had to understand, now, how profoundly different he was from the rest of us. And if you imagine the hearing impaired would be any more generous to the developmentally disabled than the rest of us, you are sadly optimistic about human nature. If anything, they were more embarrassed by the presence of Noah at their party. That this bobbing, rocking spaz—is there a sign that correlates with that insult?—could even attend the same school as they did must have seemed insulting.

I found myself hating them, these arrogant deaf fucks. Who were they to exclude my brother? I couldn't even communicate with them, of course, to tell them that they were a bunch of assholes. How do you shout at the deaf? And then I felt a familiar feeling again, that sense of embarrassment about my brother. And for the first time, I wondered if Noah felt that as well, that awareness of how he was coming across. Yes, I could see it, Noah was becoming self-conscious.

We found Noah's teachers, the wonderful Stan, Elyse, Sheila, those who had helped with Noah's speech. I thanked them, and Noah gave them each a hug. They were so proud of Noah, their success story. The progress he had made was astonishing, but it had still left him—just as I had been—among the biggest losers at his high school.

113.

The great surprise was when we were able to communicate by telephone. Halting conversations, certainly, but Noah was gradually able to listen to a disembodied voice without losing interest or focus. He could tell me about his new job, his new reading coach, his tutors. He actually enjoyed reading, he told me, liked the idea of gathering information from books; he found the accretion of sentences to be relaxing. He admitted he sometimes didn't understand what he read.

"If the story turns too much you are lost," he said to me, which is true for all of us.

He quickly progressed past the elementary school–level readers—now that my daughters are making their way through the same sorts of books, I realize that Noah went through them at about the average rate, starting with the A-level books and making his way to Z, and finally what are called "chapter books." I told him that the books he was reading, the elementary school readers, were the worst books. Boring. I remembered hardly being able to get through the easiest of them.

"Boring," he repeated to me. "That's it. Boring. I don't like boring."

"What do you like?" I asked him.

"Watches, helicopters, animal traps, fire trucks, tractors, keys, typewriters, ATVs, hydrofoils, snowmobiles, jet boats—"

"Okay, okay," I stopped him. "Get books about stuff you like, about snowmobiles or something."

He hung up on me. He would have lousy phone manners his whole life.

114.

Noah developed a curious personality, childlike yet surprisingly quick to retain facts, memorize schedules, even able to reconstruct a route after taking it just once. He is not one of those rare autistics, those who have Asperger's syndrome, who are gifted with some great mathematical or numeric ability. He will spend his life slow to calculate and unsure if he is receiving the correct change. Yet he is able to read newspapers and magazines. And surprisingly, after years of working menial jobs like delivering newspapers (his first job after high school) and helping to restock at a local stationery store—both jobs for which at first he needs supported staffing that he soon outgrows—he is a careful enough reader to secure a job as a part-time proofreader at our local newspaper, the *Palisadian Post*, where he is a procrustean adjudicator of the language and can become quite upset if a writer insists on a vernacular or colloquial usage over Noah's correct, albeit awkward-sounding fix. It remains a curiosity that his spoken language will stay awkward and stilted, his pronouns a jumble, his verb agreement capricious; yet when he reads, he notices immediately deviations from rules of grammar or spelling.

It is a perfect job for him, allowing Noah to walk from his home, our childhood home along the cliff, to the newspaper three afternoons a week, where he listens to the radio through headphones—his favorite show is the car-talk guys on NPR—and goes over the weekly newspaper's classified ads, columns, and sports stories.

The irony of both his sons ending up in journalism does not escape my father. I have begun my own peripatetic wander through professional writing—working on books, magazine articles, essays—for a wide range of magazines. My career will take me around the world, and I will achieve small successes, sporadic ups and downs. I am not a disappointment, though I still depend, to an embarrassing degree, on my parents, on their resources to bail me out, their kind words to spur me on. In that sense, I feel not so different from Noah. And, while I travel widely and live in Tokyo, New York, Southeast Asia, I return to Los Angeles frequently. My brother is a man now, in spirit and intellect as well as body; though awkward, stolid, stuttering, still rocking back and forth as he speaks, he is a grown-up and shows it.

Noah has thrived, has pulled ahead in our sibling rivalry. Not for any real worldly success—I have published a book, written dozens of stories, received some praise—but because he seems happy, satisfied; perhaps it is the bliss of the ignorant, I think to myself, but does that matter?

I am lost. And it is Noah who has found himself.

And for the first time in my life I produce a strange thought: Why can't I be more like Noah. Happy, at last, at least.

115.

These are the years of my dissolution. My adolescent marijuana and soft drugs habit has turned into an adult pills and powders habit that will, by my late twenties, leave me institutionalized. The irony of this, the autistic son living on his own, the normal son living in a rehab center, is not lost on any of my immediate family members.

There were afternoons when I was hanging out with Noah when I swear that Noah would regard me as the fuckup. I would be too loaded on heroin to make it to the dining table to share a meal with him, a meal that Noah, in an attempt to please me, had prepared. He had heated up beans, rice, chicken, flour tortillas, rolled the mixture into burritos, set down a bowl of chips and salsa. And Noah didn't even like Mexican food; he knew I did. And I had arrived, headed into the bathroom where I peeled open a few green balloons of smack and sucked the dirty powder up my nose. I came out and collapsed on Noah's sofa.

He was proud of his rudimentary cooking, having just recently become confident about using the gas stove—my mother still worried about his competence in certain areas—and had invited me over to make a meal for me, eager to show off to his brother his new skills. And I had been too loaded even to make it to the table.

He doesn't hold a grudge, and certainly missed, or ignored, the worst of my drug addiction. And anyway, he had nothing for me to steal, his life confined and contained in a mile or two of Pacific Palisades, still under the careful watch of my mother and father. "I sometimes wonder if Noah needs us more now than he did before," my father wrote in his diary a few months before I went into rehab, "if his talking allows him to make the kinds of demands that in the past, he could not have made. Today, he called us and announced that he wanted to go to see the new animated *Toy Story* movie. I was hoping to get back to work at my office and I told Noah that I would take him, but not today. He became very upset, unwilling to compromise. I finally agreed to take him in the afternoon, which meant my whole day was shot. Noah stuffed himself with popcorn and drank soda and rocked back and forth and I don't even know if he could follow the story—I barely could, or bothered to. But I did take some solace from the fact that whatever was up there on the screen had nothing to do with me. I am no longer, even aspirationally or economically, a part of the motion picture business. Which is a relief. Because I always felt a fraud, selling myself as something I wasn't. But I don't want to take Noah to any more matinees. Next time he can take a bus. But I guess I am now making up for those matinees I never had to take Noah to when he was a kid, so I am a sixty-eight-year-old father finally bringing his thirty-year-old son to the pictures. In this case, I would argue, better never than late.

"Foumi and I were talking yesterday about the irony of Noah now seeming the more settled of our two sons, the more predictable in his behavior, the more reliable in his moods. Karl has become an enigma, always so hard on himself, so easily upset when he doesn't get what he wants. He can't appreciate what he has achieved and always seems depressed, upset, pessimistic. Foumi, with her maternal instinct, says it's the drugs. But she's been saying that since Karl was in high school. (Though she was right then.) And Karl is erratic and unpredictable in a way that drugs would explain. Silka, his girlfriend, is as unable to cope with Karl as we are, and he is ultimately more her problem than ours. Foumi accuses me of being too lenient when Karl was a teenager, that I let him drink a beer or glass of wine at dinner and that has led to his becoming a drug addict and liar.

"You never get over rooting for your progeny, caring about them, and if I hung in this long with Noah, and he reciprocated by his surprising progress, then how can I walk away from Karl? Or is it easier because Karl is, at least allegedly, the normal son and therefore responsible for himself. While Noah will call demanding a lift to a movie and I will drop everything to do that, Karl, for all his problematic behavior, doesn't need me to drive him around. I can't cut off one and not the other, and we have given Noah, in some ways, so much more than Karl. So how can I resent Karl for being a pain in the ass in his own way?

"I just wish he wasn't such a depressive type and could appreciate what he has. I am proud of him. I tell him that I am proud of both my sons but I should have made that clear to him years ago."

116.

We, my girlfriend and I, lived, then, on the second floor of a Spanish-style house in the Fairfax District of Los Angeles, down the block from the Farmers Market. There was a long driveway down the side of the house and a garage in back. I never felt comfortable in that lovely apartment, the furnishings never seemed appropriate, the bedroom too bright, the living room too echoey. I used one of the bedrooms as an office, where I was writing a novel for which I had already received half my hundred-thousand-dollar advance. I had launched my career in Tokyo, writing for a wide range of magazines, published my first book about Japan, and then returned to Los Angeles, where my frequent dabbling in drugs turned into a full-fledged addiction. I withdrew from Noah; I withdrew from the world. There was a closet attached to my office where I could sit and blow out my hits of crack or crystal meth, chase that with a little heroin, and then get back to not writing my book.

I've already written about my own drug addiction, in a book and several magazine articles, but I will say that Noah became nothing more to me than another member of my family to be avoided, though he was perhaps less of an annoyance than my girlfriend, in that he demanded very little from me, and I could use going to see him as a cover for more drug taking. I would sometimes sit in the bathroom at Noah's house, taking hits from my crack stem and blowing them out the window. I would emerge and sit down with Noah, while he rocked back and forth and watched *Joker's Wild* or another of his noisy game shows, and then, after a few minutes, retreat to the bathroom for another hit.

"I'm doing BM a lot," Noah observed at one point. He meant that I was going to the bathroom frequently.

I nodded.

"I should take a Sankyo," he said, prescribing one of my mother' s Japanese stomach medicines.

I nodded, high. Whatever.

117.

When I finally did check in to a drug treatment center outside of Bend, Oregon, I expected my girlfriend to leave me, my parents to grudgingly remain in my corner, and Noah to be indifferent. The treatment center was a one-story brick bungalow, with two in-patient wings extending back from a central administrative hall, where the admissions officers sat inside a rectangular counter island. Behind them were the detox rooms, in which I spent my first two nights under the medical supervision of attending nurses. In the wards, we shared rooms with fellow addicts and alcoholics, and this particular institution specialized in treating professionals; my fellow patients were doctors, lawyers, and bankers. We discussed the Twelve Steps, had frequent meetings, listened as the counselors outlined their various sobriety strategies. There were grief groups, feedback groups, spirituality summits, family workshops, career sessions, and a lot of basketball and

Ping-Pong. I enjoyed rehab, found in the constant company and chattiness of the environment a pleasant social thrum that had been totally absent from the late stages of my addiction.

A centerpiece of this treatment center was its Family Week, held every month, during which children, parents, siblings, and spouses would visit the facility and participate in workshops with the patients. Since addiction was viewed as a disease, family members were viewed as having been exposed to the disease or, perhaps, as carriers themselves. They would go through a mini-treatment of their own, part of which was signing an agreement to consume no drugs or alcohol during their four days in town. That my girlfriend, Silka, would come to visit was a little bit surprising, since my checking in to treatment had left an open question as to whether she would stay in this relationship. My parents, no doubt employing the logic that they had already, in their time, attended hundreds of such institutional meetings relating to Noah, agreed to come up for this little symposium and discussion of my fuckups. The surprise was when I heard from my father that Noah would be joining them.

As I said, I enjoyed rehab and was not happy about this disruption in my daily treatment center routine. I had fallen in with a group of addicts my own age, and we were playing steady and competitive two-on-two basketball games on the outdoor court. The food here wasn't terrible, and I even came to tolerate all the good-natured and uplifting talking that was required of us. Most important, I became a believer in the importance of staying drug free. I was a happy consumer of sobriety, so, like a shopaholic in a mall, I was in my element.

The family sessions were meant to follow a certain arc. There would be a great deal of anger directed toward the addict, the listing of grievances and various disappointments, the lies, the stealing, the cheating, and then, at least superficially, there would be, in the subsequent days, an opportunity for reconciliation. Some parents or wives were of course so angry and so hurt they were not even interested in going through this exercise; those usually didn't show up. There were also the children of grown men and women—the daddy anesthesiologist who was hooked on Versed, the mommy lawyer who couldn't put down the Prosecco and cocaine—who would get to tell their parents how they had let them down. It wasn't forgiveness, the counselors kept reminding us. We should not be forgiven for what we had done. But our family members should know that whatever we had done, they weren't to blame, and our family members also had to learn just how sick and deceitful we were.

The heart of the program was a group of three or four families sitting around in a circle, with addicts and family members talking honestly about their feelings and their anxieties and resentments. For those unaccustomed to this culture of sharing and jargon of recovery-speak, it was all, initially, a little embarrassing. But for those of us on the inside, it was important just to let our family members know that we were so invested in this process we had even mastered slightly silly new ways of speaking. In turn, each family member would take a seat across from the addict and lay out his disappointments, hurts, and grievances, encouraged to do so in the "When you . . . I feel . . ." format that I would later find my daughter being taught in first grade. Then each person in the circle would offer his or her feedback in turn.

The sum total of all this mutual crying and admonition was love and reunion. Wives wanted their husbands back, parents wanted their sons and daughters, kids wanted their mommy or their daddy.

118.

Silka, unfamiliar with all this Twelve Step talk, this culture of recovery, was far too realistic to view me as anything but a lying idiot. But I knew and she knew that if she had bothered to make this flight up here, then she had already resigned herself to giving us another go, so our session would be little more than a formality. She had prepared her list of three resentments, writing them out on a sheet of foolscap that she unfolded, cleared her throat, and proceeded to read aloud. I was surprisingly unmoved by Silka's complaints, familiar to me as they already were: I had lied about money, I had lied about where I had been, I had disappeared for extended periods. All serious offenses, no doubt, but in the context of an addiction, really pretty clichéd, and considering that I was here, in treatment, trying to get sober, well, I could argue that we were already on our way to addressing those concerns. I didn't, of course; I sat and listened with red eyes and had to acknowledge her feelings and resentments, and I could do nothing more than tell her that I loved her and that if she could bear with me, then my behavior would improve.

The counselors kept stressing that this was for the family members, more than the patient, yet the whole format, with the addict sitting in the middle and the family members and other addicts and their families seated around them, kept the focus on the addict. Silka felt the focus of the whole event toward the addict was ultimately reinforcing an addict's fundamental selfishness, yet her reservations in this regard didn't prevent her from going through with the whole agenda. My father and mother took their turns in the chair, and I cried with my mother.

I had worried, when I heard Noah would be coming, that he would revert to body rocking, self-stimulation jags during the group sessions and might have to be removed from the group. Noah took a few sessions off—the counselors made a special exception to allow him to watch television in the nurses' station—but he hung in there for a surprising amount of the group sessions, listening even to other family's particular addiction experiences and, remarkably, offering feedback, of a sort.

He mangled his pronouns, of course, and a few times said "pass" instead of commenting. But there were instances when Noah would rock back and forth and show peculiar insight into a situation, saying of one father who was confronting his daughter, "He doesn't understand what he is saying, so he says other things." Or, when a mother said she didn't know if she could trust her son anymore, "He doesn't want to say things now because she doesn't know if they will still be true later." The crying was confusing to Noah, the tears spurting forth, first one party, then the other, and not all the tears necessarily correlating with anger or sadness. I could see Noah squinting when a mother began crying, and looking around the room, confused, because nobody had said anything. For him, the idea that the causative agent for these tears could be cumulative or in the distant past was mysterious. Why is she crying? Why is he upset? He didn't have the emotional experience to comprehend these delayed reactions. That he sat through hours of this was, I knew, a powerful demonstration of love on his part. I hadn't expected him to show up, much less actually sit through these long, confusing sessions.

There was some discussion among my parents, Noah, and me as to whether he wanted to sit in the chair and go through the "When you . . . I feel . . ." litany. First of all, I pointed out, Noah would reverse or switch the pronouns, a minor logistical concern, but there was also the larger challenge of whether Noah understood the great causal arc at work here, that this was an attempt to deal with the grief and impact an addict causes on the family, and, frankly, I really didn't feel I had done that much to harm Noah. What did I actually owe him? That wasn't for me to decide, of course, that was for Noah to say.

"I wanna go," Noah said.

We were sitting in a lousy Italian restaurant in town, having dinner together. I assumed that Noah meant he wanted to depart the restaurant or leave this town altogether and return to Los Angeles. "Soon, Noah," my father said.

"You mean you want to speak in the group," Noah corrected us. He meant that he wanted to speak in the family circle.

I looked at my father. "Okay with me."

Of course, Noah had as much right as anyone to participate, though I was surprised that he would be so eager to join in. He rarely engaged in conversation with strangers, and I had assumed that this venue, with its heavy skein of family tension, would be forbidding. Yet Noah, out of tune as he was with so much of the emotional subtext, had probably missed much of that unspoken and deep communication. But then why would he want to go through with the family session?

The afternoon of his session, he took his seat in the middle of the circle facing me and rocked back and forth while the other families shuffled in. He didn't seem nervous so much as just absent, his body here but his mind withdrawn to wherever it goes when Noah is self-stimming. We didn't look alike, but we looked like brothers, the same black hair, mixed features, full lips. I was taller, but Noah seated across from me suddenly loomed large.

I really didn't know what to expect. The family sessions with my father, mother, and girlfriend had been intense but had picked over predictable details: lies, thefts, disappointments. But Noah's role here was still confusing me.

Then it struck me, as I sat there, that here was Noah, my autistic brother, the little brother, always the needy one, who was here to help me. Our roles had been totally reversed, he was in the seat of admonishment, expressing anger, hurt, dispensing forgiveness. For the first time in our lives, I was looking to Noah as the good brother, the good boy. How had our roles become so reversed? Just a few years earlier he had been always the victim, always the problem, and I the normal son.

I don't know if he noticed the irony of the situation. But I began crying, not for myself, not for forgiveness, but for how far Noah had come. I needed to be this far down to see how high he had risen.

"You're my brother," Noah began. He had neglected to prepare a list. "I'm his brother. And I am here, you came here, because I love you." He stopped rocking back and forth and nodded his head once, and then several more times. "Karl? I need you. I need my brother."

The words came slowly, with great effort, like most of Noah's talk. He was taking great pains with his pronouns, with his conjugations. He was looking at me and rocking back and forth.

I wiped my tears away.

It was late afternoon. The air in central Oregon is clear compared to the smog of southern California. My father had commented that a persistent earache that he had at home had cleared up in Oregon. In this thin air, voices carried, and from somewhere, another room perhaps, where another family group—there were several simultaneous congregations—was in session, I heard applause and cheering, as if someone had just blown out birthday candles.

In our room, we sat silent, and for the first time between us brothers, I was the one who couldn't talk.

119.

In my recovery, in my long journey back while we were still living in Los Angeles, Noah became more and more a great supporter. We became friends for the first time, equals, finally grown-up brothers. We would spend several days in a row together and then, like so many adult siblings I know, not speak for two weeks, but there wouldn't be any tension or discomfort between us. I took Noah to movies most Monday afternoons; we both preferred matinees to evening shows. But he began to insist on buying the tickets and popcorn and soda from his own salary.

But my own role and my parents' responsibilities in his life were still disproportionately large. Noah had virtually no friends, and so we all felt obligated to spend time with him so that he would still feel a part of the world. He enjoyed his work routine and got along with everyone at his office, yet he still refused to participate in the company softball games or Fourth of July picnics. His reasons, I knew, had to do with the fact that he was embarrassed about himself. He had made fantastic progress and, as far as his employer was concerned, had become a linchpin of the copyediting desk, yet Noah could tell how far from normal he still was.

One afternoon, we were sitting at the dining room table in his house—the same table around which our family had convened and argued and fought for years—and Noah asked me if I knew anything about television dating services. He had been watching an infomercial that promised to fix up local singles and "guaranteed" results. I told him I hadn't used any of them myself and so wasn't sure about how they would work. He stood up and went to his bedroom and came back with a shiny folder with a photo of an attractive brunette in a swimsuit on the cover. I flipped through the folder and immediately could tell that this was the packet you received after you paid your membership fee. Noah didn't have a checkbook.

"Did you give them money?" I asked.

Noah nodded.

"How?"

"I sent it to them."

"Cash?" I asked.

He nodded.

"Why?"

"I want a girlfriend," he said.

I didn't know what to tell him. Who was going to love Noah? I read through the brochure, with its promises of "multiple levels of compatibility" and "relationship correlation screening," all based, apparently, on the answers Noah would provide on these documents and, eventually, a video interview. Noah had already answered all the multiple-choice questions but he was struggling with the answers that required written sentences. His answers, I supposed, were unlikely to attract a woman as comely as the one that graced the cover of the dating-service brochure, since Noah had answered honestly that his hobbies were "watching television" and "walking." He wanted help answering the more complex questions, regarding what he was looking for in a woman. So far, all he had come up with was "sex."

I told him I would take the brochure home with me to work on it. I remembered a story told by one of Noah's Regional Center case managers of another developmentally disabled man who had managed to meet up with a developmentally disabled woman, had sex with her, and then quickly broke up with her. When his case manager had asked why he had broken up with her, he explained that he didn't want to have sex with a retarded girl. He, like Noah, had joined a dating service, but since he didn't know how to read he was unable to fill in the forms. What was I supposed to do? It would be better, as my girlfriend suggested, simply to hire Noah a prostitute.

I went ahead and filled out the form, writing in careful platitudes about what Noah was looking for in a companion, but quickly realized that I wasn't actually helping Noah by doing this, since it was a video dating service and each prospective partner would see footage of Noah. When I attempted to call the service to talk about the situation, I was rebuffed. The privacy of the client, even if he was my brother, precluded any discussion about his profile or service. I explained that he was autistic, that it was outrageous that they would take his money or give him a membership.

"We have all kinds of clients," the woman who answered the phone explained. "Who knows who he might meet."

"You have developmentally disabled clients?" I asked.

"Every client is special," she said.

"But he's autistic."

"Artistic?"

"No, *autistic*, do you know what that means?"

"You would be surprised at the folks who use our service."

I erased the platitudes and wrote in honestly that Noah was a high-functioning autistic and was looking for a similar woman with whom he might have a social outing. When I showed the form to Noah, he read it and shook his head. He didn't want an autistic girl; he wanted a normal girl. He didn't want some retard, he said, some freak. Why couldn't he have a pretty girl?

"Autistic girls can be pretty," I said.

He didn't respond. We were back in his kitchen. "They're not pretty enough. She doesn't know how to dress."

This from a guy who was twiddling a rubber band in his hand as he spoke to me.

"Noah, I hate to say this, but you are being a terrible snob. I mean, we all have to take what we can get."

He began rocking back and forth again. "Take what we can get. Take what we can get."

"Okay," I said, "let's try it."

120.

The next morning I picked him up to take him to the dating service, where they were to shoot his introductory video. We were to return the forms and go over them with a dating coach, and then sit down for the shoot. Noah has never been the most thoughtful dresser, but for his video shoot, he had selected one of those long-sleeve T-shirts that had a tuxedo printed on it. Noah did not intend any irony in wearing this shirt.

I suggested that we go inside and find a better shirt, something a little more casual. He was nervous and distracted, and when I pulled out a simple blue polo shirt, he held his hands up above his head as if I should remove his T-shirt.

"I'm not going dress you, Noah," I told him.

He pulled the shirt off himself and slipped on the collared shirt. I stood before him and brushed his hair out of his face. His bangs were still cut in a straight line across his forehead, as my mother had always cut his hair. We needed to stop for hair gel. Noah was a good-looking guy, and if I were an autistic chick, why wouldn't I go for him?

The meeting at the dating-service office was held in a little carpeted room intentionally set up not to feel like an office. There was a sectional sofa in the corner beneath sealed windows set so high in the walls we couldn't see out of them. Noah and I sat on one side, and Noah's dating coach sat at a forty-five-degree angle to us. Oscar was a small Filipino man, and he managed to keep up his false enthusiasm for the first thirty seconds of our meeting. When he finally understood the profound "specialness" of this particular client, he became slightly less chipper and more measured in his promises, at one point even reminding us that they do not guarantee success, or even any dates at all.

I felt like we were at Noah's graduation dance all over again, in another venue where, no matter what progress Noah has made, he would always fall short. If only this guy could understand the great willpower Noah was demonstrating as he sat here, calm, measured, not even playing with a string or rubber band.

"He's a good guy," I explained. "He just wants to meet people."

"Normal people," Noah helpfully added.

The coach nodded and flipped through the completed paperwork we had handed him.

"Can I speak to you outside for a moment?" he asked.

I shook my head. "We can talk here."

"Okay." He shook his head. "We have a certain number of clients similar to Noah, a certain pool of singles, very nice clients—"

"Normal girls," Noah repeated.

"Look, Noah." I turned to him. "You have to be realistic here. Let's see who you see."

Oscar explained that after Noah had made his video—Noah's tier of membership entitled him to a simple interview type of video; I gathered there were more expensively produced videos available that would presumably show the client in a better light—he could sit down and watch the videos of the eligible clients and choose whom he would like to meet. If the female client agreed, then the two were free to arrange a meeting. His membership fee entitled him to seven introductions; each additional introduction would cost more.

Noah nodded. Why was he so obsessed with normal women? What exactly was normal anyway?

"Let's just see what happens? Okay?"

Noah was starting to rock back and forth. I could see that this made Oscar nervous. "Noah, Noah," I whispered, "stay still. Steady."

He calmed down.

"Okay," Oscar said, "let's go in the other room and make the tape. You know, sometimes people bring in additional footage, you know, at home doing whatever they feel shows them—"

"Don't worry about it, Oscar," I cut him off. "Let's just get through this."

We followed Oscar to another little room where a guy seated on a stool flipped through a car magazine next to a video camera on a tripod. Opposite him were a stool and an armchair before a blue curtain. Oscar walked around the stool to the curtain pulley. "What background does he like?" he asked me.

"Ask Noah," I told him.

Oscar nodded. "We have white, blue, and red. Or you can use the white wall. Most of our clients prefer that."

"Orange," Noah said.

"We don't have orange," Oscar said. "I think, um, white would suit you. Sets off your dark hair. Stool or seat?"

By now, Noah's repetitive motions, his rocking back and forth, had attracted the notice of the camera operator. He looked up and squinted.

Noah sat down at the edge of the chair. I stood before him and arranged his hair. Oscar produced some powder which he dabbed on the end of Noah's nose and his forehead. We stood back. He was a handsome fellow, and seated there, leaning forward, brows furrowed, he looked almost normal.

They had several formats. One was an informal, sort of first-person monologue; the other was a basic Q&A. Oscar offered both options, and Noah chose the latter.

Oscar would be off camera, asking questions.

"Okay, let's start by saying your name, age, and where you live and your occupation."

"Your name is Noah, you are twenty-eight and you live in Pacific Palisades." Noah still mixed up his pronouns when he was nervous.

Oscar looked at me.

"My name," I whispered.

Noah nodded. "Your name is Noah."

"Noah, just say your name."

"Noah Greenfeld."

"How old are you?"

"Twenty-eight."

"Where do you live?"

"Pacific Palisades."

And so on. By keeping his answers short, Noah came across as a taciturn, cautious fellow new to dating. No, he'd never been married. No, he hadn't recently been in a relationship. No, he didn't mind dating divorcées. Yes, he was employed. Even his job, copyeditor, sounded like a real job.

"I like rubber bands, string, word searches, and game shows," Noah said, when asked about his hobbies.

Oscar looked at me. I shrugged.

We watched the videotape playback on a monitor in another room. Noah watched himself carefully, nodding at his own words. He seemed pleased with his performance.

"Do you think I can meet a normal girl?"

I told him that normal was relative. Who was normal, after all?

Noah shook his head. "You know what I mean."

I rewound the tape, and he watched himself again.

Outside, Oscar took me aside and told me that there were actually a few "special" clients like Noah, any number of young women with various types of developmental issues, and that perhaps we should consider having Noah first review that material. I agreed with Oscar that this dating pool was more likely to put forth a candidate for my brother, but I also knew that Noah had set his sights on a normal woman.

"I'll talk to him."

The way the service worked, after you made your videotape, you were given dozens of tapes to watch, each with six little interviews or profiles of different prospective dates. There was a title sequence before each segment with a first name and client number. If you liked what you saw or heard, you wrote down the number and typed it into a computer database, along with a short note. That client would be alerted to your interest, given the option of viewing your profile, and then, if she so desired, the phone numbers of each party would be released to the other.

We sat in the gray-carpeted room and watched videos of women telling us about themselves. Noah became upset as it became apparent that these women were autistic or retarded or somehow developmentally afflicted. They seemed like nice enough girls, but all of them were, clearly, going to have a hard time securing dates with any regular guys. There were at least two in wheelchairs and another who was enormously fat and seemed to have trouble modulating her voice. There was a slender women in glasses who spoke in a high-pitched, singsongy voice that made it sound like she was always talking to herself. And perhaps it was a brother's ego, but I believed that Noah's performance on his video put him in a different class than these women.

"Karl, tell them, tell them normal," Noah was insisting. "I told you. You tell them."

"Noah," I told him. "You tell them. Okay?"

He sat there, suddenly transfixed at the screen.

I looked and saw an attractive black woman who spoke in a pleasing, deep voice. She could almost be normal, and for a moment I wondered what she was doing there, then she mentioned that she liked playing with Legos and Mr. Potato Head and riding on swings.

"I know her," Noah said.

"She's pretty," I told Noah. "Write down her client number."

"You know her," Noah said.

"Sure, you *want* to know her," I said.

"Latanya," he read the name on the screen.

"Great, write it down," I repeated.

"She went to my school," Noah said. "I remember her."

I looked closely at the girl, then read the name. This was the girl who pulled Noah around in a wagon all those years ago? He had been just ten or eleven and now he remembered *that*? So he remembered everything? Or just what he wanted to remember.

I was confused by this whole turn of events. Could this be the same girl? And, even stranger, were all of Noah's memories in there, just waiting for a catalyzing image or sound to surface?

Suddenly, Noah stopped complaining that he was in the dating pool with all the "special" clients and became typically fixated on Latanya. After we had watched a few more clients, he went out to find Oscar to tell him he wanted Latanya's phone number immediately.

"We can't do that," Oscar explained. "We give your number and a message to the client, and she chooses to respond or not."

Noah understood but was disappointed. I helped him write this note:

Dear Latanya—

You pulled me in a wagon at Westport School. I am Noah. I talk now. Do you remember me? I have my own house where we can meet in privacy.

Noah

I pointed out to Noah that such a note might be seen as a little too forward. He needed to be a little more circumspect about stating his intentions. He agreed and rewrote it, leaving off the last sentence.

He found the rest of the clients to be less attractive, and as we were leaving, he asked Oscar again if he had already been in touch with Latanya.

"It can take a while," Oscar said.

"And if she's not interested?" I asked.

"We will pass that along to the client."

Noah was pacing back and forth and bobbing his head, "Latanya. Latanya. When will she call?"

I ushered him out of there before Oscar and the staff came to the conclusion that Noah was an obsessive creep. He could get fixated on subjects, and at times like this, it was hard to shift his focus. In the car on the way to Hamburger Hamlet, which Noah liked because of the root beer, he asked me several times if I thought she would call. I told him I wasn't sure, that girls are always hard to figure out and, I reminded Noah, this might not be the same Latanya.

"Don't be stupid," he said to me.

I shook my head. "Don't call me stupid, Noah, I spent my whole morning with you at the VideoDate."

He was convinced it was Latanya, and that she would remember him. I worried that this wasn't her and, if it were, that she would not recall pulling an autistic boy around a yard in a wagon. I needed to prepare him for the possibility that his affection and fond memories were unrequited. Or would Noah have to muddle through love's travails in the same manner as the rest of us?

121.

"Latanya, Latanya, the beautiful name rang a bell instantly," wrote my father in his journal. "Of course I remembered the cute girl who used to come to Noah every morning when I dropped him off. I hadn't thought about her in years but here is what I wrote about Latanya nearly 20 years earlier. 'At school this morning he went straight to Latanya and sat down in a wagon until she began to pull him around. Noah really likes her. His first girlfriend. Adele said he'll do anything Latanya tells him to do. I wish Latanya would tell Noah to start talking. But that's beyond even her.' How amazing it would be if this were the same girl? And if she is, will she remember or want to meet Noah? Or, if she does remember him will she still agree to meet him? My heart will break for Noah if his heart breaks over Latanya, and being the sentimental old Jew that I have become I find myself rooting for happy endings despite knowing, in my bones, that a sad ending is always a better bet. Foumi, the pragmatist who sees serendipity everywhere, is sure that this is the same girl. I am not so sure but I hope for Noah's sake they can meet. He has never before shown any interest in his old Westport peers but then why would he? They were all nearly as lost as he was. In some ways we are lucky that Noah is so forward looking, that he is so focused on whatever is at hand. So it was a surprise to all of us when he not only recognized Latanya but still felt such warmth toward her.

"I hope she is she. I know Karl has been the facilitator of Noah's search for romance, and it must be a thankless job, given that Noah seems as picky in this area as he is in all others. But you never stop rooting for your children, even after the amazing comeback has happened, how quickly I take that for granted and now start selfishly dreaming of Noah married, with someone to take care of him so that, not if but when something happens to Foumi and me, Noah will be provided for and Karl won't feel too burdened.

"Of course it's unlikely but I've become more sentimental rather than less as I've watched my sons, finally, grow up."

122.

Noah was at home, typically alone, and probably, literally, sitting by the phone, as he had taken to doing since returning from VideoDate. Whenever I called, he answered practically before the phone had even rung and then didn't hesitate to show his disappointment at hearing my voice. He asked if I had heard from Latanya and when I asked why I would have heard from her he said he was just wondering.

It was an excruciating six days for all of us. I don't know why we all decided it was so important that Latanya call, that Noah find this girl with whom he had shared such a fleeting childhood friendship. Yet rather than carefully damp down his enthusiasm, we were all swept up in it, as if she would complete Noah and make him, somehow, closer to normal. He would have the job, the house, the girl, and then we could all go about our lives content that Noah was experiencing all the dimensions of human interaction.

I was trying to get my own career back on track after my stint in rehab, tentatively getting in touch with those magazines that would still have me, picking up a few assignments, and starting to travel again. The only thing harder than getting going as a writer is keeping going as a writer. And I had let down quite a few editors when I had gone off to rehab, blown assignments, spent expense money. I didn't expect forgiveness, but I still hoped for it. When it wasn't forthcoming, I had to island hop my way back into the business.

My book contract was blown. I had spent the first half of my advance, and my publisher disliked the manuscript. I couldn't bring myself to rewrite the book, so I abandoned it. This was not a terrible time to be a magazine writer. The Internet had yet to pose any great threat to print, and the optimistic, as they always used to do, were launching new magazines. I was able to write for a few of them, making a few thousand dollars for a range of articles, and then I inveigled my way back into the more lucrative Condé Nast publications, which allowed me to feel that I was at least on my way back to being a professional writer.

Silka and I still shared the spacious, three-bedroom apartment, the whole second floor of a stucco, Spanish-style house on Fourth Street off of Fairfax, with the office in the back and the small walk-in closet where I used to hide when I was smoking coke or meth. Now that I was clean, I never even went in there anymore, instead sitting at my desk and writing or lying on the sofa and reading. I was reloading, or trying to. I was not yet old, but that first exciting flush of youthful potential and energy had been dissipated, and instead of successfully reaching the next rung on the ladder I had fallen off it. That left me grasping, but still young enough to make it back up.

I don't know how much support normal sibling pairs provide each other. How much do they share? How much can they lean on each other? This has always perplexed me, even as I now watch my own daughters. But there were times, when I was going through my own rough patches, when I would have liked to have been able to talk to Noah, to tell him my troubles and worries and just have him listen or tell me to shut up or just be a younger brother who would look up to me.

But instead of asking him for support, I was instead fielding anxious calls from Noah, who was wondering about Latanya.

When she did call, and I relayed the news to my girlfriend, she said we were acting as if Noah had begun to speak all over again.

123.

Latanya, it turned out, also remembered Noah, or at least she said so. They had talked for a while over the phone. When I asked Noah what they talked about, he said they discussed movies. She wanted to meet Noah but first said that her father wanted to speak with my father. Gerrie, Latanya's dad, was an electrician and had no recollection of Noah, though he, of course, remembered Westport School. He had been against Latanya joining the dating service at all, but he couldn't stop her. She had had some difficult experiences, he explained, sexual experiences. He wanted to leave it at that. Noah, too, my father related.

Gerrie was concerned lest she fall into another situation where she was vulnerable. He didn't like the idea of her dating, or even of her leaving the house in the evenings.

"She still lives at home?" my father asked.

She did.

Gerrie said it would be fine with him if they met, but Noah would have to come over to his house.

Was Noah high functioning? Gerrie asked.

My father explained what had happened, with the augmented speech, the breakthrough, almost miraculous. Yes, Noah had made great progress. And Latanya?

"She is a real sweet girl," Gerrie explained. "They called her retarded when she was small. Now they would call her autistic. She cries real easy, always did. And has a lot of energy, too much for me and Marlo."

What race was Noah, anyway? Gerrie wondered.

My father laughed. Jewish? Japanese? Why?

Gerrie laughed. "You're right. Like we can be choosey."

124.

I drove Noah over to Latanya's house, a bungalow in Inglewood, not far from the 405 Freeway. Outfitted in his polo shirt and jeans, sneakers with Velcro straps, Noah asked me how he looked before we departed. I assured him he looked fine.

"Noah," I said, when we were driving, "do you remember about safe sex, about birth control?"

I had been steeling myself for this conversation. My father said he had brought it up with Noah several times, but he had requested that I go through it with him one more time.

"Latanya will have sex with me tonight?" Noah asked.

"No, I don't think— No," I said. "I just want to make sure you understand, in the future, if you have sex, then you have to wear a condom."

"Yes, yes, condoms," Noah said. "Here."

He pulled a few rubbers from his pockets, opened and apparently . . . used.

"Noah," I said, "where did you get these?"

"Bought them."

"Then why do they look used?"

"I opened them," Noah explained, "to play with."

They were like rubber bands, the consistency familiar and pleasing to Noah. So he had been running them between his fingers while he watched his television shows.

"They're not broken," Noah explained.

"Yeah, okay, but you kind of can't open them until you use them. In fact, that's a rule. They have to stay new."

Noah nodded.

"Didn't they tell you that?" I asked. "Didn't anyone tell you not to open them?"

Nobody had bothered, but then why would they? With Noah, you could never forecast all the contingencies.

When we arrived at the well-kept bungalow, we parked and walked up the narrow paved walk to a screened-in porch and a barred, locked screen door, Noah a few steps behind me. There was lawn gone a little yellow in patches on each side of the path, and what looked in the dim, whitish streetlight like birds of paradise and some sort of ficus growing in clumpy dirt around the porch. A yellow light glowed from behind the curtained windows.

I rang the doorbell and waited as Noah fidgeted nervously beside me. We all wanted so much for Noah to find a social life, but wasn't I putting too much onus on a match-made date? Weren't we making the same mistake as Noah, attaching so much to this casual meeting? Expectations were way out of line, I thought, as a deadbolt slid open and the door swung back. Backlit by the interior light, I could see a black man with a gray beard and behind him, thick wisps of wavy, rust-colored hair—someone, a woman, was standing back there.

Gerrie wore wire-frame glasses and a short, gray mustache. He greeted us warmly, a nasally, raspy voice, a little Texan twang, I guessed. And as I was responding and Noah stepped forward to shake his hand, I saw Gerrie looking down in surprise at Noah's hands.

He was still holding the rubbers, running a pair of pink Trojans between thumb and index fingers.

"Noah," I said.

"What the hell is this?" Gerrie said.

"He self-stims," I blurted out. "You know, with rubber bands, string, anything that he can stretch and unstretch."

"But condoms?"

"I know, this doesn't look good." I felt like a failed pimp.

I took them from Noah and, not knowing what else to do, shoved them into my pockets.

Gerrie shook his head. "I don't know what to say."

I heard a girl's voice. "Noah?"

Noah started rocking back and forth, excited, suddenly speechless.

Gerrie shrugged and stepped back. We entered.

Latanya was a lovely, large girl, with thick black hair that had obviously just been styled so that there was a sweeping curl up and back above her shiny forehead. She had full lips, dignified nose, and slightly buggy eyes. I don't know how else to put this, but she had a smile that communicated stupidity, a dumb grin, but that's not to say it wasn't lovely in a way. But it did betray her loopiness, her disability, however mild it might be.

I was surprised at how Noah took her hand, then bowed, gentlemanly, as if he had been practicing. He was taking care to speak in a measured tone, careful words, summing up his memories of their time together, twenty years ago.

If Latanya remembered Noah, she also seemed to be confusing him with other boys she had known in her childhood. She remembered pulling Noah around in a wagon, but also seemed to recall the two of them riding bicycles together, which could not possibly have happened: Noah still didn't know how to ride a bike.

Noah took this in stride, so delighted was he to be in Latanya's company. Gerrie and I sat in wing chairs across a coffee table from the two of them on a sofa, Latanya wearing black jeans and an elaborately dyed T-shirt bearing the image, when I finally got a clear look at it, of Mariah Carey. Latanya's mother was out for the evening with friends, and Gerrie offered me a beer, which I declined, newly clean and sober as I was. I accepted a glass of water and then followed Gerrie into the kitchen, where we talked about Noah and Latanya.

Her progression had been more even, and though the family had been on the verge of institutionalizing her, they had never gone through with it. She had three siblings, the youngest of whom, a boy named Chad, came into the kitchen while we were talking and poured himself a glass of orange juice. She had a job at a department store, rehanging discarded clothes. She rode the bus to work, and Gerrie picked her up when her shift was finished.

When I caught a glimpse of the two of them, Noah seated, one knee up on the sofa so that his sneaker dangled over the floor, Latanya with both hands folded over her knee, her foolish, toothy smile communicating great warmth, I couldn't help but feel hope and possibility, for Noah, for the world. There were prospects, opportunities, for Noah, for all of us, and he could, without thinking, help lead me to some understanding of that.

We agreed that the two of them should go to a movie later that week. I would drop them off; Gerrie would pick them up. The film they chose was a noisy, humans-versus-alien-invaders movie that I worried might be a little violent but that Gerrie assured me would be fine. "They aren't children," he reminded me.

Driving Noah home, I wanted to ask him if Latanya was high functioning enough, if Noah worried that she wasn't "normal" enough for him. Hadn't he been the one who wanted to meet a "normal" girl? Latanya, for all her charm, was still almost a child. But then, I had to remember, so was Noah. Who was I to find her wanting?

Noah seemed taken by the girl, pretty as she was. Perhaps presented with her pulchritude he had simply abandoned his previous metrics. Then again, couldn't Latanya have done better, if she were just a little higher functioning? Gerrie had intimated Latanya had some dating troubles in the past, and I could too easily see the good-natured girl being taken advantage of. And Noah, for all his awkwardness, actually seemed to be a gentleman, an attribute that Gerrie had detected and approved of.

As I looked over at Noah sitting in the passenger seat, a little bit smug as he grinned about his first meeting with Latanya, I couldn't resist punching him in the arm, because, you know, he's my little brother, the arrogant bastard.

125.

Over the next few years, I would wrench my career back on track. My girlfriend, Silka, who had stuck by me through my addiction and rehab, would become my wife. We would marry in the Netherlands, attended by my parents and my brother, who flew to Europe for the ceremony and party that were held at my in-laws' house in Gulpen, outside Maastricht, and then the dinner and reception at a castle in Belgium. Noah had mastered sitting quietly when he began to feel overwhelmed by the crowd and noise, and for most of the party, even while a local marching band led several rounds of awkward, cross-cultural dancing. My in-laws were gracious with Noah, both accepting him and managing to effortlessly ignore him throughout the few days we were all bivouacked throughout their village. Noah slept upstairs at Silka's parents' house, in a narrow room where once Silka's younger brother, Til, had lived. My parents were a constant presence, and my mother complained frequently about how tired she was looking after Noah. (My mother, upon arriving in Amsterdam where we met before journeying south, had been steadily lamenting the state of her stomach. Silka had spent the day before our wedding preparing soft rice—white rice boiled to a floppy, soggy death—to soothe her stomach. My parents were staying in a little hotel on one of the canals while Silka and I stayed at her sister's apartment on the Singel. In Amsterdam, Noah had stayed in a room across the hall and had been surprisingly indifferent to Amsterdam, though he was frustrated that the hotel room lacked more than basic Dutch television.)

I was ambivalent about the wedding, and had not actually invited any of my own friends. It was and remains a trait of mine that I am a failure at self-celebration.

I failed to participate in my high school, college, and graduate school graduation ceremonies, and I've allowed only one birthday party to be thrown in my honor. I approached each of life's supposed milestones with disinterest, and my wedding was no different. We had already been living together for four years, and marriage wouldn't change any part of our living arrangement. And on some level I felt this ceremony was somehow related to my drug addiction, to my getting sober, to becoming officially, at thirty-one, an adult. But I didn't see it as a joyous occasion so much as something to be gotten through, though Silka's mother, Gundi, took it upon herself to arrange a pleasing ceremony and party, among a dozen family members whom I may well never see again.

I remember sitting with Noah out on the upstairs porch. The house was perched on the side of a meadowed heights; we gazed down upon the tidy little village: the brick houses, the cobblestone streets, the orderly gardens, the *frites* shop in town with its little wooden sign advertising French fries in paper cones. We talked about marriage, about Silka and Latanya, our women. Noah had been going steady with Latanya for five months, and even Gerrie seemed to approve of the match. While he was wary of allowing Latanya to sleep over at Noah's, he seemed resigned to the fact that the two were lovers, Latanya spending her days off with Noah. They were a charming couple and had eagerly taken up cooking as a mutual hobby, preparing all manner of baked goods and exotic dishes. I sometimes gave them a ride to bookstores in Santa Monica or Brentwood, where they would buy cookbooks and culinary magazines, poring over recipes and talking about what they wanted to bake. It was curious to see, but around Latanya Noah seemed more grown-up, as if he were shouldering the role of mature man in a relationship. She doted on him, bringing him small gifts, some flowers, a shirt she had bought with her own money, an advertising display from the department store where she worked.

While the two of them were in the kitchen, carefully measuring out flour, sugar, and cinnamon, or mixing a marinade, or even reducing preserves or maple syrup, there was an earnestness about their effort that made them seem normal. They enjoyed having Gerrie and Marlo over for dinner. Finally, after months of practicing and experimenting, they cooked a feast of brisket, sweet potatoes, brussels sprouts, gravy, greens, and biscuits, and hosted my parents, her parents, two of her siblings, Silka, and me—all of us crowded around the dining table and onto another folding table I helped set up in the kitchen. They handled the preparation and serving with eager aplomb, unspilling, squinting as they sliced and ladled, all in all, a better performance than my fiancé and I could have put on.

There we were, sitting around the table in the living room, a great, multiracial gathering, Asian, black, Jewish, autistic, having our dinner, and all of us warm inside from the sense that here, these two strange kids, were making it, somehow.

126.

Now, as Noah and I sat on that Dutch veranda, over the little town where my fiancée had grown up, I think we both were pleased at our progression. Latanya hadn't been able to join us because her parents worried at the long flight and whether my parents, now almost seventy, could handle both Noah and Latanya. She had thrown a tantrum when she was told that she couldn't come, a reminder that this was not yet a perfect couple. But Noah had stayed calm, as if understanding that he had to accept certain limitations. The flight over had been trying for my parents, more from anxiety at how Noah might react than from anything he actually did. He asked me how I knew I wanted to marry. I had never confessed to him my true feelings, worrying that he wouldn't understand that I never did anything without some reluctance. How could Noah possibly understand the regrets I already felt for the women I might never know. But why did I want Noah to retain a childlike view of marriage, that it should be a perfect union, entered into without hesitation or regret?

Noah surprised me by understanding much more about my ambivalence than I expected. He himself wasn't sure he wanted to marry, but for the first time, because of Latanya, he understood what that entailed. He had changed a great deal since the two of them had reconnected, becoming, somehow, more a man, even his gait changing, his former, slightly Chaplinesque waddle straightening into more of a stride as he walked up Bowdoin to his job at the newspaper. He was becoming more taciturn, patient, less agitated, all a natural result, perhaps, of having regular sex for the first time in his life. He was more confident and knowing. But this relationship with Latanya also cast him as something else, I noticed, more an equal to me as a man. And so we sat there, talking in the long afternoon, this green, Dutch valley an unlikely place for either of us to have reached. And if you saw us there, Noah and me, you would have had a hard time guessing which was the normal brother and which the autistic one.

127.

It is half a decade later, and I have moved from Los Angeles to New York to Hong Kong, where I am running a weekly newsmagazine. I go to the airport to pick up Noah, waiting on my side of the sliding-glass doors for my brother to emerge among the other black-haired international travelers, one among them, a little ragged after more than a dozen hours in the air. I am looking forward to seeing him, my brother. After those first years of growing closer together, Noah living just a few miles from me in Los Angeles, and even when I was in New York, it was easy to stay in touch, just three time zones away. In Hong Kong, where we have been living for the past two years, it is harder to catch Noah, given the erratic hours that he keeps. He has actually moved on to an even better job, as a copyeditor at a law firm in Century City. He is well paid and receives generous benefits, and, my father proudly tells me, there isn't a whiff of doing Noah a favor in hiring him.

He is still with Latanya, a relationship that's going on five years. The two of them are together many evenings and every weekend. She sleeps over at Noah's house, an arrangement that at first made Latanya's parents uncomfortable but which they had no choice but to agree with. The two of them are in love, and they make a beautiful couple, physically attractive, delighting in each other's company, and remarkably, my father points out, almost completely self-sufficient economically. They are both entitled to SSI and Medicaid for their health care, but Noah is fully covered by his employer. Of course, Noah's housing is partially subsidized by my parents, but that seems like a petty point to make as he continues to thrive and prosper.

He emerges, and I am surprised to see him in a navy blue wool blazer. His hair is cut short, and he wears a trim, graying beard. We are both getting older, and Noah's hairline is already starting to recede. He is skinnier than I, three inches shorter, but the first thought I have is the same one I always have when I see him nowadays: how normal he looks, how much like a regular guy. If you didn't know what to look for, the occasional tics or repetitive motions, the rubber band he still often carries in his right hand, you wouldn't know how severely autistic he once was.

I drive us back to my flat on the Peak, near the end of Barker Road, where we enjoy a dazzling view of Central and beyond that Victoria Harbor and Kowloon, the city falling down and springing up from the lush green of these hills, spires of concrete, steel, glass topped with green and yellow lights, the spires of the buildings level to our own hillside aerie. I drop Noah's bags in our guest room and we sit down on our blue sofas, Noah facing the window so that he can see the view. Esmee and Lola, my two daughters, are shy at first, but Noah, for the first time since their births, makes an effort to coax them to socialize. He has brought them picture books, Legos, two little dresses, all from him and Latanya. Here, away from his parent-owned house, well-dressed, holding in his hand a class of ice water, he is so self-possessed, so together, that when he tells me that he is getting married, that he and Latanya have decided to make it official, I almost forget how complicated and tricky this issue might be.

"Have you told Mom and Dad?" I ask.

He shakes his head.

"Has she told her parents?"

No again.

But they have decided, and I have seen enough of these two to understand that no one will be able to stop them.

They will set a date and would like my family to attend.

We will be there, Noah.

My brother has come, I realize, to seek my blessing for his wedding.

"Noah," I tell him, "you don't need my approval."

And he doesn't. As we sit there, gazing out the window at the bright bauble of a city beneath us, I remember how my father ended his first book about our family, about Noah, over thirty years ago. "Now finally, he and Karl are off to sleep. The house is quiet. Foumi's put a pie in the oven, and now she's at her desk writing—lately, she's begun a new sideline career, having published two articles in two of Japan's leading magazines. And I've just gone to the bookcase to check on that first sentence of Tolstoy's, and come away shaking my head. 'Happy families,' I know, 'are *not* all alike.' "

REALITY

128.

PSYCHOLOGICAL AND
PSYCHOPHARMACOLOGICAL REVIEW

NAME: *Noah Greenfeld*
REGIONAL CENTER: *Westside*
REGIONAL FACILITY: *Avenues Navigating the Spectrum of Rights and Responsibilities*
RESIDENTIAL CLASSIFICATION: *Supported Living*
DATE OF REPORT: *07-09-06*

DIAGNOSTIC IMPRESSION

AAMD Diagnosis

80. 790 Profound to severe mental retardation associated with or due to the Following Psychiatric Disorder, Other (Autistic Disorder).

DSM—IV—TR Diagnosis

Axis I: 299.00 Autistic Disorder

292.0 Lorazepam (Ativan) Withdrawal (Provisional)

292.12 Lorazepam (Ativan)—Induced Psychotic Disorder, With Hallucination (Provisional)

292.89 Lorazepam (Ativan)—Induced Sleep Disorder, Insomnia Type (Provisional)

304.10 Lorazepam (Ativan) Dependence, With Physiological Dependence, In A Controlled Environment
(Provisional)

9 Severe Mental Retardation, with behavioral symptoms

Axis III: Status post fracture of left 5th finger (01-07-92); History of anemia; History of insomnia; Difficulty maintaining optimum weight; Status post pneumonia; Mild visual impairment (early cataracts and minimal myopia bilaterally); Allergic rhinitis; History of extrapyramidal syndrome (EPS); Skin lesions/ dry skin; Chronic constipation; Status post thyroiditis versus hyperthyroidism (02-08-01); Multiple pigmented nevi on back; History of scabies (12/01 and 12/02); Missing dentition.

BEHAVIORAL/EMOTIONAL FUNCTIONING:

Current Psychiatric Diagnosis

Noah has been diagnosed with the pervasive developmental disorder, Autistic Disorder. He displays many characteristics of this disorder which include a failure to develop peer relationships, a lack of social or emotional reciprocity, failure to develop expressive communication, repetitive, self-stimulatory motor movements, inflexible adherence to specific nonfunctional routines (e.g., difficulty in transitioning from one activity to another, and extreme agitation as manifest by self-injurious and aggressive behavior when changes are made in his routine or he is around unfamiliar staff)

Currently Identified Maladaptive Behaviors

Currently, Noah has three identified high priority maladaptive behaviors that interfere with his adaptive programming. These include banging his head against solid surfaces, pinching himself, and grabbing others. Further, his behavior of chewing on clothing identified in the Behavioral Barrier section of his Approaches and Strategies. Noah may also intentionally spit at others, pinch or scratch others, dig his fingernails into others, and/or pull others' hair. He may bite, head-butt, and hit others, throw objects at others, and hit/slap his head when he is highly agitated. These behaviors are identified as Program Alerts in Noah's Approaches and Strategies.

Aversive/Restrictive Behavioral Intervention History

Noah has medical orders for a helmet with face shield which was used contingently for management of smearing saliva and to prevent injury when he was placed in time-out for his aggressive behavior. The use of the helmet with face shield was discontinued on 03-06-96 and 11-30-95, respectively for both of these conditions. At Noah's 2001–2002 annual planning conference, it was the decision of the interdisciplinary team to reinstate the use of a secured helmet with face shield because of injury that he had sustained as a result of banging his head. Behavior management and Human Rights Committee approval was obtained on 05-01-01. The use of the contingently applied helmet was discontinued on 11-01-01 because it had not been used for six consecutive months. Noah had orders for locked time-out which was used contingently for management of his aggressive behavior. This intervention procedure was discontinued on 11-30-95.

Behavioral Emergencies

During Noah's 2004–2005 annual year he had 21 behavioral emergencies that required varying as needed (PRN) dosages of Ativan intramuscularly (IM) (either a.5 or 2 mg) and were associated with changes in his psychotropic regimen: 3 in August (08-05-04, 08-06-04); 4 in September (09-10-04, 09-16-04, 09-19-04, and 09-26-04; 2 in December (12-11-04 and 12-22-04); 6 in January (01-01-05, 01-03-05, 01-06-05, 01-10-05, 01-26-05, and 01-28-05); and 6 in March (03-08-05, 03-22-05, 03-25-05, 03-27-05, 03-30-05, and 03-31-05). Further, Noah had 4 more behavioral emergencies and received 2 mg of Ativan IM on 04-27-05, 05-08-05, 05-15-05, and 05-22-05.

129.

A middle-aged man sits by himself on brown lawn outside a run-down house in South Central Los Angeles. He seems neither to miss company nor show any eagerness to seek it. If you greet him, he will not look at you nor turn in the direction of your voice.

Noah is still alone. Noah never traveled to New York, Holland, or Hong Kong. He never reconnected with Latanya. Noah never spoke. I described the circumstances and history of our family as accurately as I could. I did go to rehab. I did get married. We did move to Hong Kong. But Noah never spoke.

I dreamed that happy outcome. I imagined the life I wanted for me, for Noah, for my parents. I conjured it, as therapy, as a study in what if, as an attempted answer to the great question in our family: What if Noah could talk? What if Noah were normal? What if? What if?

Noah is today a client of California's Regional Center system for the developmentally disabled, his life indifferently recounted in seven horizontal feet of files containing psychiatric progress notes and client location sheets and social discharge summaries and psychological evaluations. His story is told there in starker terms than in any of my father's books or in my mother's writings or in my memory. There, in the state system for the developmentally disabled, he has been a client, a ward, passed from institution to institution, damaged, hurt, roughed up. Noah's adulthood came on too fast—he was just fourteen when he was first institutionalized at BMI, eighteen when he went to his first of a succession of group homes, twenty-five when he began a fifteen-year stay at the Fairview Developmental Center, a state institution—and his has been a harder life than I like to think about. When friends ask after Noah, it is too complicated to explain the details and nuances of his suffering. The facilities where he has ended up, the careless caregivers, the cruel housemates, the abusive psych techs (as the junior-college-trained assistants working with the developmentally disabled are called) have left Noah grizzled, gaunt, angry, defensive, and lost. To spend time with Noah is to confront the uncinematic reality of madness. There is nothing quaint or charming about raving, violent lunacy, about a man in torn, ragged clothes, banging his head against a concrete floor, scratching himself, spitting, pinching. I have to be honest—he is not charming, not to me, not anymore. He is a grown man and a heavy burden, prickly, hard to love, disinclined to please, quick to lash out. I wish I could say I love him, but I'm not sure anymore. But I feel guilty that I don't love him, and that culpability causes me to act as if I do love him.

That the system failed Noah is beyond a doubt. But, of course, Noah failed the system first. You can't ask the world to provide for those who have effectively turned their back on it. And Noah, as a low-functioning autistic adult, is rejection personified. Help him, offer him a snack he likes, a pat on the back, a cool drink on a hot day, and he will as likely grab your hair or scratch your arm as smile. He wasn't always like this, of course, he used to be more gentle, occasionally loving, but much of that affection was abraded through years of harsh surroundings. He learned, the hard way, that you strike first and ask questions later. The other clients at some of his group homes learned to be wary of him. While other clients, and staff, got the better of him and sometimes had their way with him.

Noah never spoke. A high-functioning, criminally inclined autistic, or a perverted caregiver, can take advantage of that. I spent my adult life knowing terrible things were happening to Noah—in one group home he was almost certainly raped by a higher-functioning autistic male—yet somehow averting my attention just enough so that I could go on, so that I could answer, when people asked, "Noah's okay," because answering that my brother was raped, more than once, takes the conversation out of the realm of small talk.

130.

I don't know Noah. He is, I suspect, unknowable. Yet he remains the center of my life.

I hate him for that.

If I could, I would never write about him, speak about him, I would tell anyone who asked that I was an only child.

Yet he's my brother.

I dread the phone calls from my parents. He has attacked another client. He's bitten one of his psych techs. He has been beaten up. He has a black eye, a chipped tooth, another unexplained scar. Those calls remind me. They make me feel helpless because Noah is helpless.

I want to have hope. I read the books and articles about autism, the alleged scientific breakthroughs, the inspiring family stories, and they are all, ultimately, about hope. But then the reality of Noah intrudes, and I struggle to feel a similar sense of possibility. So I push it out of my mind, and after I hang up I attempt to purge Noah from my consciousness.

I don't feel sorry for myself. And I don't feel pity for Noah, though he is in every real sense pitiful. To feel pity for Noah and not anger would be letting him off too easily, I tell myself, would somehow be unfair to him. His autism doesn't preclude him from being just as responsible for his own circumstances as any of us. That is a philosophical gimmick I employ, to believe that Noah has somehow chosen his life, not consciously but biologically, which is even more ineluctable. He is where he is because of who he is, just as you or I are who we are and are doing what we are doing because of our genetic makeup, circumstances, personalities, good or bad luck or karma or whatever else you want to throw into the mix of destiny. His autism doesn't give him a free pass on ultimately being responsible for himself. Autism is his destiny.

Even as I tell myself that, I feel the reality of Noah intruding and the weight of worrying about him returning. Unless I am willing to walk away, to just close my heart to him, then understanding why he is where he is, is as useless as figuring out the exact temperature while you're freezing to death. It's information, but it's just not helpful.

131.

When I visit, he recognizes me. He knows me. Sometimes, rarely, he hugs me, or lets me hug him. Frequently he spits at me, or tries to pinch me. His spitting is perfunctory; he makes the sounds of spitting but there is very little saliva actually launched. It is a warning gesture, an attempt to establish territory—don't come too close—a gorilla beating his chest, a dog baring his teeth. He is a man—it is still shocking to think of him as a man, a corollary to society's habit of referring to all the autistic as "children," as if, somehow, they never grow up. They do, and Noah looks his forty-one years, with his receding hairline and thinning black hair, graying facial stubble, shallow furrows between his eyes and slight radiating of wrinkles beginning at their edges. He is handsome, better looking than I, his features somehow a more pleasing combination of our parents' different races: black hair, Caucasian eyes, nose shaped a little like a quartered sphere, small mouth, and chiseled cheekbones. He has small feet, is bow-legged and skinny, but with a slight pot belly. His hands and forearms always seem scabbed, self-inflicted scratches and cuts. He bruises his forehead from banging his head against walls, he picks up other bruises, scrapes, and scars at a rate that must be similar to a boxer in training, one, two a day, most of them unobserved by his various caregivers. The damage helps to make him look more wizened than me, his greeting gaze also contributes; it is a skeptic's squint: prove it, he might be saying, prove it. I make the first move. As I said, I always try to hug him.

Sometimes, when he's happy, I get the hug back. It is one armed, brief. He is going through the motions.

I cannot think of any other human relationship that would continue with so little positive feedback from one party—those whose parents suffer from severe Alzheimer's or who have had loved ones suffer traumatic brain injuries know this sense of visiting, of loving and getting so little in return. But Noah knows me. He has a memory, perhaps of those decades we lived together.

What does he make of his own childhood? A distant sense of warmth, a vague idea of more comfort then versus discomfort now? He lived with us, my mother and father and me, in a home—a family, that has to mean something, right?—where, at the very least, he had to know he was loved. He would have felt that, wouldn't he? Despite all the literature explaining the emotional distance of the autistic, they are human in the sense that they can feel good and bad based on how they are treated. It is terrible to say this, but a dog knows love, so Noah must, too. But does Noah share the almost universal memory of the familial cocoon, his mother's embrace, his father's lap, being carried, hugged, lifted up and away from danger and into safety?

I believe he does, because when he sees our parents, his reaction is often so different from when he sees me. He is more likely to hug them, even to bend his head forward so that they can kiss him on the forehead. Our parents—my father is now eighty, my mother in her late seventies—surprise me with their deep reservoir of love for Noah. Their loyalty astonishes me, and sometimes I have thought it is their weakness. If they could have gone on, somehow cut him off, as some other parents of the severely autistic do—I've seen them, these addled adults, in state institutions, ignored, never visited, wandering down linoleum hallways in their self-protective helmets, the staff at the facilities taking their cues from the outside world and ignoring them even more than they ignored Noah. Our family fought for Noah in part to show the rest of the world that Noah was loved, in the hopes that perhaps Noah would be better treated by those inside the facilities because there was family outside the facility that was watching. Those severely autistic who have no one, they have very short life expectancies.

My father walks in shuffling steps, his hands in his jacket pockets, a captain's hat or baseball cap on his head that Noah always makes him remove. He doesn't like hats. My mother is shorter, she was never more than five feet two, and in her eighth decade I believe she has lost an inch or two, and she has grown wider in the middle. When Noah was at home, she was slender, as narrow as a prepubescent boy; all the running after him kept her a flyweight. Now she is heavier and has taken to wearing the layers of dull-colored sweaters and aprons and housedresses, the kind I remember my grandmother wearing when I was small. As a boy, I called this the "*obasan* uniform," *obasan* being Japanese for grandmother. In other words, my mother is plump in the way that grandmothers often are.

The two of them, my old parents, slightly hunched, carrying their little bags of Noah's favorite goodies, California rolls and fresh-cut pineapple and rice crackers and guava punch. My mother lays out a napkin and opens the plastic supermarket sushi container, and then Noah tears into it, stuffing his mouth with crab and avocado and rice and looking warily around, lest someone would take away his food. He leans forward, his elbow around his meal, the way I imagine a convict would in prison. He gorges himself quickly, pushing more food into his mouth before he has even swallowed the previous bite. He doesn't understand, or believe, in delayed gratification. And his years in and out of group homes and California State Department of Developmental Disabilities facilities have further reinforced the notion that if something is good, now, then take as much of it as you can.

Then he starts on his fruit, his crackers, his juice, pouring this down his throat as quickly as my mother can empty the can. If he is in a good mood, he will then hang around for a while. Perhaps we will take a walk or a short drive. He will bob his head slightly and smile, a wide, open-mouthed, cheek-creasing, eye-muscle relaxing expression of uncomplicated joy that is as real as smiles get—Noah doesn't lie. He will say, "M-m-m-m-m-m-m-ommy," and then expect the reward that is always forthcoming when he uses a word.

As my father says, when Noah is in a good mood, you feel like you've won the lottery.

132.

Noah still marks his territory with saliva, spitting into his fingers and then touching a spot on the door frame or the wall or the sofa. It is exactly as a dog would do, only with spit instead of urine. When I take a walk with him, he will leave his saliva on lampposts, parking meters, bus stop shelters, even garbage cans, sometimes after we've watched a hound piss at the base of the very same object. I've never seen him return to inspect these spots nor to check if anyone else has marked this territory.

I always assumed it was some primitive, mammalian gesture asserting itself through the neurological clutter of Noah's mind, and it made me wonder if perhaps Noah was capable of animal behaviors, like hunting or catching a scent and following another animal's track, but I have never seen him go further than this curious, repetitive marking procedure. My mother, when she walks with him, still carries with her a napkin so that she can wipe his fingers before he licks them, catching up with him after he has touched a park bench and saying *"akitana,"* Japanese for "filthy."

My father shrugs and says, "What about the times we're not here?"

And unspoken is the motivation for why we do so much of what we do for Noah: it is to make ourselves feel better.

133.

A friend of mine who also has an autistic brother asked me about guilt. I reflexively told her I didn't have any, at least not about Noah.

"Bullshit," she said.

I thought for a moment; we were walking down Broadway and stopped at a corner. "I guess you're right."

I'd never thought of it before. I assumed I just felt sorry for Noah, that I would do what I could to help Noah. Actually, it made me tired thinking about Noah. There were no solutions; I had resigned myself to that so long ago I didn't even remember ever thinking there might be. So I built this static model of Noah = Problem and tried to leave it unexamined because there were no answers, right? (Remember my other equation: Autism = Destiny.)

But guilt seemed far-fetched. Yet she was right, I did feel guilty when I thought about Noah. Why was I here, normal, speaking, writing, talking, living a life, while Noah was always twice-imprisoned, in his mind *and* in an institution. It wasn't fair, but that wasn't my fault. Life isn't fair, and Noah is a living, breathing, twenty-four-hour-a-day lesson in that. I don't believe I suffer from some version of survivor's guilt. I was never at any risk of autism. The guilt has to do with a practical matter: Couldn't I be doing more? I mean, he's my brother. Shouldn't I be visiting more often, calling up his caregivers, fighting for his rights in the various supervisory and medical hearings that are held to determine his fate? Yet I had instead traveled the world, spending decades getting as far as I could from Noah: New York, Paris, Tokyo, Bangkok, Ibiza, Hong Kong. And I rarely considered how my absence affected Noah. If he could talk, then we could have spoken on the phone; he could have told me he wanted to see me. (What the hell do brothers talk about anyway? Even though I have one, I realize I have no idea.)

So his silence allowed me to wander away, to stay gone, leaving Noah in the hands of my parents, who never suggested I should stay closer because of him. Who are reluctant to even remind me that Noah will be my problem as well. We've talked about it, but never so specifically that a schedule is discussed. But I understand that Noah is there, always, on my time horizon, the destination of my journeys as sure as he was the point of embarkation.

My father has said he doesn't want me to feel burdened, that it's not fair that I should live with this obligation. How is it then that I feel it is as inevitable as hair graying? Because it is assumed that I will take care of Noah, that my parents will go on for as long as they can, and they are already faltering, forgetting appointments to meet with his doctors, losing the list of medications Noah is taking. Here is how implicit the whole arrangement has become: during a recent visit, as my father realized that of my two daughters, the older Esmee has a more gentle disposition than her more lawyerly younger sister, he said to me, "If something happens to you, then I think Esmee would take care of Noah."

So then at what point is the guilt imparted to Esmee? And will she ever feel that she's doing enough?

It is ironic that in the 1970s, my father played the heavy when autistic parents were gathered to discuss their issues on TV. Twice he appeared on Tom Snyder's *Tomorrow Show* to advocate euthanasia for the severely retarded and autistic. He did this, he said, to highlight how little was being done by the state and society for those afflicted, "to dramatize the plight of those afflicted." In truth, he was unable to stop worrying over Noah, constantly fretting over his lousy schools and his indifferent teachers. I now see my parents' devotion to Noah as a strange kind of sacrifice, a masochistic cycle they saw no way out of. As a parent now myself, I feel the great sucking force on my love and spirit emanating from my daughters; how could I ever turn my back on them? But if it were survival, I ask myself, if it were them or me, would I still sacrifice everything so that they might feel a little better?

But Noah never required one massive decision, to institutionalize him or keep him at home. It was a gradual process during which every day a small decision was made to keep him home, if only for one more day. "We keep thinking of finding a place for him," my father wrote. "We know we have to start the long weaning process. But how hard it is to wean oneself from a six-and-a-half-year test of love." Yet my mother and father were resolute in keeping him home, making, every day, that small decision to stave off Camarillo or Letchworth for one more day, while conceding that it was inevitable. What it came down to for them was this: our home was the best place for Noah, even though Noah was the worst thing that could happen to a home. My father used to tell me that he talked and wrote about killing Noah because that meant he could never do it, that the confession and motive were already there, on tape, in his books, so he could never get away with the crime.

But I was a different matter. I had never talked about it with anyone, had never written such a thought down. I think about this sometimes when I visit Noah now. I could stage the same sort of accident my father wrote about—take him out on a boat and push him overboard. Noah can barely swim. His symptoms include frequent jerky movements and erratic behavior. He would be more likely to fall overboard than stay on the boat. And then the problem would be solved and that way, if something happens to me, then perhaps poor Esmee or Lola won't have to spend their middle years bringing sushi and fruit to their crazy uncle.

He will be even more grotesque by then; the severely autistic don't groom themselves. Noah is far more likely to pick up a stray piece of trash or make sure all doors are securely closed or put any cups into the sink. He likes his surfaces pristine, even if that means picking up a piece of dog feces. This symptom is described in the *Diagnostic and Statistical Manual of Mental Disorders'* guide to autism, "inflexible adherence to specific, nonfunctional routines or rituals." (Noah, by the way, scores a perfect 17 out of 17 on that test; 6 is good enough for a diagnosis. He excels in autism.)

He has already changed so much from his boyhood self that I struggle to remember the cute child. For Esmee and Lola, who never saw the boy he was, it may well become incomprehensible why anyone ever cared for this spitting old man. The caregivers and psych techs who see him now must wonder: How was he ever loved? Why would anyone pretend that he is anything more than a freak, a broken human, a sick animal, kept alive by the taxpayers and despite himself? I can see him that way, too; I am guilty of the same rationalizations, particularly when I need to justify my going months without seeing him.

My mother, who has very little artifice, once said, "You know, if something happens to us, you have to go see him, to check up, otherwise, he will be hurt." She was near tears as she explained this to me. I was back from one of my journeys, sleeping in my teenage bedroom for a few days or weeks before setting off again. "People like Noah, they die if no one goes to look in."

So I make the drive down Interstate 10 to La Brea and then down La Brea to Chesapeake and the little house by the recycling center where he lives now in a supported-living environment. I am fueled by guilt.

Is that all there is? Can a relationship really be sustained entirely by the guilt one party feels toward the other, by a sense of obligation, never acknowledged, discussed, or even appreciated?

134.

A few years ago I traveled to Boston to write an article about the quarterback Doug Flutie. He had recently joined the New England Patriots and we were sitting in his kitchen talking about his learning a new offensive system when his autistic son, Doug Jr., loped into the room. He was eleven at the time, and I was instantly stricken by a sad recognition. The repetitive rocking back and forth, the way he held his fingers up before his eyes and twiddled them around, the slight list to the right when he walked. I hadn't intended for the story to be about Dougie's autism, yet that's what I wrote. Because once I saw Dougie, everything else in Doug and Laurie's life suddenly seemed secondary to the fact of their son's autism. I immediately saw, as clearly as I had lived my own life, their family's journey and how hard their road would be.

When the story was published, I received numerous letters, most of them flattering but a few were angry with me for not acknowledging the great gift that had been given to me. Noah, these parents asserted, was not a negative; it was my attitude toward him that was reprehensible. Initially, I reflexively dismissed these letters. But gradually, I began to wonder if perhaps my thinking about Noah had become too shaded by what I perceived to be my own responsibilities and obligations. Why couldn't I, like so many of my readers, see the positive in being Noah's brother?

I had learned from him cynicism, defeatism, negativity, and suspicion. What was wrong with me? Why didn't I see the wonderful lessons to be learned? Patience, service, generosity, and selflessness, these were certainly fine traits for a human being. Yet I had failed to learn these because, instead, I had ignored him. He was a problem, just sitting there, forever, in whatever fucked-up institution or group home he happened to be in that year. I have consigned him to a very specific territory in my mind, and I don't let him disturb me. Denial has worked for me.

And if I can stay hard and calloused, if I can go through life without caring or feeling for Noah, then I will be better off. Because there is nothing to be gained from loving Noah but those lessons in patience and service and generosity and selflessness. Maybe if he were my son or daughter I would feel differently, but he is my brother, and aren't sibling obligations different than parental? Ultimately, I tell myself, my best chance at happiness is to turn my back and walk away.

But I know I can't.

AFTERWORD

I suspected, even before I boarded the planes and rented the cars, that there were no cures for my brother's affliction. Yet the television news kept broadcasting stories of hope. A boy in Evansville, Illinois, whose parents had staged an intensive, immersive intervention when he was diagnosed at eighteen months now responded to the newscaster's questions in the same evasive, smiling manner as would any other six-year-old; a famous actress put her son on a gluten-free diet and then wrote of his remarkable return to normalcy; the families on *Oprah*, on *The View*, on *60 Minutes*; the revelations of new therapies, medicines, treatments, interventions. My bookshelf was filled with redemptive memoirs, each outlining the remarkable and moving journey of a family pulling together and restoring their child.

But as I have come to realize, there are no adult autistics featured in any of this media coverage. The pathos of the child who for the first few months of his life appears to be developing normally and then, in the words of so many of the memoirs and hope manuals, "regresses" or "vanishes," makes it seem as though autism is a tragic affliction that snatches children but ends there.

And yet there's Noah, my forty-year-old brother, an adult autistic and living proof of the obvious: autism is not a terminal disease, so each of these autistic boys, and girls, are likely to become autistic adults. But where are the well-funded programs and research papers and longitudinal studies ascertaining the state of adult autistics?

I have phoned representatives of the numerous autism advocacy groups that have arisen over the past decade looking, I suppose, for reassurance that my brother still has some kind of chance, that with all these happy endings, with all this money and focus and research—with Oprah!—Noah won't end up a member of a lost generation of autistics. What I have found out is that the focus of these organizations—the research, the grant money, the treatments—is relentlessly toward the children. There are plenty of studies being done to benefit adults with Asperger's, the highest-functioning part of the autism spectrum, but next to nothing to help low-functioning autistic adults.

I began to hear, at conferences and panel discussions, that as this current cohort of autistics, those born in the 1990s, grow into adolescence and adulthood, the research will refocus there, on treatment for the adolescent autistics. I'm not overly optimistic; certainly Noah is not going to benefit in his lifetime. For adult autistics, much is just as it was fifty years ago. State institutions for the developmentally disabled. Group homes run by those of varying qualifications. Living at home with aging parents. If there is a family involved, the boy, or man, is looked after, perhaps, or at least not willfully neglected. I also have seen many autistics whose parents have passed away, or whose families have just stopped visiting them in state hospitals, where Noah was formerly a client. Groggy-seeming men, with lazy jaws, unkempt hair, scratches, bruises. I can remember their names: Buddy, Nick, Gerald. They don't live long, these boys; who was going to make sure they were taken for routine physicals? Who would bother to X-ray their chests or wonder if they had polyps? They died in middle age. The attendants at these institutions can't help but take their cues from the families. They, like the men, are only human.

One spring day in 2007 I boarded a plane for Seattle, to attend another major conference that drew together the various arms of the autism establishment: the geneticists seeking a cause, the behaviorists seeking better therapies, the epidemiologists looking to explain prevalence, the neurologists looking to understand etiology. At these gatherings, too, were the parents. You could identify them immediately; they were the ones who leaned forward, spoke loudly, pleaded. They were shabbily dressed compared to the doctors and geneticists; years of living with an autistic boy or girl had forced spartan sartorial choices—rough durable fabrics, hair tightly coiffed, no dangling jewelry that might be pulled or twisted or yanked by an unruly and angry twelve-year-old. I knew these mothers and fathers, recognized in them my own parents' reduced lives. As they interrupted conversations between specialists, talking about random mutations and single common pathways, about strict shaping versus looser shaping contingency, about PRT versus ABA, I recognized in their eyes the desperate need for help. The specialists sometimes didn't know what to make of them and simply nodded or offered sympathy. The most empathetic of them took the time to listen, to hear for the umpteenth time a personal story about vaccines or about diet or about facilitation, about hope, really, about something the family had tried, or, more likely, had heard about and now wanted—information, data, a study.

These are parents of autistic children, of course. The parents of autistic adults have long since retreated into a kind of defensive resignation. The journey begins here, with desperate pleas, with a search for knowledge. And for many, it ends with a family just trying to figure out how to get from week to week. Every conversation with my father and mother begins with a short report about how Noah is doing, his weight is up, it's down, he scratched a caregiver, he has a large bruise on his forehead of unknown provenance, he smiled, he didn't smile. Through the bad news and the good, we try to stay optimistic, despite the obvious downward part of the arc we suspect we are now descending.

Among the nearly five thousand attendees, I believe I am the only sibling of an adult autistic. But I did not attend to find empathy or even consolation; I was there to gather information about studies and programs for adult autistics.

Amid 458 papers and presentations and three dozen talks given by the elite academics and specialists covering autism, only two dealt with low-functioning adults, and neither one included a cohort large enough to be statistically relevant. From the podium, I heard the cofounder of Cure Autism Now plead for more money and focus on autistic teens, but the call stopped there despite the fact that all of the autistic children the advocacy groups are supporting will grow up to be adults.

Of course, the great autism industrial complex wants to believe that by treating children, they are heading off the next generation of autistic adults. In reality, the success rate for these early-intervention programs, for the full-time, eight hours a day starting at eighteen months with speech therapy support, is still far lower than the glowing media reports would lead one to believe. The question for me, of course, is what would have been Noah's fate had he been diagnosed today and had the best interventions known? The answer is impossible to ascertain, but the reality is that maybe 10 percent of kids as severely autistic as Noah benefit from the current intervention to the point where they will become functioning members of society. Many autistic kids who are diagnosed and treated early will improve and should be treated, but chances are they are not really low-functioning autistics to begin with. The epidemic of diagnoses is among the most controversial aspects of autism, but early diagnosis is confusing in that a child between eighteen months and five years makes a fantastic amount of developmental progress, with or without intensive intervention, so a child who seems withdrawn at eighteen months might seem normal at five years old, even without intervention. So how do we know who is really benefiting from all this intervention? These conferences, for all the good intentions and hard work of the experts, are still selling short-term solutions to high-functioning kids, the easiest-to-treat segment of the autistic population. Where, I always find myself wondering, does Noah fit into this?

He doesn't. He was a lost boy then, and he is a lost grown-up now.

At one conference, I stand before a great man, a smart, charming geneticist with understanding eyes. "How old is your brother?" he asks. "Is he verbal? Where does he live?" I explain and immediately realize he has already slotted me into the category of "concerned family." (It is novel that a sibling is here instead of a parent, but siblings will soon become common enough, as this current swelled cohort of diagnosed autistics ages into adulthood.)

He tells me how sorry he is. It is heartfelt, but the squint of his eyes catches me off guard when I realize that he sees me as a figure to be pitied. I want to show him that I am not, that I am vital and full of life and not chained to my unfortunate brother, so when he asks how long I am going to be in town, I tell him I am leaving early the next morning, to fly to Las Vegas, to see a highly anticipated prize fight. The neurologist shakes his head. He detests boxing, he says, those blows to the brain. Terrible. Terrible.

I am left standing there, feeling foolish.

Later, he will address a vast hall, speak on the state of genetic research into autism, regret that the search is just now entering a new phase, that the "low-hanging fruit" has been plucked and that the researchers have concluded there will be no autism gene isolated. The great genetic hope of so many in the autism community, that we would find autism's location on the genome and therefore be able to more quickly diagnose and maybe prevent it, was now gone. The geneticist seemed almost contrite as he summed up what everyone in the room already knew, that "autism was not an easy disease."

It may not be one disease or condition at all, but merely a collection of behaviors and deficits stemming from a range of rare mutations. We are all comprised of far more genetic variations than we previously had imagined. Our ability to analyze the genome has shed new light on just how many so-called copy-number variations, strips of RNA proteins transcribed as GUUAGGUAGGUAUGUGUA where bits and pieces have been mislaid or dropped, we have in our DNA. The vast majority of those "mistakes" are harmless, protein dead ends that fail to express in RNA activity. Geneticists are now saying that the autistic seem to have even more than the rest of us. Still, it will only be a clue, when you consider all the other isolated genetic causes: Fragile X, Rett disorder, Williams syndrome, Gilbert syndrome, untreated fetal ketonuria. The geneticist explains that the autism diagnosis is a roundup. He calls it "the amazing heterogeneity of autism." The child doesn't respond to social stimuli, is nonverbal or echolalic, is prone to repetitive motions and stereotypical behaviors. Perhaps these are each the result of various rare variations, either mutations or deletions in the genome, mistakes and errors in genetic coding similar to what we all carry, only these somehow affect the function of the gene. All of us can answer yes to at least one or another item on a checklist of autism symptoms listed in the diagnostic criterion—are you occasionally "preoccupied with parts of objects," do you have "nonfunctional routines or rituals," do you have an interest that is "abnormal either in intensity or focus"? Any one or even several of these proclivities means nothing. Too many and you are autistic.

Portia Iversen, the author of *Strange Son* and the founder of Cure Autism Now, asks what if autism is this giant collection of various gene mutations and variations, each contributing a little behavioral tic that together add up to the condition.

That is where the research is pointing. It is a fascinating idea, this concept that autism is not a disease at all, but a trait that is expressed everywhere in the genome. Sort of like being Asian. You can't really find the gene that makes people Asian. It is expressed everywhere in the genome.

What does this mean for boys like Noah? Yes, treatment strategies have evolved since Noah went through Lovaas's UCLA program, but there has been no revolution. Intervene earlier, with more intensity, with greater focus. That is the sum of it. There are dietary therapies, yet for every child who benefits another shows no improvement. Perhaps, if Noah were born today, then diagnosis would have been earlier and Discrete Trial intervention would have started sooner. And would that have made a difference? I have met plenty of autistic boys who, as Portia Iverson describes of her son Dov, "flunked Lovaas" (or similar intensive programs), just as Noah did. Would a few seasons' head start have transformed him?

Early intervention is now the accepted and recommended course, with the diagnosis made, if possible, at five months. Are "normal" children being caught up in this early diagnostic dragnet? Of course. How many of them are among the miraculously "cured"? We will never know, but it can't hurt to start early. What we do know is that all autistic children grow up. And I wish, I really do, that they will all miraculously recover.

But I know, I really do, that not all of them will.

ACKNOWLEDGMENTS

My father, Josh Greenfeld, steadily counseled me during the writing of this book and provided me with the idea that forms its core. I talk to him frequently about what I am working on, and his advice has helped me to steer my course. His books and private journals were also an invaluable resource.

Silka, my wife, provided emotional support during the writing, reminding me, as I lamented for the hundredth time how badly all this was going, that I always bitch and moan while I'm in a book.

My mother, Foumiko Kometani, was a rock. My daughters, Esmee and Lola, continued their relatively normal childhood development.

This book changed very much from the original concept, which was to write a much more general book about autism. I spoke to dozens of scientists, specialists, and researchers, and the vast majority of them were not included in the final version. I am still grateful for the time and support of all those who met with me, especially Dan Geschwind, Matthew State, Portia Iversen, Jon Shestack, Sally Rogers, Sally Ozonoff, Irva Hertz-Picciotto, Laurie Schreibman, Bob Koegel, Lynn Kern Koegel, Ron Grinker, Kim Stagliano, Sophia Colamarino, Meredith Gibbs, and Carlos A. Pardo.

My editor, Gail Winston, never seems to doubt me. My agents, Gail Ross and Howard Yoon, are always on my team.

Thanks also to Jonathan Burnham, Terry McDonell, Bob Roe, Phillip Gourevitch, Nathaniel Rich, Joanne Lippman, Katherine Wheelock, Klara Glowsceska, Jim Impoco, Daniel Peres, George Quraishi, Barry Harbaugh, Kyle Pope, Dorinda Elliott, Adi Ignatius, Shea O'Rourke, Benjamin Percy, David Bar-Katz, Christopher Astley, Guy Aroch, John Seabrook, and Ptolemy Tompkins.

This book was conceived in part as my Henry Crown Fellowship project for the Aspen Institute.

BIBLIOGRAPHY

The following books, papers, and articles are either cited or mentioned in *Boy Alone*, or informed the writing.

Books

Greenfeld, Josh. *A Child Called Noah.* 1972.
———. *A Client Called Noah.* 1986.
———. *A Place for Noah.* 1978.
Kometani, Foumiko. *Passover.* 1989.

Bettelheim, Bruno. *The Empty Fortress.* 1967.
Buck, Pearl S. *The Child Who Never Grew.* 1950.
Carter, Rita. *Mapping the Mind.* 1998.
Chomsky, Noam. *Knowledge of Language.* 1986.
———. *Syntactic Structures.* 1957.
Dennett, Daniel C. *Consciousness Explained.* 1991.
Dunne, John Gregory. *Quintana and Friends.* 1980.
Foucault, Michel. *Madness and Civilization.* 1965.
Grandin, Temple. *Emergence.* 1986.
Grinker, Roy Richard. *Unstrange Minds.* 2007.
Haddon, Mark. *The Curious Incident of the Dog in the Night-time.* 2003.

Harris, Sandra L., and Beth A. Glasberg. *Siblings of Children with Autism.* 2003.

Iversen, Portia. *Strange Son.* 2007.

Kaufman, Barry. *Son Rise.* 1976.

Keller, Helen. *The Story of My Life.* 1903.

Kirby, David. *Evidence of Harm.* 2005.

Koegel, Lynn Kern, and Claire LaZebnik. *Overcoming Autism.* 2004.

Lane, Harlan. *The Wild Boy of Aveyron.* 1976.

LeDoux, Joseph. *Synaptic Self.* 2002.

Leighs, James. *Deception & Sanity.* 1978.

Maurice, Catherine. *Let Me Hear Your Voice.* 1993.

Newton, Michael. *Savage Girls and Wild Boys.* 2002.

Park, Clara Claiborne. *Exiting Nirvana.* 2001.

———. *The Siege.* 1967.

Pettit, Philip. *Made with Words.* 2008.

Piaget, Jean. *The Child's Conception of the World.* 1929.

———. *The Construction of Reality in the Child.* 1954.

———. *The Language and Thought of the Child.* 1926.

Pollack, Richard. *The Creation of Dr. B.* 1997.

Porter, Roy. *A Social History of Madness.* 1987.

Ramachandran, V. S. *A Brief Tour of Human Consciousness.* 2005.

Ratey, John J. *A User's Guide to the Brain.* 2001.

Richards, Julie E., and R. Scott Hawley. *The Human Genome.* 2005.

Rimland, Bernard. *Infantile Autism.* 1964.

Schreibman, Laura. *The Science and Fiction of Autism.* 2005.

Senator, Susan. *Making Peace with Autism.* 2006.

Shattuck, Roger. *The Forbidden Experiment.* 1980.

Shelley, Percy Bysshe. *Prometheus Unbound.* 1820.

Skinner, B. F. *Beyond Freedom and Dignity.* 1971.

———. *Walden Two.* 1948.

Solomon, Andrew. *The Noonday Demon.* 2001.

Volkmar, Fred R., Rhea Paul, Ami Klin, and Donald Cohen, eds. *Handbook of Autism and Pervasive Developmental Disorders*, vols. 1 and II. 2005.

Ullman, Leonard P., and Leonard Krasner. *Case Studies in Behavior Modification.* 1965.

Articles and Papers

The Autism Genome Project Consortium. "Mapping Autism Risk Loci Using Genetic Linkage and Chromosomal Rearrangements," *Nature Genetics*, March 2007.

Belmonte, Matthew K., Greg Allen, et al. "Autism and Abnormal Development of Brain Connectivity," *The Journal of Neuroscience*, October 2004.

Eisenberg, Leon. "The Autistic Child in Adolescence," *American Journal of Psychiatry*, February 1956.

———. "The Fathers of Autistic Children," *American Journal of Orthopsychiatry*, 1957.

Ferster, C. B. "Positive Reinforcement and Behavioral Deficits of Autistic Children," *Child Development*, vol. 32, 1961.

Fombonne, Eric. "Epidemiological Surveys of Autism and Other Pervasive Development Disorders: An Update," *Journal of Autism and Developmental Disorders*, August 2003.

———. "Is There an Epidemic of Autism?," *Pediatrics*, March 2007.

Greenfeld, Josh. "A Child Called Noah," *Life*, October 1970.

Gupta, Abha R., and Matthew W. State. "Recent Advances in the Genetics of Autism," *Biological Psychiatry*, June 2006.

Herbert, Martha R. "Autism: A Brain Disorder or a Disorder that Affects the Brain?," *Clinical Neuropsychiatry*, October 2005.

Kanner, Leo. "Autistic Disturbances of Affective Contact," *Nervous Child*, 1943.

———. "The Conception of Whole and Parts in Early Infantile Autism," *American Journal of Psychiatry*, July 1951.

Kiernan, Chris. "The Use of Nonvocal Communication Techniques with Autistic Individuals," *Journal of Childhood Psychology and Psychiatry*, March 1982.

Lichstein, Kenneth L., and Laura Schreibman. "Employing Electric Shock with Autistic Children," *Journal of Autism and Childhood Schizophrenia*, vol. 6, no.2, 1976.

Lord, Catherine, Ann Wagner, et al. "Challenges in Evaluating Psychosocial Interventions for Autistic Spectrum Disorders," *Journal of Autism and Developmental Disorders*, December 2005.

Lovaas, O. Ivar. "A Behavior Therapy Approach to the Treatment of Childhood Schizophrenia," *Minnesota Symposia on Child Psychology*, 1965.

Lovaas, O. Ivar, Benson Schaeffer, and James Q. Simmons. "Building Social Behavior in Autistic Children by Use of Electric Shock," *Journal of Experimental Research in Personality*, vol. 1, 1965.

Moser, Don. "Screams, Slaps and Love," *Life*, April 1965.

Neimark, Jill. "Autism: It's Not Just in the Head," *Discover*, March 22, 2007.

Rogers, Sally J., and Bruce F. Pennington. "A Theoretical Approach to the Deficits in Infantile Autism," *Development and Psychopathology*, vol. 3, 1991.

Rogers, Sally J., Susan Hepburn and Elizabeth Wehner. "Parent Reports of Sensory Symptoms in Toddlers with Autism and Those with Other Developmental Disorders," *Journal of Autism and Developmental Disorders*, December 2003.

Sebat, Jonathan, B. Lakshmi, et al. "Strong Association of De Novo Copy Number Mutations with Autism," *Science*, April 20, 2007.

Shattuck, Paul T., "The Contribution of Diagnostic Substitution to the Growing Administrative Prevalence of Autism in US Special Education," *Pediatrics*, April 2006.

Shattuck, Paul T., and Maureen Durkin. "A Spectrum of Disputes," *New York Times*, June 11, 2007.

Simon, Nicol. "Kaspar Hauser's Recovery and Autopsy: A Perspective on Neurological and Sociological Requirements for Language Development," *Journal of Autism and Childhood Schizophrenia*, vol. 8, no. 2, 1978.

Stone, Wendy, Caitlin R. McMahon, et al. "Early Social-Communicative and Cognitive Development of Younger Siblings of Children with Autistic Spectrum Disorders," *Archives of Pediatrics and Adolescent Medicine*, April 2007.

Vargas, Diana L., Caterina Nascimbene, et al. "Neuroglial Activation and Neuroinflammation in the Brain of Patients with Autism," *Annals of Neurology*, January 2005.

Wallis, Claudia. "Inside the Autistic Mind," *Time*, May 7, 2006.

Werner, Emily, and Geraldine Dawson. "Validation of the Phenomenon of Autistic Regression Using Home Videotapes," *Archives of General Psychiatry*, August 2005.

Witwer, Andrew, and Luc Lecavalier. "Treatment Incidence and Patterns in Children and Adolescents with Autism Spectrum Disorders," *Journal of Child and Adolescent Psychopharmacology*, no. 4, 2005.

ALSO BY KARL TARO GREENFELD

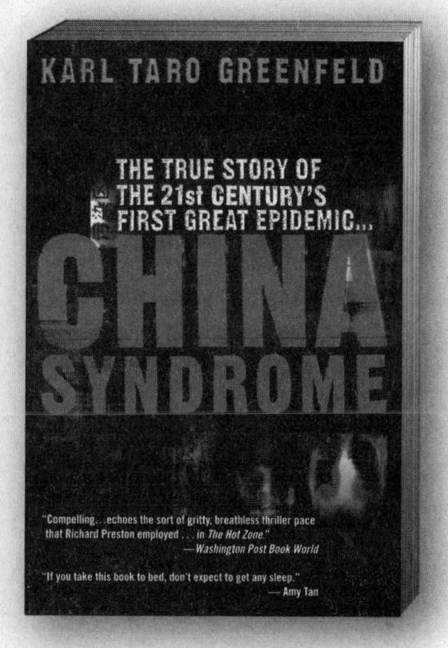

CHINA SYNDROME

The True Story of the 21st Century's First Great Epidemic

ISBN 978-0-06-058723-9 (paperback)

"A fast-moving, truth-is-stranger-than-fiction thriller that doubles as an excellent primer of emerging infections for scientists and laypeople alike. . . . A detailed look at China's culture of secrecy in the throes of a global public health crisis." —*Los Angeles Times*

"Fine reporting . . . a scientific whodunit."
—*The Financial Times*

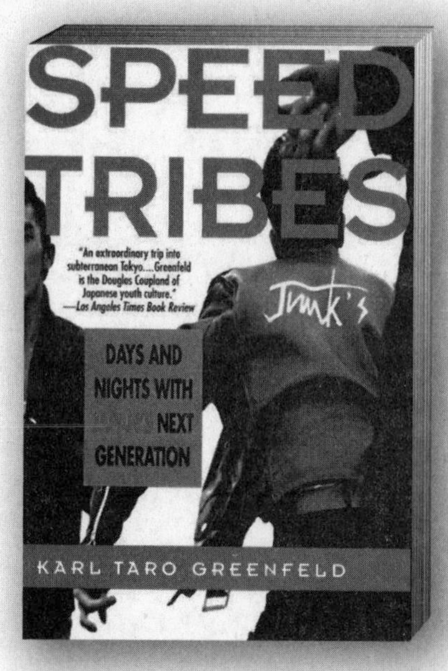

SPEED TRIBES

Days and Nights With Japan's Next Generation

ISBN 978-0-06-092665-6 (paperback)

"A grippingly fresh portrait of an unseen country. . . . As faces and stories accumulate like mosaic tiles, Japan's netherworld emerges with almost unbelievable vividness."
—*Washington Post Book World*